Bibliography of the International Arthurian Society
Volume LXVIII (2016)

Bibliography of the International Arthurian Society

Volume LXVIII (2016)

Edited by
Nathanael Busch

DE GRUYTER

INTERNATIONAL ARTHURIAN SOCIETY

Responsible Editor
Nathanael Busch
Universität Siegen
Germanistisches Seminar
Hölderlinstraße 3
57076 Siegen
Email: busch@germanistik.uni-siegen.de

ISBN 978-3-11-046676-8
e-ISBN (PDF) 978-3-11-046749-9
e-ISBN (EPUB) 978-3-11-046689-8
ISSN 2197-4616

Library of Congress Control Number: 2018961124

Bibliographic information published by the Deutsche Nationalbibliothek
The Deutsche Nationalbibliothek lists this publication in the Deutsche Nationalbibliografie; detailed bibliographic data are available on the Internet at http://dnb.dnb.de.

Printing and binding: CPI books GmbH, Leck

MIX
Papier aus verantwortungsvollen Quellen
FSC www.fsc.org FSC® C083411

www.degruyter.com

Contents

The Annual Bibliography; aims and current changes

ici fenist li premiers vers.
Erec

This volume of the *Bibliography of the International Arthurian Society (BIAS)* marks the end of a long series. Since 1949 the preceeding *Bibliographical Bulletin of the International Arthurian Society / Bulletin Bibliographique de la Société Internationale Arthurienne* draws, year by year, attention to scholarly works concerned with the *matière de Bretagne*. The Bibliography is one of the main objectives of the society that was founded after the second Arthurian Congress in Quimper in 1948. In 68 volumes about 40.000 items have been collected by hundreds of bibliographers, merged by 9 editors. Up to volume LXIV it held further material: particular articles, that have been published in *JIAS (Journal of the International Arthurian Society)* since 2013, as well as a list of officers of the society and a list of members (now online on the society's website at http://www.international-arthuriansociety.com/).
After all this time Arthurian scholarship is more vivid than ever. Therefore it is our intention to adjust *BIAS* to the needs and possibilities of our time. The last printed volume lists publications till 2015. Later publications will be published online as an open and free database at <http://bias.internationalarthuriansociety.com/> It is the society's aim to digitalise the past volumes and integrate them into the database as soon as funding will be available.

The editor would like to express his gratitude for all help during the publication of this volume. In particular I am grateful for the pleasant collaboration with the staff at De Gruyter. Niklas Kunz did magnificent work to write the database. Simon Jenke and Antonia Krihl assisted with the edition of the data. Ann Howey entered the data for the North American branch.

https://doi.org/10.1515/9783110467499-007

Editorial conventions

The *Bibliography of the International Arthurian Society (BIAS)* lists all scholarly books and articles directly concerned with the *matière de Bretagne*. Subjects which are only indirectly concerned with it, such as the origins of courtly love, are deliberately excluded. Also excluded are popular works, general surveys found in histories of literature and most studies which deal with the Arthurian tradition after the sixteenth century. Within these limits, the Bibliography aims to include all books, reviews and articles published in the year preceding its appearance, an exception being made for earlier studies which have been omitted inadvertently.

Each national branch of the Arthurian Society is responsible for its own section of the Bibliography. Each section is divided into four parts: I. Texts, Translations and Adaptations; II. Critical and Historical Studies; III. Reviews; IV. Reprints; V. Doctoral Dissertations/Higher Degree Theses. The contents of each section are arranged in the alphabetical order of authors' names. As often as possible a brief, objective account is given of the contents of each study listed in the Bibliography. For practical purposes, as well as to conform to a decision taken at the Second Triennial Arthurian Congress, these digests are given in English, French or German. Each section of the Bibliography is printed in alphabetical order according to nationality. The first publication listed for each year is given the number one; the rest follows in numerical order down to the end of the Bibliography. Any reference to the Bibliography should therefore include the number of the Bulletin, the year and the number of the individual publication, e. g. *BBIAS*, I, 1949, 20. At the end of the Bibliography are printed two indexes, one of authors and one of subject-matter. The indexes are prepared by the bibliographers of the national branches. The style of the items differs from preceding volumes due to technical reasons.

https://doi.org/10.1515/9783110467499-008

List of Abbreviations

a&e	anglistik & englischunterricht.
ABäG	Amsterdamer Beiträge zur älteren Germanistik, Amsterdam.
ABB	Archives et Bibliothèques de Belgique, Brussels.
ABR	American Benedictine Review, Atchison, Kansas.
AEF	Anuario de Estudios Filológicos, Cáceres.
AEM	Anuario de Estudios Medievales, Barcelona.
AfK	Archiv für Kulturgeschichte, Köln.
AG	Acta Germanica. Jahrbuch des Germanistenverbandes im südlichen Afrika, Frankfurt a.M., Bern, New York, Paris.
AI	American Imago, Brooklyn, New York.
AInt	Arthurian Interpretations, Southern Methodist University, Dallas, Texas.
AION	Annali Istituto Universitario Orientale di Napoli, Sezione Romanza.
AJ	Antiquaries Journal, London.
AJFS	Australian Journal of French Studies, Monash University, Clayton, Victoria.
AJP	American Journal of Philology, Johns Hopkins University, Baltimore, Maryland.
AL	Arthurian Literature, Cambridge.
Alazet	Alazet, Huesca.
Alf	Alfinge, Córdoba.
Alfa	Alfa, Sao Paolo, Brasil.
ALE	Anales de Literatura Española, Alicante.
AM	Analecta Malacitana, Málaga.
AnEF	Anuario de Estudios Filológicos, Cáceres.
ANF	Arkiv för nordisk filologi, Lund.
AnFH	Anales de Filología Hispánica, Murcia.
AnFil	Anuari de Filologia, Barcelona.
Angélica	Angélica, Lucena.
Angl	Anglia, Berlin.
AnL	Anuario de Letras, México.
AnLE	Anales de Literatura Española, Alicante.
AnMal	Analecta Malacitana, Málaga.
Annales	Annales. Economies, Sociétés, Civilisations, Paris.
Ann Bret	Annales de Bretagne, Université de Haute-Bretagne, Rennes.
ANQ	American Notes and Queries, University Press of Kentucky.
Ant	Antiquity, Cambridge.

https://doi.org/10.1515/9783110467499-009

APS	Acta Philologica Scandinavica, Copenhagen.
AQ	Arizona Quarterly, University of Arizona, Tucson.
ARBA	American Reference Books Annual, Littleton, Colorado.
Arbitrium	Arbitrium: Zeitschrift für Rezensionen zur germanistischen Literaturwissenschaft, Berlin.
Arcadia	Arcadia, Berlin.
Arch	Archivum, Oviedo.
ArchJ	The Archaeological Journal, The Royal Archaeological Institute, London.
Arch Camb	Archaeologia Cambrensis, Cardiff.
ArFA	Archivo de Filología Aragonesa, Zaragoza.
ArH	Archivo Hispalense, Sevilla.
ArL	Archivos Leoneses, León.
Arthuriana	Arthuriana, Dallas.
ASR	American Scandinavian Review, New York.
AStnSpr	Archiv für das Studium der neueren Sprachen, Berlin.
Atlantis	Atlantis, Acadia University, Wolfville, Nova Scotia.
AUMLA	Journal of Australasian Universities, Modern Language and Literature Association, Monash University, Clayton, Victoria.
AusCJ	Australian Celtic Journal, University of Sydney, New South Wales.
BANABMD	Boletín de la Asociación Nacional de Archiveros, Bibliotecarios, Museólogos y Documentalistas, Madrid.
BB	Bulletin du Bibliophile, Paris.
BBAHLM	Boletín Bibliográfico de la Asociación Hispánica de Literatura Medieval, Barcelona.
BBIAS	Bibliographical Bulletin of the International Arthurian Society, Madison.
BBMP	Boletín de la Biblioteca Menéndez Pelayo, Santander.
BBSIA	Bulletin Bibliographique de la Société Internationale Arthurienne/ Bibliographical Bulletin of the International Arthurian Society (1949–2011).
Béal	Béaloideas, Dublin.
BEC	Bibliothèque de l'École des Chartes, Paris.
Ber	Berceo, Logroño.
BF	Boletím de Filologia, Lisbon.
BHR	Bibliothèque d'Humanisme et Renaissance, Paris and Geneva.
BI	Books Ireland, Dublin.
BIAS	Bibliography of the International Arthurian Society (2012–...), replaced BBSIA/ BBIAS
BIEA	Boletín del Instituto de Estudios Asturianos, Oviedo.

BIEG	Boletín del Instituto de Estudios Giennenses, Jaén.
Bien dire et bien aprandre	Bulletin du Centre d'Etudes Médiévales et Dialectales de l'Université de Lille-III.
BJRL	Bulletin of the John Rylands University Library of Manchester.
BNa	Beiträge zur Namenforschung, Heidelberg.
BoJB	Bonner Jahrbücher des Rheinischen Landesmuseums in Bonn, Darmstadt.
BRABL	Boletín de la Real Academia de Buenas Letras, Barcelona.
BRAC	Boletín de la Real Academia de Córdoba, Córdoba.
BRAE	Boletín de la Real Academia Española, Madrid.
Brit	Britannia, London.
Bro	Broteria, Lisbon.
BSCC	Boletín de la Sociedad Castellonense de Cultura, Castellón.
BTAM	Bulletin de théologie ancienne et médiévale.
BWAS	Bulletin de l'École des Hautes Etudes, Tokyo, Université Waseda.
CAIEF	Cahiers de l'Association Internationale des Etudes Françaises, Paris.
CA	Current Archaeology, London.
Caligrama	Caligrama, Palma de Mallorca.
Castilla	Castilla, Valladolid.
CCM	Cahiers de civilisation médiévale, Poitiers.
CE	College English, Wesleyan University, Middleton, Connecticut.
Celt	Celtica, Dublin.
CentR	The Centennial Review, Cdt critica del Testo Roma, Michigan State University, East Lansing, Michigan.
CF	Cuadernos de Filología, Ciudad Real.
CF-III	Cuadernos de Filología-III, Valencia.
CFF	Cuadernos de Filología Francesa, Univ. Extremadura.
CFMA	Classiques français du moyen âge, Paris.
CFR	Cuadernos de Filología Románica, Barcelona.
ChauR	The Chaucer Review, Pennsylvania State University, University Park, Pennsylvania.
CHis	Cuadernos Hispanoamericanos, Madrid.
ChLA	Children's Literature Association Quarterly, Baltimore, MD.
Choice	Choice, American Library Association, Chicago, Illinois.
CHR	Catholic Historical Review, Catholic University of America, Washington, D.C.
CIF	Cuadernos de Investigación Filológica.

CILH	Cuadernos de Investigación de Literatura Hispánica, Madrid.
Cithara	Cithara, Saint Bonaventure University, Saint Bonaventure, New York.
CJIS	Canadian Journal of Italian Studies.
CL	Comparative Literature, University of Oregon, Eugene, Oregon.
Clio	Clio, Indiana University-Purdue University at Fort Wayne, Indiana.
CLS	Comparative Literature Studies, Pennsylvania State University, University Park.
CMCS	Cambrian Medieval Celtic Studies, Aberystwyth.
CML	Classical and Modern Literature, Terre Haute, Indiana.
CMLR	Canadian Modern Language Review, Welland, Ontario.
CN	Cultura Neolatina, Rome.
Codices manuscripti	Codices manuscripti & Impresi, Wien.
ColG	Colloquia Germanica, Bern.
Com	Comitatus, University of California, Los Angeles.
Cosmos	Cosmos, The Journal of the International Cosmology Society, Edinburgh.
CP	Classical Philology, University of Chicago, Illinois.
CRCL	Canadian Review of Comparative Literature, Edmonton, Alberta.
CrI	Critical Inquiry, University of Chicago, Illinois.
Crit	Criticism, Wayne State University, Detroit, Michigan.
Critique	Critique: Studies in Modern Fiction, Washington, D.C.
CRM	Cahiers de Recherches Médiévales et Humanistes, Orléans.
Crotalón	Crotalón: Anuario de Filología, Madrid.
CS	Cornish Studies, Exeter.
CSANA Yearbook	Celtic Studies Association of North America Yearbook, Dublin.
CTI	Cuadernos de Traducción e Interpretación, Bellaterra, Barcelona.
DAI	Dissertation Abstracts International, University Microfilms, Ann Arbor, Michigan.
DAM	Deutsches Archiv für Erforschung des Mittelalters, Köln.
DanS	Dante Studies, Dante Society of America, Cambridge, Massachusetts.
DFS	Dalhousie French Studies, Halifax, Nova Scotia, Canada.
Dia	Diacritics, Cornell University, Ithaca, New York.
Digraphe	Digraphe, Paris.
DJJ	The David Jones Journal, Swansea.
DR	Dalhousie Review, Dalhousie University, Halifax, Nova Scotia, Canada.
Du	Der Deutschunterricht, Stuttgart.

DVj	Deutsche Vierteljahrsschrift für Literaturwissenschaft und Geistesgeschichte, Stuttgart.
EC	Essays in Criticism, Oxford.
EHR	English Historical Review, Harlow, Essex.
Éigse	Éigse: A Journal of Irish Studies, Dublin.
EL	Estudis Lulianos, Palma de Mallorca.
ELH	Journal of English Literary History, Johns Hopkins University, Baltimore, Maryland.
ELN	English Language Notes, University of Colorado, Boulder, Colorado.
EME	Early Medieval Europe, Oxford.
EMS	English Manuscript Studies, 1100–1700, London.
Encomia	Encomia: Bibliographical Bulletin of the International Courtly Literature Society, Salt Lake City, Utah.
English	English: The Journal of the English Association, Leicester.
Epos	Epos, Madrid.
ER	Estudis Romànics, Barcelona.
Ériu	Ériu, Dublin.
ES	English Studies: A Journal of English Letters and Philology, Amsterdam.
ESC	English Studies in Canada, University of Alberta, Edmonton.
EsMedS	Essays in Medieval Studies, Illinois Medieval Association.
Esp	L'Esprit créateur, Louisiana State University, Baton Rouge.
EstRom	Estudios Románicos, Murcia.
Ét. Angl	Études anglaises, Paris.
Ét. Celt	Études celtiques, Paris.
Ét. Germ	Études germaniques, Paris.
Études de lettres	Études de lettres, Lausanne.
Euph	Euphorion, Heidelberg.
Exemplaria	Exemplaria: A Journal of Theory in Medieval and Renaissance Studies, Leeds.
Exp	Explicator, Richmond Professional Institute, Richmond, Virginia.
Fabula	Fabula: Zeitschrift für Erzählforschung, Berlin.
FCS	Fifteenth-Century Studies, Marygrove College, Detroit, Michigan.
FF	French Forum, Lexington, Kentucky.
FFRSH	Futsugo-Futsubungaku-Ronshu, Tokyo.
Fil	Filología, Buenos Aires.
FM	Filología moderna, Madrid.
FMLS	Forum for Modern Language Studies, St. Andrews.

FMSt	Frühmittelalterliche Studien: Jahrbuch des Instituts für Frühmittelalterforschung der Universität Münster, Berlin.
Folklore	Folklore, the journal of The Folklore Society, London.
ForI	Forum Italicum.
FR	French Review, American Association of Teachers of French, Champaign, Illinois.
FS	French Studies, Oxford.
FSB	French Studies Bulletin, Oxford.
GAG	Göppinger Arbeiten zur Germanistik, Göppingen.
GenL	General Linguistics, Pennsylvania State University, University Park.
Genre	Genre, University of Oklahoma, Norman.
Germanistik	Germanistik: Internationales Referatenorgan mit bibliographischen Hinweisen, Berlin.
GLL	German Life and Letters, Oxford.
GN	Germanic Notes, Lexington, Kentucky.
GQ	German Quarterly, American Association of Teachers of German, Chapel Hill, North Carolina.
GR	Germanic Review, Columbia University, New York.
Grial	Grial, Vigo.
GRM	Germanisch-romanische Monatsschrift, Heidelberg.
GSR	German Studies Review, German Studies Association, Arizona State University, Tempe.
HAB	Humanities Association Bulletin, University of Alberta, Edmonton, Alberta.
HerA	The Heroic Age. A Journal of Early Medieval Nortewestern Europe, Memorial University of Newfoundland.
Hispania	Hispania: Journal of the American Association of Teachers of Spanish and Portuguese, University of Southern California, Los Angeles.
History	History: The Journal of the Historical Association, Oxford.
HJ	Hispanic Journal, Indiana University of Pennsylvania, Indiana, Pennsylvania.
HJb	Heidelberger Jahrbücher, Berlin.
HLB	Harvard Library Bulletin, Cambridge, Massachusetts.
HLQ	Huntington Library Quarterly, San Marino, California.
Hort	Hortculis. The Online Graduate Journal of Medieval Studies, University of California Press.
HR	Hispanic Review, University of Pennsylvania, Philadelphia, Pennsylvania.
HTh	History and Theory.

IASdL	Internationales Archiv für Sozialgeschichte der deutschen Literatur, Berlin.
Iberoromania	Iberoromania, Berlin.
IHE	Indice Historico Español, Barcelona.
Incipit	Incipit, Buenos Aires.
Islandica	Islandica, Cornell University, Ithaca, New York.
Italica	Italica, American Associaiton of Teachers of Italian, University of Wisconsin, Madison.
Itin	Itinerarium: Revista Trimestral de Cultura, Lisbon.
ItQ	Italian Quarterly, Rutgers University, New Brunswick, New Jersey.
JAF	Journal of American Folklore, University of Texas, Austin, Texas.
JBAA	Journal of the British Archaeological Association, London.
JBS	Journal of British Studies, University of Chicago.
JCL	Journal of Celtic Linguistics, Cardiff.
JEGP	Journal of English and Germanic Philology, University of Illinois, Urbana, Illinois.
JFLS	Journal of French Language Studies, Cambridge.
JFR	Journal of Folklore Research, Indiana University Folklore Institute, Bloomington.
JIAS	Journal of the International Arthurian Society.
JIES	Journal of Indo-European Studies.
JMEMS	Journal of Medieval and Early Modern Studies, Duke University, Durham, North Carolina.
JMH	Journal of Medieval History, Headington & Exeter.
JMRC	Journal of medieval religious cultures, University Park, PA.
JPC	Journal of Popular Culture, Bowling Green State University, Ohio.
JWMS	The Journal of William Morris Studies, The William Morris Society, London.
KE	Kansas English.
KrLitt	Kritikon Litterarum, Darmstadt.
L&P	Literature and Psychology, University of Hartford, West Hartford, Connecticut.
L&S	Language and Style.
LB	Leuvense Bijdragen, Leuven.
LD	Letras de Deusto, Bilbao.
Lendemains	Lendemains, Köln.
Letras	Letras, Lima, Peru.
Library	The Library: The Transactions of the Bibliographical Society, Oxford.
LiLi	Zeitschrift für Literaturwissenschaft und Linguistik, Stuttgart.

Lingua e stile	Lingua e stile, Roma.
LitR	Literary Review, Fairleigh-Dickinson University, Madison, New Jersey.
Littérature	Littérature, Paris.
LJb	Literaturwissenschaftliches Jahrbuch, Berlin.
LL	Language and Literature: Journal of the Poetics and Linguistics Association, London.
LP	Literature and Psychology, Fairleigh Dickinson University, Keaneck, New Jersey.
LR	Lettres Romanes, Louvain.
LlC	Llên Cymru, Cardiff.
LSE	Leeds Studies in English, Leeds.
LT	Levende Talen, Groningen.
MA	Moyen Age, Bruxelles.
Madoc	Madoc, tijdschrift over de Middeleeuwen, Utrecht.
Man	Manuscripta, St. Louis University, Missouri.
M&H	Medievalia et Humanistica.
Med	Medievalia, UNAM, Méjico.
MedArch	Medieval Archaeology, Leeds.
Med. Aev	Medium Aevum, Oxford.
Mediaevalia	Mediaevalia, Center for Medieval and Early Renaissance Studies, State University of New York, Binghamton.
Mediaevistik	Mediaevistik: Internationale Zeitschrift für interdisziplinäre Mittelalterforschung, Frankfurt a.M., Bern, New York, Paris.
Médiévales	Médiévales, Université de Paris-VIII.
MedPer	Medieval Perspectives.
MélCV	Mélanges de la Casa de Velázquez, Madrid.
MF	Moyen Français, Université de Montréal, Canada.
MGRS	Meijigakuin-Ronso, Tokyo.
MichA	Michigan Academician, University of Michigan, Ann Arbor.
Millennium	Millennium, tijdschrift voor middeleeuwse studies, Nijmegen.
MisMM	Miscelánea Medieval Murciana.
MLJ	Modern Language Journal, University of Wisconsin, Madison.
MlJb	Mittellateinisches Jahrbuch, Stuttgart.
MLN	Modern Language Notes, Johns Hopkins University, Baltimore, Maryland.
MLQ	Modern Language Quarterly, University of Washington, Seattle, Washington.
MLR	Modern Language Review, Leeds.

Monats	Monatshefte, University of Wisconsin, Madison.
Mosaic	Mosaic, University of Manitoba, Winnipeg.
MP	Modern Philology, University of Chicago, Illinois.
MR	Medioevo Romanzo, Naples.
MRom	Marche Romane, Liège.
MS	Medieval Studies, Pontifical Institute of Medieval Studies, Toronto, Canada.
Mytl	Mythlore (Journal of the Mythopoeic Society), Fredonia, New York.
N&Q	Notes and Queries, Oxford.
NdJb	Niederdeutsches Jahrbuch, Neumünster.
NdW	Niederdeutsches Wort, Münster.
Neophil	Neophilologus, Amsterdam.
NFS	Nottingham French Studies, Nottingham.
NL	Nederlandse Letterkunde, Groningen.
NLH	New Literary History, Charlottesville, Virginia.
NLWJ	National Library of Wales Journal, Aberystwyth.
NM	Neuphilologische Mitteilungen, Helsinki.
NML	New Medieval Literatures, Oxford.
NMS	Nottingham Mediaeval Studies, Nottingham.
NRFH	Nueva Revista de Filología Hispánica, Mexico.
NZZ	Neue Zürcher Zeitung, Zürich.
Ogam	Ogam: Tradition celtique, Rennes.
Olifant	Olifant, Société Rencesvals, American Canadian Branch, University of Virginia, Charlottesville.
Ornicar	Ornicar, Paris.
PAPS	Proceedings of the American Philosophical Society, Philadelphia, Pennsylvania.
PBA	Proceedings of the British Academy, London.
PBB	Du zur Geschichte der deutschen Sprache und Literatur.
Parergon	Parergon, University of Sydney, Australia.
Peritia	Peritia: Journal of the Medieval Academy of Ireland, Cork/Turnhout
Perspectives médiévales	Perspectives médiévales, Paris.
PhL	Philosophy and Literature, Johns Hopkins University, Baltimore, Maryland.
PhR	Philosophy and Rhetoric, Pennsylvania State University, University Park.
PIMA	Proceedings of the Illinois Medieval Association.
PLL	Papers on Language and Literature, Southern Illinois University, Edwardsville.

PMAM	Publications of the Medieval Association of the Midwest, Emporia, Kansas.
PMASAL	Papers of the Michigan Academy of Science, Arts and Letters, University of Michigan, Ann Arbor.
PMLA	Publications of the Modern Language Association of America, New York.
PQ	Philological Quarterly, University of Iowa, Iowa City.
PRF	Publications Romanes et Françaises, Genève.
PRIS-MA	PRIS-MA, C. E. S. C. M. de l'Université de Poitiers.
Proh	Prohemio, Madrid-Pisa.
PrV	Príncipe de Viana, Pamplona.
PSAS	Proceedings of the Society of Antiquaries of Scotland, Edinburgh.
QFLRM	Quaderni di Filologia e di Lingue Romanze, Università di Macerata.
QFR	Quaderni di Filologia Romanza, Bologna.
QI	Quaderni d'Italianistica, Canadian Society of Italian Studies.
QL	Quinzaine littéraire, Paris.
Queeste	Queeste, tijdschrift over middeleeuwse letterkunde, Leiden.
Quidditas	Journal of the Rocky Mountain Medieval and Renaissance Association, Northern Arizona University, Flagstaff, Arizona (formerly JRMMRA).
Razo	Razo: Cahiers du Centre d'Etudes Médiévales de Nice.
RBPH	Revue Belge de Philologie et d'Histoire, Bruxelles.
RChL	Revista Chilena de Literatura, Santiago, Chile.
RCPhR	Revue Critique de Philologie Romane, Alessandria
Rech. Germ	Recherches Germaniques, Université des Sciences Humaines, Strasbourg.
RefR	Reference Reviews, Bingley.
REH	Revista de Estudios Hispánicos, Alabama.
REI	Revue des Études Italiennes, Bordeaux.
RES	Review of English Studies, Oxford.
ResPL	Res Publica Litterarum, University of Kansas, Lawrence.
RF	Romanische Forschungen, Frankfurt a.M.
RFE	Revista de Filología Española, Madrid.
RFLCR	Revista de Filología y Lingüística de la Universidad de Costa Rica, San José, Costa Rica.
RFLL	Revista de Filología de La Laguna, La Laguna.
RFR	Revista de Filología Románica, Madrid.
Rh	Rhetorica, University of California, Berkeley.
RHT	Revue d'Histoire des Textes, Paris.
RhVjbl	Rheinische Vierteljahrsblätter, Bonn.

RIO	Revue Internationale d'Onomastique, Paris.
RJ	Romanistisches Jahrbuch, Berlin.
RLC	Revue de Littérature Comparée, Paris.
RLe	Revista de Letras, Säo Paulo, Brazil.
RLit	Revista de Literatura, Madrid.
RLM	Revista de Literaturas Modernas, Mendoza, Argentina.
RLMed	Revista de Literatura Medieval, Madrid.
RLR	Revue des Langues Romanes, Paris.
RLiR	Revue de Linguistique Romane, Paris.
RMAL	Revue du Moyen Age Latin, Lyon.
RMR	Reading Medieval Reviews, Reading, e-journal at: http://www.reading.ac.uk/AcaDepts/ln/Medieval/rmr.htm
RMRLL	Rocky Mountain Review of Language and Literature
RMS	Reading Medieval Studies, Reading.
Rom	Romania, Paris.
RomN	Romance Notes, University of North Carolina, Chapel Hill.
RomQ	Romance Quarterly, University of Kentucky, Lexington.
RPF	Revista Portuguesa de Filosofía, Braga.
RPFil	Revista Portuguesa de Filología, Coimbra.
RPh	Romance Philology, University of California, Berkeley.
RQ	Renaissance Quarterly, Renaissance Society of America, New York.
RR	Romanic Review, Columbia University, New York.
RSI	Rivista di Studi Italiani, Toronto.
RSH	Revue des Sciences Humaines, Paris.
RUB	Reclam Universal-Bibliothek, Stuttgart.
RZLG	Romanistische Zeitschrift für Literaturgeschichte/Cahiers d'Histoire des Littératures Romanes, Heidelberg.
SAC	Studies in the Age of Chaucer, University of Oklahoma, Norman.
SAQ	South Atlantic Quarterly, Duke University, Durham, North Carolina.
SAR	South Atlantic Review, University of North Carolina, Chapel Hill.
SATF	Société des Anciens Textes Français, Paris.
Scan	Scandinavica, University of East Anglia, Norwich.
ScHR	Scottish Historical Review, Glasgow.
SCJ	Sixteenth Century Journal, Kirksville, Missouri.
ScotSt	Scottish Studies, University of Edinburgh.
SCR	South Central Review, South Central Modern Language Association, Texas A & M University, College Station, Texas.
Script	Scriptorium, Bruxelles.
SEL	Studies in English Literature 1500–1900, Rice University, Houston, Texas.

Sem	Seminar, Canadian Assocaition of University Teachers of German, University of Toronto.
Semiotica	Semiotica, The Hague.
Senefiance	Senefiance, Aix-en-Provence.
SF	Studi Francesi, Turin.
SGS	Scottish Gaelic Studies, University of Aberdeen.
SHR	Southern Humanities Review, Auburn University, Alabama.
SLI	Studies in Literary Imagination, Georgia State College, Atlanta.
SM	Studi Medievali, Spoleto.
SMART	Studies in Medieval and Renaissance Teaching, Wichita, Kansas.
SMC	Studies in Medieval Culture, Western Michigan University, Kalamazoo.
SMV	Studi mediolatini e volgari, Pisa.
SN	Studia Neophilologica, Uppsala.
SoQ	The Southern Quarterly, University of Southern Mississippi, Hattiesburg, Mississippi.
SoR	Southern Review, Louisiana State University, Baton Rouge.
SP	Studies in Philology, University of North Carolina, Chapel Hill.
Spec	Speculum, Medieval Academy of America, Cambridge, Massachusetts.
Spicilegio moderno	Spicilegio moderno, Bologna.
SpL	Spiegel der Letteren, Antwerp and The Hague.
Sprk	Sprachkunst, Wien.
SR	Scandinavian Review, American-Scandinavian Foundation, New York.
SS	Scandinavian Studies, University of Wisconsin, Madison.
SSF	Studies in Short Fiction, Newberry College, Newberry, South Carolina.
SSL	Studies in Scottish Literature, University of South Carolina, Columbia.
StC	Studia Celtica, Cardiff.
StMed	Studies in Medievalism, Cambridge, D.S. Brewer.
STS	Shi-to-Sambun, Tokyo.
StudH	Studies in the Humanities, Indiana University of Pennsylvania, Indiana, Pennsylvania.
StudHib	Studia Hibernica, Dublin.
Style	Style, Northern Illinois University, DeKalb.
StZ	Studia Zamorensia, serie philologica, Zamora.

Sub-Stance	Sub-Stance: A Review of Theory and Literary Criticism, University of Wisconsin, Madison.
Symp	Symposium, Syracuse University, Syracuse, New York.
Taliesin	Taliesin, Academi, Cardiff.
TATE	Tategoto, Tokyo.
Text	Text, Society for Textual Scholarship, Queensborough Community College, Bayside, New York.
Thalia	Thalia, Studies in Literary Humor.
Thes	Thesaurus: Boletín del Instituto Caro y Cuervo, Bogotà.
THES	Times Higher Education Supplement, London.
Thoth	Thoth, Syracuse, New York.
Thought	Thought, Fordham University, New York.
THSC	Transactions of the Honourable Society of Cymmrodorion, London.
TLF	Textes Littéraires Français, Genève.
TLS	Times Literary Supplement, London.
TMR	The Medieval Review (formerly Bryn Mawr Medieval Review), Medieval Institute at Western Michigan University.
TNTL	Tijdschrift voor Nederlandse Taal- en Letterkunde, Leiden.
Tocher	Tocher, School of Scottish Studies, University of Edinburgh.
Topic	Topic, Washington and Jefferson College, Washington, Pennsylvania.
Trad	Traditio, Fordham University, New York.
Traliphi	Travaux de linguistique et de philologie, Centre de Philologie et de Littératures Romanes de l'Université de Strasbourg.
TRB	Tennyson Research Bulletin, Lincoln, England.
TrD&G	Transactions of the Dumfriesshire and Galloway Natural History and Antiquarian Society, Dumfries.
Tris	Tristania, University of Tennessee, Chattanooga.
Trivium	Trivium, St. David's University College, Lampeter.
TrR	Translation Review, University of Texas, Dallas.
TS	Tolkien Studies: An Annual Scholarly Review, West Virginia University Press
TSL	Tennessee Studies in Literature, University of Tennessee, Knoxville.
TSLL	Texas Studies in Language and Literature, University of Texas, Austin.
TSWL	Tulsa Studies in Women's Literature, University of Tulsa, Oklahoma.
UTQ	University of Toronto Quarterly, Toronto.
UWR	University of Windsor Review, Windsor, Ontario, Canada.

Verba	Verba, Santiago de Compostela.
Viator	Viator, University of California, Los Angeles.
VR	Vox Romanica, Bern.
WB	Weimarer Beiträge, Wien.
WF	Western Folklore, Los Angeles, California.
WHR	The Welsh History Review, Cardiff.
WHumR	Western Humanities Review.
WS	Women's Studies.
WW	Wirkendes Wort, Trier.
YES	Yearbook of English Studies, Leeds.
YFS	Yale French Studies, New Haven, Connecticut.
YREAL	Yearbook of Research in English and American Studies.
ZAA	Zeitschrift für Anglistik und Amerikanistik.
ZBL	Zeitschrift für bayerische Landesgeschichte, München.
ZfcPh	Zeitschrift für celtische Philologie, Tübingen.
ZfdA	Zeitschrift für deutsches Altertum und deutsche Literatur, Stuttgart.
ZfdPh	Zeitschrift für deutsche Philologie, Berlin.
ZfG	Zeitschrift für Germanistik, Neue Folge, Berlin.
ZfSL	Zeitschrift für französische Sprache und Literatur, Wiesbaden.
ZfvglSpr	Zeitschrift für vergleichende Sprachforschung, Göttingen.
ZgL	Zeitschrift für germanistische Linguistik, Berlin, New York.
ZGORh	Zeitschrift für die Geschichte des Oberrheins, Stuttgart.
ZrP	Zeitschrift für romanische Philologie, Berlin.
1616	1616. Sociedas Española de Literatura General y Comparada.

Australia and New Zealand

Bibliography for 2015 compiled by Sarah Randles

II Critical and Historical Studies

1 LEITCH, Megan G., "'grete luste to slepe'. Somatic Ethics and the Sleep of Romance from *Sir Gawain and the Green Knight* to Shakespeare," *Parergon*, 32.1 (2015), 103–28.

Literary sleep in Middle English literature can be read productively alongside instructions about sleep in courtesy books and dietaries, and in the light of Galenic medical understandings of sleep. Literary sleep often operates as an ethical discourse in late medieval secular literature, especially romance.

2 OVENS, Michael, "Violence and Transgression in Chrétien de Troyes's *Yvain, le Chevalier au Lion*," *Parergon*, 32.1 (2015), 53–76.

By defining violence in terms of violation and reading the text through the Augustinian-Bernardian frame of the 'inner disposition' (intention, emotion), new parallels and recursions emerge within Yvain which undermine the supposed phenomenological separation of violence and non-violence in the medieval period.

III Reviews

3 *Arthur in Medieval Welsh Literature*, ed. O.J. PADEL. Cardiff: University of Wales Press, 2013, 111 p. (cf. *BIAS*, LXVI, 2014, 435).

Rev. by MCDONALD, Roderick, *Journal of the Australian Early Medieval Association*, 11 (2015), 118–20.

https://doi.org/10.1515/9783110467499-023

4 Halsall, Guy, *Worlds of King Arthur. Facts and Fictions of the Dark Ages*. Oxford: Oxford University Press, 2013, 384 p. (cf. *BIAS*, LXVI, 2014, 339).

Rev. by Denison, Jane-Anne, *Journal of the Australian Early Medieval Association*, 11 (2015), 103–4.

5 *The Arthur of the Italians. The Arthurian Legend in Medieval Italian Literature and Culture*, ed. Gloria Allaire and F. Regina Psaki. Cardiff: University of Wales Press, 2014, 352 p. (cf. *BIAS*, LXVII, 2015, 376).

Rev. by Harty, Kevin J., *Parergon*, 32.1 (2015), 214–6.

Belgium and the Netherlands

Bibliography for 2015 compiled by Frank Brandsma, Marjolein Hogenbirk, and Jacqueline Wessel, with the help of Lauren Hoogen Stoevenbeld and Roos Brands

II Critical and Historical Studies

6 ALAMICHEL, Marie-Françoise, "*The Boke of Brut* attribué à Thomas Castleford. Une affaire de droit," *MA*, 120 (2014), 299–314.

The Boke of Brut, attributed to Thomas Castleford and completed soon after 1327, was handed down in the form of a single fifteenth-century manuscript. It is in the long and flourishing Brut tradition, but has its own specific characteristics. One of the most interesting is its insistence on the idea of the law. This long text of 39,439 verses defines a good king, his political power, and the form his actions should take. It outlines what concerns he should have at all times – specifically the common good – and underscores the indispensable collaboration between royal and sacerdotal power. Castleford also concerns himself with the Breton/English people (the question of national identity features prominently in the chronicle), who are supposed to find peace and prosperity within their vast territory. This can be assured by each person respecting his position, observing the law and its rules and ensuring that one's own rights as well as those of others prevail. In the view of Thomas of Castleford, unity and a single authority were essential to avoid chaos. They justified a call for a nationalistic crusade, with Castleford taking up the idea of a just war, which several theologians had helped to define. "Faith, Law, Country": this, it seems, was Castleford's credo throughout the chronicle. (M.-F.A.)

7 ATKINSON, Stephen, "'They ... toke their shyldys before them and drew oute their swerdys ...'. Inflicting and Healing Wounds in Malory's *Morte Darthur*," in *Wounds and Wound Repair in Medieval Culture*, ed. Larissa TRACY and Kelly DEVRIES. Amsterdam: Brill/Rodopi, 2015, pp. 519–34.

https://doi.org/10.1515/9783110467499-025

S.A. analyses Malory's picture of chivalric prowess as a crucial element in an ideal Arthurian kingdom. The stability of the Arthurian world is defended by knights for whom stability was first a matter of physical balance maintained despite wounds to the victorious knight.

8 BESAMUSCA, Bart, Gareth GRIFFITH, Matthias MEYER, and Hannah MORCOS, "Author Attributions in Medieval Text Collections. An Exploration," *ABäG*, 74 (2015), 89–122.

This article examines the role and function of author attributions in multi-text manuscripts containing Dutch, English, French or German short verse narratives. The findings represent one strand of the investigations undertaken by the cross-European project 'The Dynamics of the Medieval Manuscript', which analysed the dissemination of short verse narratives and the principles of organisation underlying the compilation of text collections. Whilst short verse narratives are more commonly disseminated anonymously, there are manuscripts in which authorship is repeatedly attributed to a text or corpus. Through six case studies, this article explores medieval concepts of authorship and how they relate to constructions of authority, whether regarding an empirical figure or a literary construction. In addition, it looks at how authorship plays a role in manuscript compilation, and at the effects of attributions (by author and/or compiler) on reception. The case studies include manuscripts from the thirteenth to fifteenth centuries, produced in a range of social and cultural contexts, and featuring some of the most important European authors of short verse narratives: Rutebeuf, Baudouin de Condé, Der Stricker, Konrad von Würzburg, Willem of Hildegaersberch, and Geoffrey Chaucer. The preliminary findings contribute to our understanding of author attributions in text collections from across northern Europe and point towards future lines of enquiry into the role of authorship in medieval textual dissemination.

9 BONAFIN, Massimo, "Intersezioni di motivi tradizionali nel *Cantare di Liombruno*," *RPh*, 68 (2014), 221–30.

Bonafin discusses the 15th century *Cantare di Liombruno*. He analyzes types and motives derived from international folklore, paying particular attention to the "schema narrativo morganiano così presente nei romanzi di materia bretone e di sfondo celtico" (p. 224) as defined by Laurence Harf-Lancner.

10 BRATU, Cristian, "*Translatio*, autorité et affirmation de soi chez Gaimar, Wace et Benoît de Sainte-Maure," *The Medieval Chronicle*, 8 (2013), 135–164.

C.B. discusses the strategies of twelfth-century writers such as Geoffrey Gaimar, Wace, and Benoît de Sainte-Maure to assert themselves as translators and historians. The authors elaborate on the persona of a highly knowledgeable clerk as translator, they quote from well-known and established authors and texts and they present their works as translations while posing as de facto authors. Finally, they portray themselves as the terminus ad quem of a translatio studii. C.B. argues that patterns of translatio studii can be found in the longer epilogue to Gaimar's *Estoire des Engleis*, in the *Roman de Brut* as well as in the prologue to the *Roman de Troie*.

11 BROKAMP, Bertus, "Walewein in Archeon," *Madoc*, 29 (2015), 22–35.

The article describes the reconstruction process of the murals in one of the medieval houses in open air museum 'Archeon'. These are based on the murals found in 'Klein Drakenburg' in Utrecht, which are interpreted by Erwin Mantingh as dealing with the story of the *Roman van Walewein*. This theme has been elaborated upon in the Archeon house by taking inspiration from manuscripts, medieval paintings and other murals.

12 BROWN, James H., *Imagining the Text*. Amsterdam: Brill/Rodopi, 2015, 279 p. Visualising the Middle Ages, 10.

J.B. examines *ekphrasis* – the verbal representation of a visual representation – in Wirnt von Gravenberg's thirteenth-century Arthurian romance *Wigalois*. Through close reading of the text and examining illustrated *Wigalois* manuscripts, early print editions, and frescoes, Brown explores how *ekphrasis* structures the narrative, harmonizes potential conflicts in the text, and contributes to the construction of courtly identity. This study demonstrates that the vibrant symbiosis of word and image is crucial to the poem's sustained popularity for more than six hundred years, and contributes to the history of the book and to the study of medieval and modern modes of perception. (J.B.)

13 FABRY-TEHRANCHI, Irène, "La fontaine bouillonnante et la tombe de Lancelot l'Ancien. Modalités textuelles et iconographiques de la construction cyclique dans le *Lancelot-Graal*," *MA*, 120 (2014), 331–65.

The head of King Lancelot the Elder, Sir Lancelot's ancestor who was assassinated by the Duke of Belle Garde, was plunged into a miraculous, boiling fountain, while his body, guarded by two lions, was preserved in a special tomb from which drops of blood with curative properties leached. On a textual level, the references to the marvels that followed the death of Lancelot the Elder in the *Estoire del saint Graal*, the *Lancelot propre*, and the *Queste del Saint Graal* attest to the construction of the Lancelot-Graal cycle, integrating a dimension that is both historical and genealogical. Yet, the iconography of the illuminated manuscripts of the Lancelot-Grail concentrates more on creating a series out of related episodes than on constructing a truly cyclical structure. Re-using composition and iconographic motifs strengthens the coherence of the chivalrous, marvelous universe thus created, without necessarily implying a circular effect. (I.F.-T.)

14 FABRY-TEHRANCHI, Irène, "La représentation du règne d'Arthur dans le manuscrit enluminé du *Brut* en prose, Londres, Lambeth Palace 6 (c.1480)," in *The Medieval Chronicle 9*, ed. Erik KOOPER. Amsterdam: Rodopi, 2014, pp. 117–60.

I.F. studies the representation and integration of the reign of Arthur in the historical framework of the *Brut* en prose or *Chronicles of England* in Ms. Londres, Lambeth Palace 6. The analysis covers the miniatures of the manuscript, ranging from the plot leading to the conception of Arthur to the end of his reign. The textual and iconographic choices of the prose *Brut* are highlighted by comparisons with Geoffrey of Monmouth's *Historia Regum Britanniae*, Wace's *Brut* and later prose rewritings in the *Lancelot-Grail* romance cycle, especially *Merlin* and its *Vulgate Sequel*.

15 GEVREY, Françoise, Alexis LEVRIER, and Bernard TEYSSANDIER, *Ethique, poétique et esthétique du secret sous l'Ancien Régime*. Leuven: Peeters, 2015, 560 p. La république des lettres, 59.

Alors que notre époque semble ne laisser aucune place au secret, il est difficile d'imaginer quelle fut son importance dans la pensée et la pratique sous l'Ancien Régime. Le présent volume, issu d'un colloque international qui s'est tenu à Reims, examine ce que fut le secret durant les XVIIe et XVIIIe siècles, tout en ouvrant l'étude à des textes originels comme le *Roman du Graal*, à la période romantique avec Senancour, Chateaubriand et Stendhal, voire au XXe siècle. Les contributions déclinent les diverses formes du secret: discrétion, dissimulation, énigme, mystère, implicite, clandestinité, espionnage. Dans la première partie, elles touchent à l'anthropologie et au rapport qu'entretiennent le politique et la morale. Une esthétique du secret s'affirme quand les poètes, les peintres et les dramaturges sollicitent la participation du spectateur. Le "plaisir secret" se charge alors de valeur positive. Les auteurs, les libraires et les journalistes n'ignorent pas la valeur pragmatique du secret.

16 GIANNINI, Gabriele, Jean-François NIEUS, and Giovanni PALUMBO, "Un nouveau fragment du *Merlin* en prose et de sa *Suite Vulgate* (Namur, Archives de l'État, Arch. eccl. 1664)," *MA*, 120 (2014), 673–711.

The ms. Namur, Archives de l'État, Arch. eccl. 1664, contains the income and expense account of the chapter of the canonesses of noble birth in Moustier-sur-Sambre for the period of August 5, 1563, to August 4, 1564. In the XVIth century, a section of this register was protected with three leaves of parchment (one bifolio leaf and one plain leaf) from a manuscript datable to the XIIIth century. The bifolio leaf, of which only the central portion remains, contains excerpts from the *Roman de Merlin* (ed. A. Micha, ch. 76, l. 49–59; ch. 77, l. 1–26; ch. 78, l. 63–70; ch. 79, l. 1–55; ch. 80, l. 58–64; ch. 81, l. 1–26), while the simple leaf, which is better preserved, contains an excerpt from the *Suite Vulgate* (ed. I. Freire-Nunes, from § 210, l. 11, to § 213, l. 25). The purpose of this paper is to publish this original fragment, describing it in detail, and to provide a linguistic and philological analysis. This discovery opens interesting perspectives on the distribution of Arthurian literature in Wallonia. (G.G., J.-F.N. & G.P.)

17 GIRARD, Robin William, "Simulation and Dissimulation in the *Folie Tristan* d'Oxford," *Neophil*, 99 (2015), 539–52.

Girard analyses the *Folie Tristan* in MS Douce d. 6 in the Bodleian Library in Oxford in conjunction with Béroul's *Roman de Tristan*, the *Roman de Tristan* by Thomas d'Angleterre and the Berne *Folie Tristan*. The madness of Tristan is read in light of Baudrillard's theory of simulation. The author argues that when Tristan displays the symptoms of madness in the Oxford *Folie Tristan*, the distance between Tristan's original state and the simulated state approaches zero.

18 GOODMAN, Barbara A., "Women's Wounds in Middle English Romances," in *Wounds and Wound Repair in Medieval Culture*, ed. Larissa TRACY and Kelly DEVRIES. Amsterdam: Brill/Rodopi, 2015, pp. 544–71.

B.G. studies patterns of sexual transgression, the loss of voice and societal suspicions in Middle English romances in which social tensions are aroused by ungoing sexual transgressions and ensuing punitive wounds. These patterns reveal a society in disrepair. B.G. elaborates on the *Alliterative Morte Arthur*, several of Chaucer's romances, Gower and *The Awntyrs of Arthur.*

19 HILLENBRAND VARELA, Sarah, "Origins of Misfortune. Sympathetic Magic and the Transference of Animality in Thüring von Ringoltingen's *Melusine* (1456)," *Neophil*, 99 (2015), 271–85.

The author argues that the intersection of animals and magic in *Melusine* serves the text's aim of educating its readers about moral behaviour. She first discusses the medieval tradition of interpreting the characteristics of animals in a moral manner. The concept of "sympathetic magic" is then used to analyse the examples of the convergence of animals and magical transference of their qualities in the *Melusine.*

20 LÖFSTEDT, Leena, "Notes on the Beginnings of Law French," *RPh*, 68 (2014), 285–337.

It is well known, Löfstedt states, that the Norman conquerors introduced their own language into England´s law and administration. This, however, obscures the fact that at the time of the Conquest, French was not used in legal writing on the Continent, and that, as a consequence, French legal writing was "born" in England. Based on a selection of texts spanning more than two centuries, Löfstedt studies "the early development of Law French, the creation of its vocabulary, some cha-racteristic features of its grammar, and the coexistence and function of the language used in creating it" (p. 289). Tristran´s readiness to wage a judicial battle, for instance, is briefly discussed from a legal perspective (p. 320) as is the use of the verb *arenare* (Old French *araisnier* 'to arraign') in Béroul´s *Romance of Tristran* (p. 326).

21 MARVIN, Julia, "Latinity and vernacularity in the Tradition of Geoffrey of Monmouth. Text, Apparatus and readership," *The Medieval Chronicle*, 9 (2014), 1–41.

J.M. examines the Latinity and vernacularity of several works in the Brut tradition: the *Historia regum Britanniae*, Wace's *Roman de Brut*, Laȝamon's

Brut, the Anglo-Norman prose *Brut* chronicle, and Robert Mannying's *Story of England*. She considers the role of Latin in the manuscripts as well as the evidence for what their authors and scribes thought appropriate or necessary for a vernacular work. Finally she suggests how the evidence may affect our views of the significance of vernacular translation in England as well as the role of the Brut tradition in the spread of vernacular literacy.

22 MIERKE, Gesine, "Genealogie und Intertextualität. Zu Wolframs von Eschenbach *Parzival* und Wirnts von Grafenberg *Wigalois*," *ABäG*, 74 (2015), 180–200.

Der Beitrag untersucht den genealogischen Zusammenhang zwischen Wolframs *Parzival* und Wirnts *Wigalois*. Genealogie wird als textverbindendes und -übergreifendes Konzept verstanden, das Bezüge zwischen den Romanen herstellt. In beiden Texten werden die Themen Verwandtschaft und Genealogie paradigmatisch durchgespielt. Unter dieser Prämisse erscheint das Herrschaftskonzept im *Wigalois* als Gegenentwurf zum Gralskönigtum Wolframs.

23 REYNAERT, Joris, "Tekst en opvoering van de abele spelen. Het kopieerwerk in het handschrift-Van Hulthem en de geïntendeerde voorstellingen," *SpL*, 56 (2014), 453–75.

"In the Van Hulthem manuscript (ca. 1407), the only document in which the so-called abele spelen, four very early courtly secular plays have survived, each of these plays is followed by a farce (sotternie), with which it clearly constitutes a pair, as in each case the sotternie is already announced in the rubric introducing the abel spel. The serious play and the sotternie are often also textually linked by means of a transitional passage at the end of the abel spel, in which the audience is directly addressed and informed of the fact that a farce will follow. It has been justly argued by Hans van Dijk that these links must have been added for the purpose of a specific performance and do not, as such, indicate that the pairs of serious play and ensuing farce were originally conceived as a unit at the same time. Van Dijk, and others meanwhile, have also advanced that not only these transitional passages, but other passages as well in which the audience is addressed directly, mainly the prologues and the concluding lines spoken by a 'last' character in the serious plays, may well be later additions. This view is challenged here. A close examination of the possible arguments pro and against leads to the conclusion that there is no reason to doubt the authenticity of these addresses to the public and – as a consequence – to discard them as representatives of the originally intended form and tenor of the plays." (J.R.)

24 RICHMOND, Andrew M., "'The broken shippus he ther fonde.' Shipwrecks and the Human Costs of Investment Capital in Middle English Romance," *Neophil*, 99 (2015), 315–33.

Focusing on *Sir Amadace*, the article investigates the seashore in Middle English romance as a source of perilous and problematic material bounty. The ship-wreck is a source of capital, while it is also a site of human suffering. The author looks at legal and historical records, as well as comparing the shipwreck in *Sir Amadace* to those in the romance *Emaré* and the ones in Chaucer's and Gower's versions of the Constance-narrative (Chaucer's *Man of Law's Tale*).

25 TRACY, Larissa, "'Into the hede, throw the helme and creste'. Head Wounds and a Question of Kingship in the *Stanzaic Morte Arthur*," in *Wounds and Wound Repair in Medieval Culture / Explorations in Medieval Culture 1*, ed. Larissa TRACY and Kelly DEVRIES. Amsterdam: Brill/Rodopi, 2015, pp. 496–518.

The proliferation of head wounds throughout the Stanzaic *Morte Arthur* marks the progression of the narrative towards its end. Lancelot's wounds heal, but ignite the events that lead to Gawain's three-fold head wound, from which he eventually dies. Gawain's death foreshadows the final killing blow inflicted on Arthur by his own kin. Embedded in this progression of wounds is a poignant criticism of unstable kingship and the effects of decapitating the State. L.T. argues that while Richard II may have governed badly the author of the Stanzaic *Morte Arthur* potentially questioned the methods of removing him.

26 VERGAUWEN, David, "Wagner en Brussel. Over Henri La Fontaines wagnerverering en haar banden met de Brusselse culturele wereld (1870–1900)," *Belgisch Tijdschrift voor Filologie en Geschiedenis/Revue Belge de Philologie et d'Histoire*, 92 (2014), 1173–210.

"Peu après la mort de Richard Wagner en 1883, Bruxelles se développait et devenait, grâce au théâtre de la Monnaie, une des plus importantes scènes wagnériennes en dehors de l'Allemagne. Les wagnériens bruxellois se réunissaient dans le cadre d'une association qui avait pour but la propagation de l'œuvre wagnérienne. Le wagnérisme constituait un courant sous-jacent dans les milieux maçonniques, socialistes et symbolistes dès les années 1880. Le président de l'Association wagnérienne, Henri La Fontaine, était à la fois franc-maçon et socialiste. Bon nombre de membres de l'Association étaient actifs dans le monde culturel en tant que chef d'orchestre, chanteur, écrivain, homme d'État ou artiste. En tant qu'administrateur de ce réseau ramifié, La Fontaine entretenait de nombreux contacts avec des wagnériens étrangers, ce qui fit que Bruxelles prit les devants dans la propagation de l'œuvre wagnérienne au sein du monde francophone. À Bruxelles, le wagnérisme était le domaine d'une élite, bourgeoise, intellectuelle et francophone qui ne partageait pas l'intérêt que portaient les wagnériens flamands au nationalisme. Cette étude de réseau cherche non seulement à montrer qui était actif au sein de la scène wagnérienne à Bruxelles, mais aussi de quelle façon le wagnérisme était compris par les membres de ce réseau." (D.V.)

27 VONDENHOFF, Chloé, "Een leeuw met menselijke trekjes," *Madoc*, 29 (2015), 2–10.

The article compares the characterisation of the lion in two episodes in Chrétien de Troyes' *Yvain* with that in its translations in Middle High German, Old Norse, Old Swedish and Middle English. Where Chrétien depicts the lion in human (and feudal) terms, the lion in the translations seems to behave more like a dog. The differences are due to conscious decisions on the part of the translators and are not an indication of lesser quality.

28 WOOD, Lucas, "The Ethics of Election in the *Queste del Saint Graal*," *NML*, 15 (2015), 183–224.

Galaad (Galahad), the saintly hero of the thirteenth-century Old French *Queste del Saint Graal*, is from one perspective an abstract Christ-figure whose actions and meaning are predetermined by divine providence and allegorical interpretation. However, throughout Galaad's Grail quest, the romance also cultivates an antithetical resistance to totalizing allegoresis. It insists that the hero's exploits and their sacred significance are contingent on his ethical agency and therefore on a personal virtue that remains constantly at stake, especially in the readerly activity of negotiating between the material surface of the world (and the text) and its possible meanings. The *Queste* thus uses Galaad to emplot, in a way characteristic of fictional romance narrative, the theological aporia of divine grace's coexistence with human free will. (L.W.)

III Reviews

29 BIESHEUVEL, Ingrid, and John RABOU, *Ferguut, de ridder met het Witte Schild*. Rijswijk: De vier windstreken, 2014, 88 p.

Rev. by LENTEREN, Pjotr van, *Madoc*, 29 (2015), 54–56.

30 CALIN, William, *The Lily and the Thistle. The French Tradition and the Older Literature of Scotland – Essays in Criticism*. Toronto: U of Toronto P, 2014, 413 p. (cf. *BIAS*, LXVI, 2014, 566).

Rev. by DOUGLAS, Blaise, *Moyen Âge, revue d'histoire et de philologie*, 120 (2014), 784–85.

31 *Chances du roman. Charmes du mythe. Versions et subversions du mythe dans la fiction francophone depuis 1950*, ed. Marie-Hélène BOBLET. Paris: Presses Sorbonne Nouvelle, 2013, 220 p.

Rev. by OLAH, Myriam, *Les Lettres Romanes*, 68 (2014), 669–75.

32 *Chaucer in Context. A Golden Age of English Poetry*, ed. Gerald MORGAN. Oxford / Bern / Berlin / Brussels / Frankfurt / New York / Vienna: Peter Lang, 2012, 307 p.

Rev. by YVERNAULT, Martine, *Moyen Âge, revue d'histoire et de philologie*, 120 (2014), 493–95.

33 Christie's Auction House, *Valuable Manuscripts and Printed Books. Auction Catalogue*. London: Christie's Auction House, 2014.

Rev. by DUBOIS, A., *Script*, 69 (2015), 71.

34 *Cloches et horloges dans les textes médiévaux*, ed. Fabienne POMEL. Rennes: P. U. Rennes, 2012, 314 p.

Rev. by VISSIÈRE, Laurent, *Moyen Âge, revue d'histoire et de philologie*, 120 (2014), 490–91.

35 CRAHAY, Isolde, *Aux sources féériques du Conte du Graal. Peronnik l'idiot et Perceval le nice*. Berne: Peter Lang, 2013, 441 p. (cf. *BIAS*, LXVI, 2014, 745).

Rev. by BERTHELOT, Anne, *Moyen Âge, revue d'histoire et de philologie*, 121 (2015), 189–91.

36 DE LORRIS, Guillaume, and Jean DE MEUN, *Le Roman de la Rose*, ed. Armand STRUBEL. Paris: Classiques, 2012, 139 p. Recherches littéraires médiévales, 10.

Rev. by VALENTINI, Andrea, *MA*, 120 (2014), 518–20.

37 EIFLER, Matthias, Christoph MACKERT, and Michael STOLZ, "Handschriftenfunde zur Literatur des Mittelalters, 220. Beitrag. Leipziger Handschriftenfunde I. Ein neu aufgefundenes Fragment von Wolframs 'Parzival' aus Naumburg," *ZfdA*, 143 (2014), 306–32.

Rev. by BACHER, R., *Script*, 69 (2015), 35.

38 *Essays on the Lancelot of Yale 229*, ed. Elizabeth MORE WILLINGHAM. Turnhout: Brepols, 2007, 144 p.

Rev. by SZKILNIK, Michelle, *MA*, 121 (2015), 254–58.

39 FABRY-TEHRANCHI, Irène, "La représentation du règne d'Arthur dans le manuscrit enluminé du *Brut* en prose, Londres, Lambeth Palace 6 (c.1480)," in *The Medieval Chronicle 9*, ed. Erik KOOPER. Amsterdam: Rodopi, 2014, pp. 117–60. (cf. *BIAS*, LXVII, 2015, 7).

Rev. by VAN DEN ABEELE, B., *Script*, 69 (2015), 57–58.

40 *Finden – Gestalten – Vermittlen. Schreibprozesse und ihre Brechungen in der mittelalterlichen Überliefering*, ed. Eckart Conrad LUTZ, Susanne KÖBELE, and Klaus RIDDER. Berlin: Freiburger Colloquium, 2012, 664 p.

Rev. by LANGBROEK, Erika, *ABäG*, 74 (2015), 265–73.

41 FROISSART, Jean, *L'Épinette amoureuse*, transl. Nathalie BRAGANTINI-MAILLARD. Paris: Classiques Garnier, 2014, 191 p. Moyen Âge en traduction, 1.

Rev. by LAGOMARSINI, Claudio, *Moyen Âge, revue d'histoire et de philologie*, 121 (2015), 204–05.

42 HALSALL, Guy, *Worlds of Arthur. Facts and fictions of the Dark Ages*. Oxford: Oxford UP, 2013, 384 p. (cf. *BIAS*, LXVI, 2014, 339)

Rev. by RHYS, Guto, *Mededelingen van de Stichting A.G. van Hamel voor Keltische Studies*, 65 (2015), 10–11.

43 HOFFMANN, Ulrich, *Arbeit an der Literatur. Zur Mythizität der Artusromane Hartmanns von Aue*. Berlin: Akademie Verlag, 2012, 401 p. Beiträge zu einer kulturwissenschaftlichen Mediävistik, 2. (cf. *BIAS*, LXVI, 2014, 42).

Rev. by CLASSEN, Albrecht, *ABäG*, 74 (2015), 253–55.

44 *Image et Images du Moyen Âge. Mélanges en l'honneur de Jacques Charles Lemaire*, ed. Alain GOLDSCHLÄGER. Orléans: Éditions Paradigme, 2014, 186 p.

Rev. by GUENOVA, V., *Script*, 69 (2015), 58–59.

45 KESTEMONT, Mike, *Het gewicht van de auteur. Stylometrische auteursherkenning in Middelnederlandse literatuur*. Gent: Koninklijke Academie voor Nederlandse Taal- en Letterkunde, 2013, 342 p. Studies op het gebied van de oudere Nederlandse letterkunde, 5.

Rev. by VAN DRIEL, Joost, *SpL*, 57 (2015), 83–85.

46 *La Formule au Moyen Âge*, ed. Élise LOUVIOT. Turnhout: Brepols, 2012, 362 p.

Rev. by CACOUROS, M., *Script*, 69 (2015), 43–44.
Rev. by MORRISON, Stephen, *Moyen Âge, revue d'histoire et de philologie*, 120 (2014), 507–508.

47 *La Mort le Roi Artu (The Death of Arthur) from the old French Lancelot of Yale 229*, ed. Elizabeth MORE WILLINGHAM. Turnhout: Brepols, 2008, ix-332 p. The Illustrated Lancelot Prose, 1.

Rev. by SZKILNIK, Michelle, *MA*, 121 (2015), 254–58.

48 *La Queste del Saint Graal (The Quest of the Holy Grail) from the old French Lancelot of Yale 229*, ed. Elizabeth MORE WILLINGHAM. Turnhout: Brepols, 2012, xviii + 344 p. The Illustrated Prose Lancelot, 3.

Rev. by SZKILNIK, Michelle, *MA*, 121 (2015), 254–58.

49 *Le Moyen Âge en musique. Interprétations, transpositions, inventions*, ed. Élisabeth GAUCHER-REMOND. Rennes: P.U. Rennes, 2013, 157 p. (cf. *BIAS*, LXVI, 2014, 194.222).

Rev. by MUSSOU, Amandine, *MA*, 121 (2015), 220–22.

50 *Les translations d'Ovide au Moyen Âge. Actes de la journée d'études internationale à la Bibliothèque royale de Belgique le 4 décembre 2008*, ed. An FAEMS, Virginie MINET-MAHY, and Colette VAN COOLPUT-STORMS. Louvain-la-Neuve: Université catholique de Louvain, 2011, 317 p.

Rev. by BAKER, Craig, *RBPH*, 92 (2014), 793–97.

51 *Lire en contexte. Enquête sur les manuscrits de fabliaux*, eds. Olivier COLLET, Francis GINGRAS, and Richard TRACHSLER. Montréal: PU Montréal, 2013, 195 p. Études françaises, 48.

Rev. by VELISSARIOU, Alexandra, *MA*, 121 (2015), 249–51.

52 *Math uab Mathonwy. The fourth branch of the Mabinogi*, ed. Ian HUGHES. Dublin: Dublin Institute for Advanced Studies, 2013, cxvi + 154 p.

Rev. by BRAND-DIJKSTRA, Linus, *Mededelingen van de Stichting A.G. van Hamel voor Keltische Studies*, 74 (2014), 5–6.

53 *Medieval & Renaissance Manuscripts. Auction Catalogue*, ed. Sotheby's Auction House. London: Sotheby's Auction House, 2014.

Rev. by DUBOIS, A., *Script*, 69 (2015), 71–73.

54 MUSARRA, Franco, *L'antiqua damigella. Dell'ironia nell'Orlando Furioso*. Firenze: Franco Cesati editore, 2013, 273 p. Resoconti di Letteratura Italiana, 8.

Rev. by GROOTVELD, Emma, *LR*, 68 (2014), 619–22.

55 PAVLEVSKI, Joanna, "Une esthétique du motif de la femme-serpent. Recherches ontologiques et picturales sur Mélusine au XVe siècle," in *L'Humain et l'Animal dans la France médiévale (XIIe-XVe s.)/Human and Animal in Medieval France (12th-15th c.)*, ed. Irène FABRY-TEHRANCHI and Anna RUSSAKOFF. Amsterdam / New York: Rodopi, 2014, pp. 73–94.

Rev. by VAN DEN ABEELE, B., *Script*, 69 (2015), 96.

56 *Perceforest. Cinquième Partie*, ed. Gilles ROUSSINEAU. Genève: Droz, 2012, 2 vol., I: vii-clxxii + 1–701, II: 702–1328, ill., index. p. Textes littéraires français, 615. (cf. *BIAS*, LXV, 2013, 676).

Rev. by FERLAMPIN ACHER, Christine, *MA*, 120 (2014), 540–43.
Rev. by PALUMBO, G., *Script*, 69 (2015), 97.

57 *Pour un nouveau répertoire des mises en prose. Roman, chanson de geste, autres genres*, ed. Maria COLOMBO TIMELLI, Barbara FERRARI, and Anne SCHOYSMAN. Paris: Cla, 2014, 387 p. (cf. *BIAS*, LXVII, 2015, 311).

Rev. by LAMBERT, Adélaïde, *MA*, 121 (2015), 177–80.

58 RADULESCU, Raluca L., *Romance and its Contexts in Fifteenth-Century England. Politics, Piety and Penitence*. Woodbridge: D.S. Brewer, 2013, 252 p. (cf. *BIAS*, LXVI, 2014, 362).

Rev. by NIEVERGELT, M., *Script*, 69 (2015), 102–04.

59 *Shaping Courtliness in Medieval France. Essays in Honour of Matilda Tomaryn Bruckner*, ed. Daniel E. O'SULLIVAN and Laurie SHEPARD. Woodbridge: D.S. Brewer, 2013, 309 p. (cf. *BIAS*, LXVI, 2014, 373).

Rev. by VELISSARIOU, Alexandra, *MA*, 120 (2014), 775–77.

60 Spangenberger, Nina, *Liebe und Ehe in den erzählenden Werken Hartmanns von Aue*. Frankfurt am Main u.a: Lang, 2012, 350 p. Kultur, Wissenschaft, Literatur, 26. (cf. *BIAS*, LXV, 2013, 59).

Rev. by Bayard, Florence, *MA*, 120 (2014), 529–30.

61 Strittmatter, Ellen, *Poetik des Phantasmas. Eine imaginationstheoretische Lektüre der Werke Hartmanns von Aue*. Heidelberg: Universitätsverlag Winter, 2013, 422 p. Studien zur historischen Poetik, 15. (cf. *BIAS*, LXVII, 2015, 151).

Rev. by Andersen-Vinilandicus, Peter H., *MA*, 121 (2015), 188–89.

62 Strohschneider, Peter, *Höfische Textgeschichten*. Über Selbstentwürfe vormoderner *Literatur*. Heidelberg: Universitätsverlag Winter, 2014, 370 p. GRM Beiheft, 55. (cf. *BIAS*, LXVI, 2015, 151).

Rev. by Kreft, A, *Script*, 69 (2015), 119–20.

63 Taylor, Jane H.M., *Rewriting Arthurian Romance in Renaissance France. From Manuscript to Printed Book*. Cambridge: Brewer, 2014. (cf. *BIAS*, LXVII, 2015, 414).

Rev. by Marchal, Matthieu, *RBPH*, 92 (2014), 812–14.

64 *Texte et contre-texte pour la période pré-moderne*, ed. Nelly Labere. Paris-Pessac: Ausonius Éditions-De Boccard, 2013, 256 p. (cf. *BIAS*, LXVI, 2014, 260).

Rev. by Bennet, Philip E., *RBPH*, 92 (2014), 799–801.
Rev. by Tabard, Laetitia, *MA*, 121 (2015), 269–71.

65 Venning, Timothy, *The kings and queens of Wales*. Gloucestershire: Amberley Publishing, 2012, 224 p.

Rev. by Lemmen-Friedrich, Karianne, *Mededelingen van de Stichting A.G. van Hamel voor Keltische Studies*, 64 (2014), 11–12.

Deutschland und Österreich

Bibliographie für 2015 zusammengestellt von Nathanael Busch, Cora Dietl, Markus Greulich, Angelica Rieger, Daniel David Weis und Lena Zudrell

I Texte

66 DENOYELLE, Corinne, "Un nouveu fragment inédit du Merlin en prose," *ZrP*, 131 (2015), 3–12.

Die Edition eines Fragments (Doppel-Pergamentblatt) des Merlin-Prosaromans aus dem 14. Jh. der T. Fisher Rare Books Library (Toronto), das als Unterfütterung eines Kommentarbands zum Sextus Liber decretalium Papst Bonifaz' VIII. (16. Jh.) diente, gibt in nordfranzösisch-pikardischer Sprache Uthers Hochzeit mit Igerne und deren Schwangerschaft wieder (Micha: Handschriftenfamilie x3 nach CDG). (A.R.)

67 DER STRICKER, *Daniel von dem blühenden Tal*, hg. von Michael RESLER. 3. Aufl., Berlin / Boston: De Gruyter, 2015, 322 p. Altdeutsche Textbibliothek, 92.

Während die in den 1980er Jahren entdeckte Hs. b die umfassend neubearbeitete zweite Auflage des *Daniel* von 1996 erforderlich machte, hat sich seither in textkritischer Hinsicht wenig verändert. Die grundlegende Neuerung der vorliegenden dritten Auflage ist stattdessen der zweite Apparat, ein Stellenkommentar mit sprachlichen, syntaktischen und lexikalischen Erläuterungen. Damit soll vor allem für ungeübte Leser Abhilfe bei potentiellen Verständnisschwierigkeiten geboten werden. Unübliche Satzkonstruktionen und Begriffe werden dort erläutert, wenn die Ermittlung der entsprechenden Lexeme in den mittelhochdeutschen Wörterbüchern problematisch sein könnte. Kurze grammatikalische Erklärungen und Übersetzungsvorschläge stellen vor allem für Studierende eine hilfreiche Ergänzung des bestehenden Apparats dar und sollen die Lektüre des Daniel wesentlich erleichtern. Zudem bietet die Edition eine aktualisierte Auswahlbibliographie. (L.Z.)

https://doi.org/10.1515/9783110467499-040

II Untersuchungen

68 BÄRNTHALER, Günter, "Parzival, Gawan und Feirefiz. Unterhaltung und Entlastung im Lese- und Literaturunterricht," in *Literatur-Erlebnisse zwischen Mittelalter und Gegenwart. Aktuelle didaktische Konzepte und Reflexionen zur Vermittlung deutschsprachiger Texte*. Unter Mitarbeit von Andrea HOFMEISTER-WINTER, hg. von Wernfried HOFMEISTER und Ylva SCHWINGHAMMER. Frankfurt am Main: Peter Lang, 2015, pp. 225–50.

Der Beitrag verfolgt das Ziel, Wolframs *Parzival* als "Teil eines alltäglichen Lese- und Literaturunterrichts zu etablieren", um "die mangelnde Lesekompetenz männlicher Jugendlicher zu beheben" (225). Der *Parzival* verbindet das Abenteuerliche mit dem Komischen und entspricht so besonders den Lesebedürfnissen von Burschen. Der Verf. schlägt zur Beschäftigung mit dem Komischen im *Parzival* fünf Phasen forschenden Lernens vor. (L.Z.)

69 BERTELSMEIER-KIERST, Christa, und Benedikt KLEIN, "Die Krakauer "Wigalois"-Fragmente (q). Eine weitere Handschrift im Umkreis der Cgm 19-Gruppe?" *ZfdA*, 144 (2015), 150–77.

Die Krakauer "Wigalois"-Fragmente werden erstmals ausführlich in den Blick genommen. Anhand paläografischer und schreibsprachlicher Charakteristika sowie der Einrichtung des Fragments konnte eine Verbindung zur sog. Cgm 19–Gruppe wahrscheinlich gemacht werden. Ein diplomatischer Abdruck des Fragments rundet den Beitrag ab. (D.D.W.)

70 BESAMUSCA, Bart, und Frank BRANDSMA, "État presènt. Arthurian Literature in Middle Dutch," *JIAS*, 3.1 (2015), 4–31.

Bestandsaufnahme der Forschung zur mittelniederländischen Artusliteratur, in welcher zunächst die Texte mitsamt Ausgaben und Übersetzungen genannt werden. Daran schließt sich ein Überblick zu den wichtigsten Arbeiten der letzten Jahre an, die geprägt sind einerseits von den Möglichkeiten digitaler Medien andererseits von einer europäisch-komparatistischen Perspektive. Zuletzt umreißt ein Ausblick Forschungsdesiderate. (N.B.)

71 BIRKHAN, Helmut, "*Iwein* auf dem Papiertheater," in *Historische Räume. Erzählte Räume. Gestaltete Räume*, hg. von Georg HOFER, Robert SCHÖLLER und Gabriel VIEHHAUSER. Wien: Praesens, 2015, pp. 267–307.

Eine Ausgabe von Rudolf Heinrich Greinz' Schauspiel *Iwein der Ritter mit dem Löwen* (1890) mit Überlegungen zur Darstellung auf dem Papptheater. Die Eingriffe in die Handlung des *Iwein* stellen sich im Vergleich mit der *Iwein*-Oper August Klugharts (1878) und Felicitas Hoppes *Iwein Löwenritter* (2008) als gattungs-, zielgruppen- und epochenbedingt heraus. (C.D.)

72 BLEULER, Anna Kathrin, *Essen – Trinken – Liebe. Kultursemiotische Untersuchungen zur Poetik des Alimentären in Wolframs 'Parzival'*. Tübingen: Narr/Francke/attempto, 2015, 351 p. Bibliotheca Germanica, 62.

Eine Besonderheit von Wolframs *Parzival* gegenüber Chrétien ist die Rolle, die dem Alimentären in seinem Roman zuwächst. Ausgehend von der bisherigen Forschung entfaltet die Verf.in die komplexen kulturellen und poetologischen Kontexte, in denen dieses Thema eingebettet ist. Neben differenzierten semiotischen Überlegungen bilden kulturgeschichtliche Ansätze zur Nahrungsaufnahme, insbesondere aber zum Konnex von Minne und Nahrung, die Basis der Arbeit. Diese werden im Anschluss auf unterschiedlichen Ebenen für ein vertiefendes Verständnis der Interaktion von Essen und Liebe innerhalb des *Parzival* fruchtbar gemacht und führen schließlich zum spezifischen Umgang mit Sprachbildern sowie zur Poetik des Textes. (M.G.)

73 BLEUMER, Hartmut, "Zum Begriffsproblem in der germanistischen Mediävistik – am Beispiel von Wolframs *Parzival*," in *Autorschaft und Autorität in den romanischen Literaturen des Mittelalters*, hg. von Susanne FRIEDE und Michael SCHWARZE. Berlin / Boston: De Gruyter, 2015, pp. 13–40.

Am Beispiel des *Parzivals* Wolframs von Eschenbach wird Autorschaft als komplexe Form der Metapher verstanden. Sie ist Ergebnis und Voraussetzung einer Erzählpraxis, die auf der narrativen Verfasstheit von Schriftkulturen beruht. In ihr sind die metonymisch getrennten Positionen von Autor und Erzähler aufeinander angewiesen. (N.B.)

74 BÖHN, Andreas, "Mittelalterrezeption im frühen Film," in *Das Mittelalter des Historismus. Formen und Funktionen in Literatur und Kunst, Film und*

Technik, hg. von Mathias HERWEG und Stefan KEPPLER-TASAKI. Würzburg: Königshausen & Neumann, 2015, pp. 347–63.

Der Beitrag fokussiert die Rezeption mittelalterlicher Stoffe im Film zwischen 1895 und 1927. Damit geraten insbesondere diejenigen cinematographischen Zeugnisse in den Blick, die von den heute bekannten überdeckt werden. Der Verf. stellt insbesondere die Bedeutung der zum großen Teil unbekannten Kurzfilme für die Entwicklung der späteren Langfilme heraus. (M.G.)

75 BREEZE, Andrew, "The Name of King Arthur," *Mediaevistik*, 28 (2015), 23–35.

Der Beitrag konzentriert sich auf die Belege über den historischen König Artus. Dabei geht es zunächst um die grundsätzliche Frage nach Artus' Historizität. Anschließend wendet sich Breeze den Quellen zu, die Artus' Existenz wahrscheinlich machen. Breeze Schlussfolgerung lautet: "Arthur really existed" (S. 33). (D.D.W.)

76 BRÜGGEN, Elke, "*swie ez ie kom, ir munt was rôt.* Zur Handhabung der *descriptio* weiblicher Körperschönheit im *Parzival* Wolframs von Eschenbach," in *Literarischer Stil. Mittelalterliche Dichtung zwischen Konvention und Innovation. XXII. Anglo-German Colloquium Düsseldorf*, hg. von Elizabeth ANDERSEN, Ricarda BAUSCHKE-HARTUNG, Nicola MCLELLAND und Silvia REUVEKAMP. Berlin / Boston: De Gruyter, 2015, pp. 391–411.

Charakteristisch für die Beschreibung weiblicher Körperschönheit in Wolframs Parzival ist der selektive Modus, der dem weiß-roten Farbklang besondere Relevanz verleiht. Anhand der Beschreibung der Jeschute wird gezeigt, wie die als schön geltende Kombination aus Weiß und Rot in epische Zusammenhänge gebracht wird, die auf gestörte Ordnungen und Gewalt verweisen. (L.Z.)

77 BRUNNER, Horst, *Mittelalterliche Literatur lesen. Eine Einführung*. Stuttgart: Reclam, 2016, 336 p. RUB, 17688.

Obwohl es der Titel nahe legt: Das ist keine Anthologie, sondern, das verrät erst der Untertitel: Eine Einführung, gut lesbar geschrieben für interessierte Laien oder Studierende. Sie bietet einen Überblick über bekannte Texte und empfiehlt deren Lektüre in Themenblöcken; der Artus-Block umfasst Hartmanns von Aue *Erec* und *Iwein* (Kapitel I, 15–46) und Wolframs von Eschenbach *Parzival* (Kapitel VI, 137–177). Im Hartmann-Kapitel werden der Autor, beide Romane und deren Inhalte vorgestellt, ihr französischer Ursprung angesprochen, ebenso das Prinzip des Artus-Romans und die Protagonisten werden vorgestellt. Besonderheiten und Vergleiche stützen einige Zitate in neuhochdeutscher Übersetzung. Das Wolfram-Kapitel folgt dem gleichen Muster. (A.R.)

78 BUHR, Christian, "*Îsôt nâch Îsôte*. Lyrisches im *Tristan* Gottfrieds von Straßburg," *AStnSpr*, 252 (2015), 1–22.

Ob Gottfried von Straßburg auch als Lyriker arbeitete, ist in der Forschung umstritten. Dagegen verdichten sich in Tristans Lobpreis der Isolde (8257–8304) Formen literarischer Kommunikation, die sich auf zeitgenössische Aspekte lyrischen Dichtens beziehen. Es handelt sich nicht um einen veritablen Frauenpreis, sondern um dessen zitathafte Verarbeitung. (N.B.)

79 BUNTE, Iris, *Der Tristan Gottfrieds von Straßburg und die Tradition der lateinischen Rhetorik. Tropen, Figuren und Topoi im höfischen Roman*. Marburg: Tectum, 2014, 115 p. Wissenschaftliche Beiträge aus dem Tectum Verlag. Reihe Literaturwissenschaft, 34.

Gottfried von Straßburg zeigt sich im *Tristan* als geschulter Rhetoriker. Die Arbeit stellt den Redeschmuck systematisch vor. Sortiert nach Tropen, Figuren (Sinn-, Wort-, Syntaktisch) und Topik werden knapp 40 Phänome jeweils aus der lateinisch-rhetorischen Tradition – meist Matthäus von Vendôme – erklärt und dann die Verwendung bei Gottfried aufgezeigt. Die Einleitung informiert zur Rhetorik und zum Bildungshintergrund von Gottfried sowie zur Stofftradition des Tristan im Mittelalter. (N.B.)

80 BÜRKLE, Susanne, "Der Meister-Diskurs in der volkssprachlichen Literatur um 1200. Handwerkliche Kompetenz und artistische Valorisierung," in *Literarischer Stil. Mittelalterliche Dichtung zwischen Konvention und Innovation. XXII. Anglo-German Colloquium Düsseldorf*, hg. von Elizabeth ANDERSEN, Ricarda BAUSCHKE-HARTUNG, Nicola MCLELLAND und Silvia REUVEKAMP. Berlin / Boston: De Gruyter, 2015, pp. 119–39.

Während jüngere Studien über den Meisterschaftsdiskurs vornehmlich Lyrik und Spruchdichtung in den Blick nehmen, konzentriert sich die Verf. auf epische Texte. Ausgehend von Kuhns Arbeiten wird der interartifizielle

Aspekt von Meisterschaft im Tristan analysiert. Als Spezifikum des Textes wird der "forcierte Diskurs von Meisterschaft und artes, der in der Figur Tristans kulminiert" (128) genannt. (L.Z.)

81 CHASE, Carol J., "Un manuscrit mesconnëu de l'Estoire del Saint Graal. Bourg-en-Bresse, Médiathèque Vailland 55. Le programme paratextuel," *JIAS*, 3.1 (2015), 72–101.

Die untersuchte Handschrift enthält eine Abschrift der *Estoire del Saint Graal*, die mit eng auf den Text abgestimmten Miniaturen versehen wurde (zahlreiche Abbildungen). Oft findet sich eine Miniatur zu Beginn eines Abschnitts und wird von einer standardisiert formulierten Rubrik begleitet. Die Rubriken sind nicht bloß Bildbeschreibung, sondern bieten als Lektürehilfe Orientierung. (N.B.)

82 CHEN, Yen-Chun, *Ritter, Minne und der Gral. Komplementarität und Kohärenzprobleme im "Rappoltsteiner Parzifal"*. Heidelberg: Winter, 2015, 370 p. Studien zur Historischen Poetik, 18.

Nach ausführlicher Darstellung der narrativen Linienführung in Chrétiens *Perceval*, Wolframs *Parzival* und den ersten drei Fortsetzungen des *Perceval* untersucht die Verf. die Komposition des *Rappoltsteiner Parzifal*. Der Text sei auf eine Erzeugung von Widersprüchen ausgerichtet; Brüche zwischen den Vorlagen würden nicht harmonisiert, sondern zum Teil sogar exponiert. Zugleich werde die Komplementarität von Minne- und Gralsthematik, von Irdischem und Göttlichem betont: Die Unergründlichkeit der Gnade Gottes und der Gnade der Minnedame werden ineinander verschränkt; menschliches Streben und göttlicher Wille kreuzen sich ständig. (C.D.)

83 CLASON, Christopher R., "A "Courtly" Reading of Natural Metaphors. Animals und Performance in Gottfried's "Tristan"," *Mediaevistik*, 28 (2015), 141–59.

Der Beitrag geht der Frage nach, inwiefern der Hirsch, der Eber und die Hunde in Gottfrieds 'Tristan' Bedeutungsträger sind. Clasons These ist, dass die Tiere sowohl auslegungsbedürftig sind als auch ihre Darstellung "forges connections between the individual and the universe the text presents" (S. 142). (D.D.W.)

84 Classen, Albrecht, "Die Herausforderungen des Begriffs *minne* im Translationsprozess," *Mediaevistik*, 27 (2014), 45–58.

Classen diskutiert anhand von Liedern Walthers v. d. Vogelweide und Wolframs 'Titurel' die Schwierigkeiten des *minne*-Begriffs für den modernen Übersetzer. *minne* bei Walther und Wolfram bedeutet nicht zwingend eine sexuell konnotierte Liebe, sondern ist sowohl als soziale als auch individuelle Kategorie in der höfischen Welt des Mittelalters zu verstehen. (D.D.W.)

85 *Das Mittelalter des Historismus. Formen und Funktionen in Literatur und Kunst, Film und Technik*, hg. von Mathias Herweg und Stefan Keppler-Tasaki. Würzburg: Königshausen & Neumann, 2015, 435 p.

Dieser Sammelband widmet sich mit dem Humanismus, dem 19. Jahrhundert und dem frühen 20. Jahrhundert in drei Abschnitten drei historischen Zeiträumen und deren Zugriffen auf und ihrer Interaktion mit mittelalterlicher Kunst, Literatur und Geschichtsbildern. Ein ausführliches Vorwort der Herausgeber führt in die Thematik ein und gibt einen Überblick aktueller Forschungspositionen zur Mittelalterrezeption in Geschichtswissenschaften, Kunstgeschichte und Germanistik. Die Beiträge des Bandes ergeben ein weitreichendes Spektrum, das sich von spätmittelalterlicher Handschriftenkultur, Literatur der frühen Neuzeit, des 19. und frühen 20. Jahrhunderts, über Technikkultur bis hin zum Tourismus erstreckt. Der Band ermöglicht damit, unterschiedliche Spektren kulturgeschichtlicher Aneignung und Interaktion nachzuvollziehen. (M.G.)

86 Däumer, Matthias, "'Artus ex machina'. Theatrale (Re-)Mythisierung in Eduard Stuckens Artusdramen," in *Das Mittelalter des Historismus. Formen und Funktionen in Literatur und Kunst, Film und Technik*, hg. von Mathias Herweg und Stefan Keppler-Tasaki. Würzburg: Königshausen & Neumann, 2015, pp. 295–320.

In seinem Beitrag geht der Verf. zunächst allgemein auf die Mittelalterrezeption um 1900 ein, bevor er auf die in der Forschung verhältnismäßig wenig untersuchten Theaterstücke Stuckens kommt, die im ersten Viertel des 20. Jahrhunderts (zwischen 1901 und 1924) entstanden. Dabei zeichnet er die unterschiedlichen Schaffensphasen ebenso nach wie Konzeption und kulturelle Kontextualisierung der Dramen. (M.G.)

87 DEL DUCA, Patrick, "Vom *Iwein* Hartmanns von Aue zum *Iban* Ulrich Füetrers. Ein Vereinfachungs- und Neu-Gestaltungsprozess," in *Die Bedeutung der Rezeptionsliteratur für Bildung und Kultur der Frühen Neuzeit (1400–1750) III*, hg. von Peter Hvilshøj ANDERSEN-VINILANDICUS und Barbara LAFOND-KETTLITZ. Bern: Peter Lang, 2015, pp. 13–37.

Der Verf. beobachtet drei Tendenzen in Füetrers *Iban* im Vergleich zur Vorlage: zunächst die Tilgung von Spannung, dann der Verzicht auf ideologische Aspekte und schließlich Ulrichs Originalität, sichtbar bspw. in der Bearbeitung der Ginoverentführung. Während Hartmann mit dem Ideal des 'miles christianus' "seinem Publikum einen ethischen Spiegel" (35) vorhält, verkörpert Iban schlicht einen adligen Krieger. (L.Z.)

88 DETMERS, Ines, "Annäherung an das 'temporale Imaginäre'. Christoph Heins 'dekadentes Zeitspiel' (in) *Die Ritter der Tafelrunde*," in *Mittelalterrezeption in der DDR-Literatur*, hg. von Gesine MIERKE und Michael OSTHEIMER. Würzburg: Königshausen & Neumann, 2015, pp. 146–68.

Die Verf. versucht, Heins *Ritter der Tafelrunde* nicht als Wendeliteratur oder als Niedergangsparabel, sondern vor dem Hintergrund des Historikerstreits der 1980er-Jahre als Plädoyer für Modernisierung zu lesen. Ein Vergleich der Behandlung von Zeit bei Hein und in Thomas Malorys *Morte Darthur* lenkt den Blick auf erinnerungspolitische Fragestellungen im Text. (C.D.)

89 DILLIG, Jana, und Sabrina HUFNAGEL, "'Under helm und under schilde'. Inszenierungen von Maskulinität in Kunst und Literatur des Mittelalters," in *Geschichten sehen, Bilder hören. Bildprogramme im Mittelalter*, hg. von Andrea SCHINDLER und Evelyn MEYER. Bamberg: Bamberg University Press, 2015, pp. 157–78.

Eine Reflexion über die Bedeutung von Helmen (und Maskenhelmen) für die Konstruktion von Männlichkeitskonzepten im Mittelalter. Erwähnt werden u.a. Helme im *Erec* und im *Prosa-Lancelot*. (C.D.)

90 DIMPEL, Friedrich Michael, "*Daz safer ime golde*. Der "Parzival"-Prolog zwischen Wiedererzählen und Anderserzählen," *ZfdA*, 144 (2015), 294–324.

Anhand des "Parzival"-Prologs spielt Dimpel das Verhältnis zwischen Wiedererzählung und Anderserzählen durch. Der Sinn der Erzählung wird bei Wolfram im Prolog nicht vorgegeben, sondern offenbart sich in den erzählten Situationen (vgl. S. 313). (D.D.W.)

91 DRAGOUN, Michael, Václav BOK, Kathrin CHLENCH und Michael STOLZ, "Ein neues "Parzival"-Fragment in der Bibliothek des Nationalmuseums Prag (Sammlung Adolf Patera: 1 H A 144)," *ZfdA*, 144 (2015), 77–90.

Das neu entdeckte Fragment eines Doppelblattes aus der Sammlung Patera enthielt ursprünglich 336 Verse, von denen noch 218 vollständig erhalten sind. Stemmatisch gehört das Fragment in die Nähe zur Fassung *G. (D.D.W.)

92 EILERS, Helge, "Sprachbewusstsein und Sprachreflexion bei Hartmann von Aue (Gregorius, Der arme Heinrich, Erec, Iwein)," in *Studien zu Sprache und Stil in alt- und mittelhochdeutscher Literatur*, hg. von Helge EILERS. Frankfurt am Main: Peter Lang Edition, 2015, pp. 115–29.

Eilers zeigt anhand von Sprache und Rhetorik die unterschiedlichen Lebenswelten in den jeweiligen Texten Hartmanns auf. Im "Gregorius" verwendet der Held afrz. Ritterbegriffe, die dem Abt unverständlich bleiben; im "Iwein" ist es die âventiure, die den Waldmensch irritiert; im "Armen Heinrich" eröffnet die Maierstochter ihren Eltern – unter Einfluss des Heiligen Geistes – für Heinrich den Opfertod sterben zu wollen. (D.D.W.)

93 EMING, Jutta, "'unsippiu gesellescaft'. Paradigmen von Freundschaft und Konkurrenz in Hartmanns *Iwein*," in *Freundschaftszeichen. Gesten, Gaben und Symbole von Freundschaft im Mittelalter*, hg. von Marina MÜNKLER, Antje SABLOTNY und Matthias STANDKE. Heidelberg: Winter, 2015, pp. 103–23.

Der Beitrag untersucht die Freundschaft zwischen Iwein und Gawein in ihrem Verhältnis zu Identitätskonstruktionen und Männlichkeitsentwürfen im Roman. Freundschaft und Rivalität, Ebenbürtigkeit und Hierarchie stehen in diesem Verhältnis unverbunden nebeneinander. (C.D.)

94 EMING, Jutta, *Emotionen im Tristan. Untersuchungen zu ihrer Paradigmatik*. Göttingen: V & R unipress, 2015, 234 p. Berliner Mittelalter- und Frühneuzeitforschung, 20.

Der Monographie wird die These vorangestellt, dass Gottfrieds *Tristan* "eine Sonder- und 'Schwellen'-Position zwischen verschiedenen historischen Konventionen der literarischen Darstellung und Beschreibung von Emotionen einnimmt" (7). Dazu gehören Introspektionen auf Figurenebene ebenso wie Reflexionen auf Erzählebene und nach außen gerichtete Formen von Emotionalität. In sieben Kapiteln werden verschiedene Aspekte von Emotionsdarstellungen und Emotionalität behandelt, oft mit einem Seitenblick auf die Bearbeiter des Tristanstoffes vor Gottfried. Dabei werden moderne Emotionstheorien ebenso zu Rate gezogen wie literaturtheoretische Konzepte des paradigmatischen Erzählens und philosophisch-theologische Affektlehren. Während die Verf. bspw. in Bezug auf die Marke-Figur feststellt, dass "über Emotionen eine paradigmatische Ordnung" (59) gestiftet wird, zeigt sich in der Baumgartenszene, dass Tristan und Isolde "auch über das Gewicht ihrer Emotionen [miteinander kommunizieren]" (154). Passend zum fragmentarischen Charakter des Textes endet die Studie ohne Schlusswort, dafür mit einer Analyse zu *trûren*, Abschied und Verlust. (L.Z.)

95 FASBENDER, Christoph, "Schlaflos in Sankt Wendelin. Versuch über die Einbürgerung (1969) von Lily Hohensteins Wolfram-Roman (1943)," in *Mittelalterrezeption in der DDR-Literatur*, hg. von Gesine MIERKE und Michael OSTHEIMER. Würzburg: Königshausen & Neumann, 2015, pp. 218–34.

Lily Hohensteins *Wolfram von Eschenbach* (1943) erschien 1969 unter dem Titel *Die Nächte in Sankt Wendelin* und galt als DDR-Literatur. Der Roman verbindet den Stand der Wolfram-Forschung der 1920/30-er Jahre mit scharfer Kritik an einer schwächlichen Kirche und zynischen Gesellschaftsstrukturen. Das machte ihn für die DDR akzeptabel. (C.D.)

96 FEISTNER, Edith, und Katja PUTZER, "Unbekannte Fragmente des "Jüngeren Titurel" in der Staatlichen Bibliothek Regensburg," *ZfdA*, 144 (2015), 203–12.

Die neu aufgefundenen "Titurel"-Fragmente stammen aus dem "Regensburger Karmeliterkloster" und gehören im Kontext der "Titurel"-Überlieferung wahrscheinlich der Überlieferungsgruppe I an (S. 203). Die Verfasserinnnen liefern eine ausführliche Beschreibung der Fragmente sowie Hintergründe zu deren Trägerbänden sowie einen Abdruck der Fragmente. (D.D.W.)

97 *Freundschaftszeichen. Gesten, Gaben und Symbole von Freundschaft im Mittelalter*, hg. von Marina MÜNKLER, Antje SABLOTNY und Matthias STANDKE. Heidelberg: Winter, 2015, 355 p.

Vgl. Einzeleinträge zu den Beiträgen des Bands.

98 FRIEDE, Susanne, "Die Stimme(n) der Chronik," in *Autorschaft und Autorität in den romanischen Literaturen des Mittelalters*, hg. von Susanne FRIEDE und Michael SCHWARZE. Berlin / Boston: De Gruyter, 2015, pp. 147–67.

In der Brut-Rezeption überlagert die Autorfunktion die Wahrnehmung des Texts deutlich. Dies analysiert die exemplarische Aufzeigung der Dominantsetzung der Autorfunktion und Inszenierung der herrschenden Erzählstimme, ergänzt durch die Hypothese der Herrschaft konkurrierender Stimmen, die Darstellung unterschiedlicher Autorisierungsstrategien, Überlegungen zur diesbezüglichen Rolle der matières (France, Bretagne) und zur Autorität der Handschriften. (A.R.)

99 FUCHS-JOLIE, Stephan, "Metapher und Metonymie bei Wolfram. Überlegungen zum 'Personalstil' im Mittelalter," in *Literarischer Stil. Mittelalterliche Dichtung zwischen Konvention und Innovation. XXII. Anglo-German Colloquium Düsseldorf*, hg. von Elizabeth ANDERSEN, Ricarda BAUSCHKE-HARTUNG, Nicola MCLELLAND und Silvia REUVEKAMP. Berlin / Boston: De Gruyter, 2015, pp. 413–26.

Kennzeichnend für die Werke Wolframs ist ein Zusammenspiel von Metonymien und Metaphern, wodurch Tiefenstrukturen und Oberflächen miteinander verbunden werden. Erst wenn die Bezüge der einzelnen Signifikanten gefunden werden, kann die Wildheit und Gebrochenheit von Wolframs Bildern gebändigt werden. Dabei ist die Simultanität der Signifikanten kein Mittel zur Sinnstiftung des Erzählens, sondern mehr eine "Reflexion auf das 'Wie' des Erzählens einer Geschichte" (424). (L.Z.)

100 FUCHS-JOLIE, Stephan, und Philipp GILLER, "'wie Gahmuret schiet von Belakânen'. Titurel und die Tragödie des Erzählens," in *Tragik vor der Moderne. Literaturwissenschaftliche Analysen*, hg. von Regina TOEPFER und Gyburg RADKE-UHLMANN. Heidelberg: Universitätsverlag Winter, 2015, pp. 27–46.

Am Beispiel des Titurel versuchen die Verf. Begriffe des Tragischen auf einen mittelalterlichen Text anzuwenden, wobei das "Tragische [...] nicht auf der Ebene des Erzählten, auf der Ebene der Handlung und ihrer Figuren zu suchen [ist], sondern auf der Ebene des Erzählens respektive des Erzählers" (28). (L.Z.)

101 *Geschichten sehen, Bilder hören. Bildprogramme im Mittelalter*, hg. von Andrea SCHINDLER und Evelyn MEYER. Bamberg: University of Bamberg Press, 2015, 214 p.

Vgl. Einzeleinträge zu den Beiträgen des Bands.

102 GRUBMÜLLER, Klaus, "*cristallîniu wortelîn.* Gottfrieds Stil und die Aporien der Liebe," in *Literarischer Stil. Mittelalterliche Dichtung zwischen Konvention und Innovation. XXII. Anglo-German Colloquium Düsseldorf*, hg. von Elizabeth ANDERSEN, Ricarda BAUSCHKE-HARTUNG, Nicola MCLELLAND und Silvia REUVEKAMP. Berlin / Boston: De Gruyter, 2015, pp. 179–90.

Der Beitrag stellt drei Forschungsfragen zu Gottfrieds *Tristan* in den Fokus. Zunächst wird nach der Art des Stils gefragt, den Gottfried rühmt, dann danach, ob dieser dabei von seinem eigenen Stilideal spricht und schließlich nach dem Zusammenhang von Sprachauffassung, sprachlicher Praxis und der "gedanklichen Faktur" (181) des Werkes. Der Verf. widerspricht der Lesart, den Preis Hartmanns und das Bligger-Lob als Ironie aufzufassen, und zeigt stattdessen die Aporie des Textes auf, "unbedingte Liebe [...] zu verwirklichen [...] und [...] ein unbezweifelt gültiges (rhetorisches) Ideal [...] zu erreichen" (190). (L.Z.)

103 HAMANN, Christof, und Seraina PLOTKE, "Iwein der Löwenritter. Felicitas Hoppe auf den Spuren Hartmanns von Aue," in *Text + Kritik 207*, hg. von Peer TRILCKE. München: Richard Boorberg Verlag GmbH & Co KG, 2015, pp. 17–25.

Der Aufsatz arbeitet die zentralen Merkmale von Felicitas Hoppes Bearbeitung von Hartmanns "Iwein" heraus. Obwohl sich die Autorin mit ihrem Werk an die Poetik mittelalterlicher Dichter anbindet, präsentiert sie eine moderne Bearbeitung, die als Kinder- und Jugendliteratur konzipiert ist. (D.D.W.)

104 HAMMER, Andreas, "Hartmann von Aue oder Hans Ried? Zum Umgang mit der Text- und Stilkritik des 'Ambraser Erec'," in *Literarischer Stil. Mittelalterliche Dichtung zwischen Konvention und Innovation. XXII. Anglo-German Colloquium Düsseldorf*, hg. von Elizabeth ANDERSEN, Ricarda BAUSCHKE-HARTUNG, Nicola MCLELLAND und Silvia REUVEKAMP. Berlin / Boston: De Gruyter, 2015, pp. 427–48.

Im Beitrag wird gezeigt, dass oftmals nicht bewiesen werden kann, ob der Stil des Ambraser *Erec* Hartmann von Aue oder dem Schreiber und Bearbeiter Hans Ried aus dem 16. Jahrhundert zuzurechnen ist. Dabei werden die zahlreichen Konjekturen der verschiedenen Editionen in den Blick genommen und eine stilistische und inhaltliche Analyse des Mantel-Fragments unternommen. (L.Z.)

105 HANUSCHKIN, Katharina, *Intrigen – Die Macht der Möglichkeiten in der mittelhochdeutschen Epik*. Wiesbaden: Reichert, 2015, 328 p. Trierer Beiträge zu den Historischen Kulturwissenschaften, 16.

Die Verf.in widmet sich in ihrer – aus ihrer Dissertation – hervorgegangenen Monographie dem Motiv der Intrige in höfischen Epen und Romanen vom 12.–14. Jahrhundert. Auf eine knappe Einleitung (1–11) und methodische Reflexion (13–24) folgen im Hauptteil der Arbeit Kapitel, die sich systematisch anhand einzelner Texte mit den unterschiedlichen Ausgestaltungsmöglichkeiten von Intrigenhandlungen sowie deren jeweiliger Funktion für Erzählung und Figurenkonzeption auseinandersetzten. Neben dem 'Nibelungenlied', dem 'Rolandslied' des Pfaffen Konrad und Strickers 'Karl', dem 'Herzog Ernst B', den Troja-Romanen Herborts von Fritzlar und Konrads von Würzburg sowie dem 'Friedrich von Schwaben' widmen sich mehrere Kapitel auch arthurischen Texten: Gottfrieds von Straßburg 'Tristan', Hartmanns von Aue 'Iwein' sowie Heinrichs von dem Türlin 'Diu Crône'. (M.G.)

106 HARTMANN, Heiko, *Einführung in das Werk Wolframs von Eschenbach*. Darmstadt: WBG, 2015, 134 p. Einführung Germanistik.

Dem Prinzip dieser Einführungsreihe folgend, wird in komprimierter Weise Studienanfängern ein schneller Einstieg in das Oeuvre Wolframs von Eschenbach ermöglicht. Auf drei einführende Kapitel, die sich der Epoche, wichtigen Forschungsfragen und der historischen Situierung des Dichters widmen, folgen überblicksartige Kapitel, die Einblick in Thema, Aufbau und Struktur der Lieder, des *Willehalm*, des *Parzival* und des *Titurel* (der hier als "Liebesroman" bezeichnet wird) geben. Eingefügt in die Kapitel sind Bildmaterialien und Grafiken, die sich u. a. der handschriftlichen Überlieferung widmen. Eine Zeittafel am Ende des Buches verortet Dichter und Werk innerhalb des historischen und literarischen Kontexts. (M.G.)

107 HAUSMANN, Albrecht, "Stil als Kommentar. Zur inhaltlichen Funktion des Sprachklangs in Gottfrieds von Straßburg Tristan," in *Literarischer Stil. Mittelalterliche Dichtung zwischen Konvention und Innovation. XXII. Anglo-German Colloquium Düsseldorf*, hg. von Elizabeth ANDERSEN, Ricarda BAUSCHKE-HARTUNG, Nicola MCLELLAND und Silvia REUVEKAMP. Berlin / Boston: De Gruyter, 2015, pp. 205–23.

Die Kontingenz der Tristan-Handlung und die Gerichtetheit im Text sollen als Suggestion verstanden werden, so eine These des Beitrags. Dabei werden die Rezipienten zur Bewertung eines Geschehens aufgefordert, das selbst keinen Sinn erzeugt. Ebenfalls in den Bereich der Rezeptionssteuerung gehört der Sprachklang, der dem Text einen klanglichen Kommentar zur Seite stellt und dadurch betont, "was stimmt und was zusammengehört: Tristan Îsolt, Îsolt Tristan" (223). (L.Z.)

108 HAUSTEIN, Jens, "Vorwärts ins Mittelalter! Rekonstruktion, Ausbau und Funktionalisierung der Wartburg in der zweiten Hälfte des 19. Jahrhunderts," in *Das Mittelalter des Historismus. Formen und Funktionen in Literatur und Kunst, Film und Technik*, hg. von Mathias Herweg und Stefan Keppler-Tasaki. Würzburg: Königshausen & Neumann, 2015, pp. 209–24.

Der Aus- und Umbau der Wartburg im Auftrag von Carl Alexander in der Mitte des 19. Jahrhunderts ist ein Großprojekt des Weimarer Hofs. Der Verf. geht gestützt auf zahlreiche historische Quellen auf dieses Unternehmen ein und zeigt die Verbindungen zu Malerei, Architektur und Literatur der Zeit auf, die letztlich der Selbststilisierung des Großherzogs dienen. (M.G.)

109 *Historische Räume. Erzählte Räume. Gestaltete Räume. Festschrift für Leopold Hellmuth zum 65. Geburtstag*, hg. von Georg HOFER, Robert SCHÖLLER und Gabriel VIEHHAUSER. Wien: Praesens, 2015, 316 p.

Vgl. Einträge zu den Beiträgen des Bands.

110 HOMEYER, Susanne, und Inta KNOR, "Zu einer umfassenden Untersuchung der Schreibsprache Hans Rieds im Ambraser Heldenbuch," *ZfdPh*, 134 (2015), 97–103.

Die Verfasserinnen plädieren – in Anlehnung an Kurt Gärtner und Martin Schubert – dafür, alle Schriftzeugnisses Hans Rieds sorgfältig zu untersuchen, um neue Erkenntnisse über dessen Arbeitsweise (Um- bzw. Bearbeitungen der Vorlage) im Umgang mit den meist nur im Ambraser Heldenbuch überlieferten Texte zu gelangen. (D.D.W.)

111 HUBER, Christoph, "Kristallwörtchen und das Stilprogramm der perspicuitas. Zu Gottfrieds Tristan und Konrads Goldener Schmiede," in *Literarischer Stil. Mittelalterliche Dichtung zwischen Konvention und Innovation. XXII. Anglo-German Colloquium Düsseldorf*, hg. von Elizabeth ANDERSEN, Ricarda BAUSCHKE-HARTUNG, Nicola MCLELLAND und Silvia REUVEKAMP. Berlin / Boston: De Gruyter, 2015, pp. 191–204.

Die Rede von den *cristallînen wortelîn* steht im Zentrum des Beitrags. In der Gottfried-Forschung oft dem rhetorischen Stilideal der perspicuitas zugeschrieben, nennt der Verf. jedoch die "kristalline Qualität nicht 'Klarheit', sondern 'Transparenz'" (200). Wie der Kristall in der mittelalterlichen Wahrnehmung das Licht modifiziert, bringt der kristalline Stil Gottfrieds das Andere hervor, um es gleichzeitig uneindeutig werden zu lassen. (L.Z.)

112 KERTH, Sonja, "Wolframs Greise. Alter(n) im "Parzival", "Titurel" und "Willehalm"," *ZfdA*, 144 (2015), 48–76.

Kerth arbeitet in Anlehnung an die Intersektionalitätsforschung die Figurenzeichnung der Alten in drei Texten Wolframs heraus. Mit den Begriffen disability und gender soll der sozialen Funktion der älteren Figuren in der erzählten Welt nachgegangen werden. Die Methode ermöglicht "den Blick für ambivalente Bewertungen von scheinbar eher randständigen Figuren", wodurch sie ihr "eigenständiges narratives Potential entfalten" können (S. 76). (D.D.W.)

113 KNAPP, Fritz Peter, "Hochmittelalterliche Literaturwerkstätten?" *ZfdA*, 144 (2015), 28–47.

Knapp diskutiert Bumkes und Heinzles These von den mittelalterlichen Literaturwerkstätten anhand der Fassungen des "Nibelungenliedes" und des "Prosalancelot". Der Verf. spricht sich zwar für die These aus, ein abschließender Beweis lässt sich aber nicht erbringen (S. 47). (D.D.W.)

114 KNAPP, Fritz Peter, "Komparatistische Überlegungen zur hochmittelalterlichen Blüte großepischer Kunstprosa," in *Historische Räume. Erzählte Räume. Gestaltete Räume*, hg. von Georg HOFER, Robert SCHÖLLER und Gabriel VIEHHAUSER. Wien: Praesens, 2015, pp. 23–40.

Der Verf. untersucht, wie sich der Erzählstil des *Lancelot en prose* von dem der lateinischen Historiographie unterscheidet. Zwar könne man dem *Lancelot* keinen 'hohen Stil' zusprechen, aber einen 'aus- und eindrucksvoll[en]' (30). Ein Vergleich mit altnordischen Sagas deckt einige stilistische Ähnlichkeiten auf, an denen alle komparatistischen Erklärungsversuche scheitern. (C.D.)

115 KNÄPPER, Titus, "'Darumb ist besser das man des zornes meister sy'. Zur Ambiguität von 'vreude' und 'zorn' in Konfliktdarstellungen des *Erec* und des *Prosa-Lancelot*," in *Gewaltgenuss, Zorn und Gelächter. Die emotionale Seite der Gewalt in Literatur und Historiographie des Mittelalters und der Frühen Neuzeit*, hg. von Claudia ANSORGE, Cora DIETL und Titus KNÄPPER. Göttingen: V&R unipress, 2015, pp. 89–106.

In Hartmanns *Erec* werden ritterliche Kämpfe v.a. als Zerstörung von Waffen dargestellt, Kämpfe gegen unhöfische Wesen aber als Zerstörung von Körpern. Im *Prosa-Lancelot* dagegen 'fließt das Blut in ritterlichen Kämpfen geradezu in Strömen' (96), bis der Gral in den Vordergrund tritt und eine stärkere Orientierung an christlichen Werten bedingt. (C.D.)

116 KRAGL, Florian, "Die Entzauberung der Welt. 'Realismus' als Kategorie mittelalterlichen Romanerzählens am Beispiel von Pleiers *Meleranz*," in *Historische Räume. Erzählte Räume. Gestaltete Räume*, hg. von Georg HOFER, Robert SCHÖLLER und Gabriel VIEHHAUSER. Wien: Praesens, 2015, pp. 87–104.

Der Pleier ersetzt im *Meleranz* mythische Logiken, Märchenhaftes und Monokausales der älteren Artusromane durch ein 'Gewusel an motivationalen Elementen' (101) der subjektiven Figurenstimmen. Dies könnte man nach Auffassung des Verf. 'realistisch' nennen. (C.D.)

117 Lagomarsini, Claudio, "Le cas du compilateur compilé. Une œuvre inconnue de Rusticien de Pise et la réception de Guiron le Courtois," *JIAS*, 3 (2015), 55–71.

Vorgestellt wird die Rustichello da Pisa zugeschriebene *Compilation guironienne*. In einem ersten Teil zeigt sich, dass die Sprache der Handschrift einem weiteren von Rustichello zusammengestellten Text gleicht. Im zweiten Teil werden Stemma und Überlieferung des Textes erläutert; er wurde in späterer Zeit in je unterschiedlichen Funktionen weiter abgeschrieben. (N.B.)

118 Lembke, Astrid, "Aventiuren in Aschkenas. Jüdische Aneignungen nichtjüdischer Texte und Erzählstoffe im vormodernen Europa," *Aschkenas*, 25.1 (2015), 1–10.

Die Einführung zum Themenheft gibt überblicksartig Auskunft zum "Reservoir kultureller Güter" jüdischer sowie christlicher Gemeinschaften, wozu "eine Reihe von Erzählungen, Stoffen und Motiven" gehört (5). Dabei lässt sich entgegen früherer Annahmen feststellen, dass "jüdische und christliche Autoren und ihre jeweiligen Rezipienten gleichermaßen an bestimmten Formen des Erzählens wie auch an bestimmten Inhalten Gefallen fanden" (5). (L.Z.)

119 Lembke, Astrid, "Ritter außer Gefecht. Konzepte passiver Bewährung im Wigalois und im Widuwilt," *Aschkenas*, 25.1 (2015), 63–82.

Passivität und Ohnmacht kennzeichnen sowohl den Helden des Wigalois Wirnts von Grafenberg als auch den Protagonisten seiner anonymen jiddischen Bearbeitung Widuwilt. Anders als der Held der Vorlage unterliegt Widuwilt jedoch in seinem Hauptkampf. In ihrem Beitrag untersucht die Verf. Gemeinsamkeiten und Differenzen der beiden Texte, vor allem in Bezug auf die Darstellung von Geschlechterverhältnissen und Gemeinschaft. (L.Z.)

120 Manuwald, Henrike, "Der *Mantel* im *Ambraser Heldenbuch* und die Frage nach dem Stil," in *Literarischer Stil. Mittelalterliche Dichtung zwischen Konvention und Innovation. XXII. Anglo-German Colloquium Düsseldorf*, hg. von Elizabeth Andersen, Ricarda Bauschke-Hartung, Nicola McLelland und Silvia Reuvekamp. Berlin / Boston: De Gruyter, 2015, pp. 449–68.

Die Verf. untersucht die kurze Versdichtung "in Bezug auf ihren 'Schnitt', d. h. auf eine stilistische Einordnung hin" (450f) und kommt zum Befund, dass die Machart des Textes vor allem im Aufzeigen intertextueller Bezüge besteht. Die These, dass Brüche und Disproportioniertheit des Textes dem Mantel, der nicht passt, entsprechen, hat auch Auswirkungen auf den Mantel-Erec-Verbund, der auf seine inhaltlichen und stilistischen Aspekte befragt wird. (L.Z.)

121 MASSE, Marie-Sophie, "Frühe Neuzeit und Mittelalter zwischen Alterität und Kontinuität. Memoria und translatio im Ambraser Heldenbuch," in *Das Mittelalter des Historismus. Formen und Funktionen in Literatur und Kunst, Film und Technik*, hg. von Mathias HERWEG und Stefan KEPPLER-TASAKI. Würzburg: Königshausen & Neumann, 2015, pp. 43–63.

Das im Auftrag von Maximilian I. entstandene Ambraser Heldenbuch stellt eine literaturgeschichtlich exzeptionelle Leistung dar. Auf einleitende Teile zur kulturgeschichtlichen Kontextualisierung der Handschrift folgt ein luzider Abschnitt zum Mittelalterverständnis der Humanisten im Umfeld des Herrschers, bevor sich der letzte Teil den Werken Hartmanns und der Anlage der Handschrift widmet. (M.G.)

122 MATSUURA, Jun, "Körper vs. Sprache. Zu poetologisch-anthropologischen Konzepten der Tristandichtungen Eilharts von Oberg und Gottfrieds von Straßburg," *Neue Beiträge zur Germanistik*, 14.1 (2015), 25–53.

Eilhart betont im *Tristrant* das Körperliche (vgl. Waldleben, Geburts- und Minnetrankszene, Brautnacht, Wiederkehrabenteuer). Bei Gottfried wird dem Wort größere Bedeutung zugemessen als dem Körper (vgl. Gottesurteil, Minnegrotte, Namensverwirrung um die beiden Isolden). Diese Wendung 'von Körper und Ding zu Name und Sprache' hängt mit dem Fiktionalitätsbewusstsein um 1200 zusammen. (C.D.)

123 MATTHEWS, Alastair, "Wolfram als Chronist. 'Chronikstil' und Sprecher in den Schlussstrophen des *Lohengrin*," in *Literarischer Stil. Mittelalterliche Dichtung zwischen Konvention und Innovation. XXII. Anglo-German Colloquium Düsseldorf*, hg. von Elizabeth ANDERSEN, Ricarda BAUSCHKE-HARTUNG, Nicola MCLELLAND und Silvia REUVEKAMP. Berlin / Boston: De Gruyter, 2015, pp. 339–52.

Die Schlussstrophen des Lohengrin werden in der Forschung als Chronikstrophen beschrieben, bieten sie doch einen Abriss über die Kaisergeschichte. Der Verf. zieht stilistische Vergleiche mit möglichen Quellentexten, um zu erkennen, dass im Lohengrin verschiedene Techniken kombiniert werden, "um den Erzähler zu profilieren und Abschnitte voneinander abzugrenzen" (351). Dabei wird die Stimme Wolframs als Erzähler der Schwanrittergeschichte von der Stimme des Dichters als Erzähler des Chronikteils unterschieden. (L.Z.)

124 MERTENS, Volker, "'Musikalischer Stil' in mittelalterlicher Literatur," in *Literarischer Stil. Mittelalterliche Dichtung zwischen Konvention und Innovation. XXII. Anglo-German Colloquium Düsseldorf*, hg. von Elizabeth ANDERSEN, Ricarda BAUSCHKE-HARTUNG, Nicola MCLELLAND und Silvia REUVEKAMP. Berlin / Boston: De Gruyter, 2015, pp. 287–301.

Im Beitrag wird demonstriert, wie in Gottfrieds Tristan durch klangliche Mittel, Klang- und Wortbrücken, aber auch durch die Uneindeutigkeit des Sprachklangs Struktur und Bedeutung gestiftet werden. Am Beispiel der musikalisch verdichteten Jüngeren-Titurel-Strophe wird gezeigt, wie durch Sprachmusik im Text – ähnlich wie im Tristan – Kontingenz generiert wird. Schließlich wird die Ambiguität der Poetik der Musikalität betont, die einerseits Kontingenz, andererseits Korrespondenzen und Strukturen erzeugt. (L.Z.)

125 MERTENS-FLEURY, Katharina, "Allegorische Vermittlungen. Zugänge zum Gralstempel in Albrechts "Jüngerem Titurel"," *ZfdPh*, 134 (2015), 47–76.

Mertens-Fleury zeigt anhand der allegorischen Darstellung des Graltempels die Sinnebenen des Bauwerkes. Einerseits markiert die "semiotische Komplexität" der Tempelbeschreibung die menschliche Unfähigkeit, Gottes Wirken in der Welt ganz zu erfassen (S. 74f.), andererseits werden damit die "Grenzen der Bezeichenbarkeit" "eines allegorischen Sprechens von Gott in der Welt" aufgezeigt (S. 75). (D.D.W.)

126 MEYER, Evelyn, "'Der Maler konnte oder wollte nicht lesen' – oder vielleicht doch? Die Text-Bild-Bezüge der Blutstropfenepisode in den illustrierten 'Parzival'-Handschriften," in *Geschichten sehen, Bilder hören. Bildprogramme im Mittelalter*, hg. von Andrea SCHINDLER und Evelyn MEYER. Bamberg: Bamberg University Press, 2015, pp. 191–214.

Ein Vergleich von fünf Illuminationen der Blutstropfenszene in *Parzival*-Handschriften zeigt, dass Abweichungen der bildlichen Darstellungen von Text und Rubrikaturen nicht auf ein Falschverstehen hinweisen müssen, sondern eher als Neuinterpretationen der Szene und als Spiel mit der Semantik der Bilder zu verstehen sind. (C.D.)

127 MIEDEMA, Nine, "'vriunt' als Anrede in mittelhochdeutschen Erzähltexten," in *Freundschaftszeichen. Gesten, Gaben und Symbole von Freundschaft im Mittelalter*, hg. von Marina MÜNKLER, Antje SABLOTNY und Matthias STANDKE. Heidelberg: Winter, 2015, pp. 209–28.

Untersucht wird die Verwendung und unterschiedliche Bedeutung von 'vriunt' als Anrede gegenüber dem Freund, Geliebten, Ehemann, Verwandten oder auch Fremden in mhd. Erzähltexten, u.a. in Gottfrieds *Tristan*. Als Anrede hat 'vriunt' eine deutliche Appellfunktion, oft als Erinnerung an Verpflichtungen. (C.D.)

128 MIERKE, Gesine, und Christoph SCHANZE, "Im Schatten des Baumes. Zur Semantisierung des Schattens im höfischen Roman," *LiLi*, 180 (2015), 12–44.

Nach einem ersten Überblick über Textbelege zum Schatten im höfischen Roman des 12. und 13. Jh. gehen die Verf. ausführlicher auf Wirnts von Gravenberg *Wigalois* sowie *Wolframs* Parzival und *Willehalm* ein. Abschließend ordnen sie die unterschiedlichen Ausprägungen und Funktionen und bestimmen die verschiedenen Semantiken. (M.G.)

129 *Mittelalterrezeption in der DDR-Literatur*, hg. von Gesine MIERKE und Michael OSTHEIMER. Würzburg: Königshausen & Neumann, 2015, 273 p.

Vgl. Einzeleinträge zu den Beiträgen des Bands.

130 MURRAY, Alan V., "Wernher der Gartenaere and the Arthurian Romance. The Intertextuality of Helmbrecht's Cap." *Mediaevistik*, 28 (2015), 161–73.

Murray geht zunächst auf die vielfältigen intertextuellen Bezüge ein, die an Helmbrechts Haube nachgewiesen worden sind. Dabei hat der Verfasser die großen Schnittmengen zu Wolframs 'Parzival' herausgestellt. Murray hat auf dieser Basis gezeigt, dass Wernher Helmbrecht bewusst als "antithetical Parzival" gezeichnet habe (S. 170). (D.D.W.)

131 NORRIS, Ralph, "Once Again King Arthur und the Ambassadors. A Textual Crux in Malory's Morte Darthur," *JIAS*, 3.1 (119), 102.

Fields neue Ausgabe rekonstruiert Malory anhand des Winchester-Manuskripts und Caxtons. Die Textstelle um Artus und Lucius stellt vor methodische Schwierigkeiten. Field nimmt alternierende Kürzungen an. Vermutlich aber sind beide Textzeugen unabhängige Bearbeitungen einer gemeinsamen Vorlage. (N.B.)

132 OBERMAIER, Sabine, "Zur Poetik der Tiereigennamen in der deutschen Literatur des Mittelalters," *BNa*, 50.3 (2015), 407–50.

Der Beitrag widmet sich den Tiereigennamen der deutschen mittelalterlichen Literatur, unter anderem der Artusepik. Dabei werden sowohl Benennungsmotive als auch -kontexte und literarische Funktionen der Tiere untersucht. Von einer "Poetik der Tiereigennamen" zu sprechen ist jedoch – als Resultat der Analyse – "nur in einer sehr eingeschränkten Form möglich" (427). Dem Beitrag ist ein "Kleines Lexikon der Tiereigennamen" (428–446) angehängt. (L.Z.)

133 OHLENDORF, Wiebke, "Figurengruppen in Schrift und Bild am Beispiel der Berner *Parzival*-Handschrift Cod. AA91," in *Geschichten sehen, Bilder hören. Bildprogramme im Mittelalter*, hg. von Andrea SCHINDLER und Evelyn MEYER. Bamberg: Bamberg University Press, 2015, pp. 179–90.

Eine Beschreibung der verschiedenen Bildtypen in der illustrierten *Parzival*-Handschrift der Berner Burgerbibliothek. Durch die Bildung von stereotypen Figurengruppen fordert der Illuminator den Betrachter auf, 'sich selbst in diese Skala der höfischen Welt einzuordnen' (189). (C.D.)

134 OTTE, Nicole, "Ein Sprung ins Ungewisse. Tabus und ihre narrative Realisierung im *Rappoltsteiner Parzifal*," in *Texte und Tabu. Zur Kultur von Verbot und Übertretung von der Spätantike bis zur Gegenwart*, hg. von Alexander DINGELDEIN und Matthias EMRICH. Bielefeld: transcript, 2015, pp. 91–104.

Die Besonderheit spätmittelalterlicher Artusromane wird an ausgewählten Szenen aus dem *Rappoltsteiner Parzifal* demonstriert. Während im 'klassischen Artusroman' klare Handlungsanweisungen und Verbote bestehen, wissen die Figuren im spätmittelalterlichen Roman nicht, was sie falsch machen. Es gibt 'magische' Ver- und Gebote, welche die Helden zum Scheitern und zur Anerkennung ihrer Fehlbarkeit zwingen. (C.D.)

135 QUADRELLI, Paola, "'Ein Turm von Vätern'. Generationenkonflikte in Tankred Dorsts *Merlin oder das wüste Land* und Christoph Heins *Die Ritter der Tafelrunde*," in *Mittelalterrezeption in der DDR-Literatur*, hg. von Gesine MIERKE und Michael OSTHEIMER. Würzburg: Königshausen & Neumann, 2015, pp. 127–45.

Dorst und Hein finden nach 1968 in beiden deutschen Ländern einen neuen Zugang zur Artusliteratur: Sie demonstrieren im Bild von Krise und Zerfall des Artusreichs die Vorläufigkeit von Weltentwürfen sowie die Relativität jeden Fortschritts und warnen vor der Verhärtung von Ideen, denn nur Erneuerung kann eine Gesellschaft lebendig erhalten. (C.D.)

136 RAYNER, Samantha, "The Case of the 'Curious Dosument'. Malory, William Matthews und Eugène Vinaver," *JIAS*, 3.1 (2015), 120–138.

Ein 1975 posthum vorgetragener Vortrag von William Matthews, der sich gegen die Ausgabe von Vinaver richtete, trat die sog. Malory-Debatte los. Anhand unveröffentlichter Dokumente wird die Vorgeschichte der Debatte rekonstruiert, in der Matthews auf die zweite Auflage der Ausgabe Einfluss zu nehmen versuchte und Vinaver durchaus dessen Kritik berücksichtigte. (N.B.)

137 REICHERT, Hermann, "Wolfram von Eschenbach, Chrestien de Troyes und Guiot von Provins. 'Lüge', 'Irrtum', 'Fiktion', 'Wahrheit'," in *Historische Räume. Erzählte Räume. Gestaltete Räume*, hg. von Georg HOFER, Robert SCHÖLLER und Gabriel VIEHHAUSER. Wien: Praesens, 2015, pp. 63–86.

Wolfram hat vermutlich neben dem *Perceval* Chrétiens eine zweite Fassung gekannt. Diese hielt er für ein Werk des Guiot de Provins. Es handelt sich bei 'Kyot' also nicht um eine Quellenfiktion, sondern um einen Irrtum Wolframs, und Gottfrieds Kritik an Wolfram hat nichts mit der Erfindung des 'Kyot' zu tun. (C.D.)

138 RICHTER, Julia, *Spiegelungen. Paradigmatisches Erzählen in Wolframs "Parzival"*. Berlin / Boston: De Gruyter Verlag, 2015, 324 p. Münchner Texte und Untersuchungen zur deutschen Literatur des Mittelalters, 144.

Richter unternimmt es in ihrer Studie, die Poetik Wolframs anhand der zahlreichen Wiederholungen, die immer neue Verknüpfungen ergeben, aufzuzeigen. Sie bedient sich dabei der Theorie von "paradigmatischem Erzählen", wie sie von Jurij Lotman und Rainer Warning in anderen Zusammenhängen durchgespielt wurden (S. 7–40). Für Richter ist ein rein paradigmatischer Text im Mittelalter "unwahrscheinlich" (S. 34), daher stellt sie das "Oszillieren" zwischen syntagmatischer und paradigmatischer Ebene dar (S. 38). Die Verfasserin zeigt mit ihrer Methode das "komplexe System von Verweisen und Bezügen" des 'Parzival' (S. 266) auf. (D.D.W.)

139 SCHANZE, Christoph, "Gold, Unerlogen. Zum Verständnis von "Erec", v. 373," *ZfdA*, 144 (2015), 141–49.

Schanze analysiert die Verse 368–385 des *Erec* Hartmanns von Aue. Hartmann reflektiert geschickt Fragen der Poetik, indem der geschilderte Sachverhalt nur auf der rezeptionsästhetischen Ebene zwischen Erzählen und Rezipient präsent ist. Daran zeigt sich Hartmanns Spiel mit ficta (S. 149). (D.D.W.)

140 SCHEUER, Hans Jürgen, "Schach auf Schanpfanzûn. Das Spiel als Exempel im VIII. Buch des "Parzivâl" Wolframs von Eschenbach," *ZfdPh*, 134 (2015), 29–45.

Der Verfasser untersucht die Funktionen des Exemplums im VIII. Buch des "Parzival". Von der Überlegung des exemplum ausgehend, sieht Scheuer im Schachspiel eine Allegorie, die individuelle Konfliktlösungen in der höfischen Welt dem Rezipienten vor Augen stellen soll. (D.D.W.)

141 SCHMIDT, Siegrid, "*Parzival* in Ost und West. Ein Beispiel ideologischer und kulturhistorischer Potentiale epischer Texte des Mittelalters," in *Mittelalterrezeption in der DDR-Literatur*, hg. von Gesine MIERKE und Michael OSTHEIMER. Würzburg: Königshausen & Neumann, 2015, pp. 12–25.

Eine vergleichende Analyse von Werner Heiduczeks *Die seltsamen Abenteuer des Parzival* (1973) und Auguste Lechners *Parzival* (1965) deckt in beiden Werken sehr deutlich Ideologisierungstendenzen und Deutungshoheiten ihrer jeweiligen Zeit bzw. ihres jeweiligen politischen Kontextes auf. (C.D.)

142 Schöller, Robert, "'Ahî'-Effekte. Zur Interjektionalisierung vormoderner Texte," in *Historische Räume. Erzählte Räume. Gestaltete Räume*, hg. von Georg Hofer, Robert Schöller und Gabriel Viehhauser. Wien: Praesens, 2015, pp. 41–61.

Interjektionen besitzen weitergehende Funktionen als nur den Ausdruck von Emotionen. Sie bringen in das distanzsprachliche Phänomen des schriftlichen Textes nähesprachliche Elemente ein, rufen mimetische Effekte hervor, dienen dem Klangspiel (vgl. *Tristan*), der Memorierbarkeit (vgl. *Parzival*) oder der Strukturierung von Texten. Auffällig ist die unterschiedliche Verteilung von Interjektionen in verschiedenen Textsorten. (C.D.)

143 Schwembacher, Manuel, "Parzival reloaded. Der rezpetionsästhetische Modellversuch ALIENA ("Alte Literatur im Erlebnisraum neu ästhetisiert")," in *Literatur-Erlebnisse zwischen Mittelalter und Gegenwart. Aktuelle didaktische Konzepte und Reflexionen zur Vermittlung deutschsprachiger Texte*, hg. von Wernfried Hofmeister und Ylva Schwinghammer. Frankfurt am Main: Peter Lang Edition, 2015, pp. 193–205.

Im Zentrum des Aufsatzes steht das Projekt ALIENA sowie dessen Erträge unter der Leitung von Manfred Kern (Universität Salzburg), das in Zusammenarbeit mit dem Musischen Gymnasium Salzburg von 2010–2012 in zwei Phasen stattgefunden hat. 1. Phase 2010–2011: Vorbereitung und Durchführung einer szenischen Aufführung von Wolframs "Parzival"; 2. Phase: Vermittlung und Erarbeitung der Minnelyrik durch die SchülerInnnen und Studierende. (D.D.W.)

144 Seidel, Katharina, *Textvarianz und Textstabilität. Studien zur Transmission der "Ívens saga", "Erex saga" und "Percevals saga"*. Tübingen: A. Francke Verlag, 2014, 248 p. Beiträge zur nordischen Philologie, 56.

Katharina Seidel rückt erstmals die auf den afrz. Vorlagen Chrestiens de Troyes fußenden "übersetzten Riddarasögur", das sind die "Ívens saga", "Erex saga" und "Percevals saga", ins Zentrum. Überliefert sind sie in 20 Handschriften des 14.–19. Jahrhunderts. Ziel der Arbeit ist es, die Fassungsunterschiede zu vergleichen (vgl. S. 10f.). Nicht nur die Bedeutung des Artusstoffes wird skizziert, sondern zugleich dessen Überlieferung, dessen Bearbeitung und nicht zuletzt dessen "Entstehungskontexte" (S. 41–45) im nordischen Raum. Dabei nimmt die Beschreibung sowie die

Systematisierung der handschriftlichen Überlieferung einen Großteil der Arbeit ein. Im vergleichenden Teil wird herausgearbeitet, dass die Texte, obwohl über fünf Jahrhunderte überliefert, nicht verändert wurden. (D.D.W.)

145 STAMPFER, Helmut, und Oskar EMMENEGGER, *Die Ywain-Fresken von Schloss Rodenegg*. Bozen: Athesia, 2016, 87 p.

Dieser, das Bildprogramm der Südtiroler Burg Rodenegg aus dem frühen 13. Jahrhundert reproduzierende Band zeigt die ältesten Artusfresken überhaupt, einen Zyklus nach Hartmann von Aue (1180/90) – das belegt die Namensgebung. Er offenbart ein einmaliges Zeugnis früher Artus-Rezeption. Trotz Schäden durch den Einbau eines Gewölbes, bei dessen Abbruch man dieses in den 1970er-Jahren entdeckte, ist es um ein ausführliches Bildprogramm, das von Yvains Ausritt, der Quellenepisode, anschließendem Kampf, der Tarnszene und der vergeblichen Suche nach Yvain bis zu dessen Heiratsantrag an Laudine geht (wobei die Schlussszene verloren ist). Über ausführliche technischen Details hinaus vermittelt der Band ein außerordentliches Beispiel Entstehungszeit-naher Ywain-Rezeption. (A.R.)

146 STEINKE, Robert, *Verhinderte Ritter in der deutschen Literatur des Mittelalters. Scheitern als Gelingen fiktionaler Identitätskonstruktionen*. Wiesbaden: Reichert Verlag, 2015, 256 p. Imagines Medii Aevi, 35.

Steinke untersucht anhand von Wolframs “Parzival”, Ulrichs v. Türheim “Rennewart”, Hartmanns “Gregorius” und Wernhers “Helmbrecht” das Spannungsfeld zwischen “Identität und Individualität” mittelalterlicher Romanhelden (S. 62). Dabei steht vor allem die Figur des gescheiterten Ritters im Vordergrund. Diesem misst der Verfasser den größten Erkenntniswert zu, da jene mit den “Einschränkungen und Widerstände[n]” (S. 63) der erzählten Welt zu kämpfen haben und die Figurenzeichnungen zugleich deutlich machen, “dass eine erfolgreiche Ausbildung ritterlicher Identität kein Selbstläufer ist” (S. 63). (D.D.W.)

147 SUMMERFIELD, Thea, “The Function of Fiction. King Edward I, King Arthur und Velthem’s Continuation,” *JIAS*, 3.1 (2015), 32–54.

In Lodewijg van Velthems Fortsetzung des *Spiegel Historiael* wird König Edward I. als begeisterter Arthurianer beschrieben, obgleich dafür weitere

Belege fehlen. In den bisher unbeachteten eduardisch-arthurischen Einschüben zeigt sich Velthem als ausgezeichneter Kenner der Materie. Er verwendet Artus, um staatspolitische Überzeugungen zum Ausdruck zu bringen. (N.B.)

148 SWIDSINSKI, Anja, "Freundschaft als Orientierung. Narrative Transzendenz in Wolframs *Parzival*," in *Freundschaftszeichen. Gesten, Gaben und Symbole von Freundschaft im Mittelalter*, hg. von Marina MÜNKLER, Antje SABLOTNY und Matthias STANDKE. Heidelberg: Winter, 2015, pp. 229–50.

Die Freundschaft von Gawein und Parzival wird gerade durch die Leerstellen in Wolframs Erzählung, in denen Gawein an die Stelle Parzivals tritt, zum Ausdruck gebracht. Diesem Phänomen nähert sich die Verf. mithilfe der Frame-Theorie von Katherine Young und der Idee der 'narrativen Transzendenz', wonach Leerstellen auf nicht Darstellbares verweisen. (C.D.)

149 TAX, Petrus W., "Stellvertretendes Rittertum, *buoze* und die Schuldfrage in Hartmanns "Iwein", "Gregorius" und Kreuzzugslyrik," *ZfdA*, 144 (2015), 442–60.

Anhand zentraler Stellen des "Iwein" geht Tax der Frage nach Iweins "stellvertretenden Rittertums" nach. Damit ist vor allem im zweiten Teil die "Wiedergutmachung" gemeint, und zwar nicht nur der eigenen Fehler, sondern auch die Versäumnisse anderer (bsp. Gawein), die Iwein zu richten versucht (S. 442f.). Vom Iwein wird der Bogen zum "Gregorius" sowie zu den Kreuzliedern Hartmanns gespannt. (D.D.W.)

150 TRACHSLER, Richard, "Auteurs et noms d'auteurs. Ce qu'on lit dans les manuscrits," in *Autorschaft und Autorität in den romanischen Literaturen des Mittelalters*, hg. von Susanne FRIEDE und Michael SCHWARZE. Berlin / Boston: De Gruyter, 2015, pp. 137–46.

Trachsler kommentiert die Wende von der Suche nach der Identität mittelalterlicher Autoren hin zum Text. Den Verzicht auf den empirischen Autor begleitet jedoch oft die These der Vertrautheit des mittelalterlichen Publikums mit der Autorfigur. Konkrete Beispiele demonstrieren jedoch die Veränderung von Autornamen und den Verlust der mit ihnen verbundenen Konnotationen. (A.R.)

151 VOLFING, Annete, "*Leien mund nie baz gesprach*. Wolfram als stilistisches Vorbild im *Jüngeren Titurel*, im *Lohengrin* und im *Göttweiger Trojanerkrieg*," in *Literarischer Stil. Mittelalterliche Dichtung zwischen Konvention und Innovation. XXII. Anglo-German Colloquium Düsseldorf*, hg. von Elizabeth ANDERSEN, Ricarda BAUSCHKE-HARTUNG, Nicola MCLELLAND und Silvia REUVEKAMP. Berlin / Boston: De Gruyter, 2015, pp. 323–38.

Am Beispiel des *Jüngeren Titurel*, des *Lohengrin* und des *Göttweiger Trojanerkrieges* zeigt die Verf. auf, inwieweit Texte mit einem Wolfram-Erzähler durch stoffliche und stilistische Merkmale Bezug auf Wolfram nehmen. Während stilistische und syntaktische Wiederholungen von Schlüsselelementen und Verbformen den *Jüngeren Titurel* kennzeichnen, ist der *Lohengrin* stilistisch heterogen. Im Fall des *Göttweiger Trojanerkriegs* schließlich findet Nachahmung "auf dem Niveau einer zur Schau gestellten Verspieltheit" (338) statt. (L.Z.)

152 WAGNER, Silvan, *Erzählen im Raum. Die Erzeugung virtueller Räume im Erzählakt höfischer Epik*. Berlin / Boston: De Gruyter, 2015, 385 p. Trends in Medieval Philology, 28.

Die Arbeit fragt nach einem kommunikativen Raumverständnis in der mhd. höfischen Epik, nach Erzählräumen, Wahrnehmungs- und Erinnerungsräumen sowie nach musikalischen Räumen. Es soll bewiesen werden, dass die Raumdarstellungen im höfischen Roman dahingehend ein modernes kulturwissenschaftliches Verständnis von virtuellen Räumen noch übertreffen, dass hier virtuelle Räume in wechselnder Perspektive erzählt werden. Nach Auffassung des Verf. ist es 'eine der vornehmlichen Aufgaben höfischer Literatur im Mittelalter, virtuelle Räume der Verhandlung von Inklusion und Exklusion zu kommunizieren' und dabei 'ordenunge', 'mâze' und 'herschaft' beobachtbar zu machen. Untersucht werden u.a. Räume in in Hartmanns *Iwein* und *Erec*, in Gottfrieds *Tristan* und im *Prosa-Lancelot*. (C.D.)

153 WERNER, Karen, "Zur gesinnungsbildenden Funktion von Adaptionen mittelalterlicher Erzählstoffe im Deutschunterricht. Am Beispiel von Werner Heiduczeks *Die seltsamen Abenteuer des Parzival*," in *Mittelalterrezeption in der DDR-Literatur*, hg. von Gesine MIERKE und Michael OSTHEIMER. Würzburg: Königshausen & Neumann, 2015, pp. 26–41.

Der Beitrag untersucht, welche Nacherzählungen mittelalterlicher Literatur in DDR-Lehrplänen verortet waren. Artusromane wurden 'als Exempel früher Ideologie- und Gesellschaftskritik' (32) betrachtet. Heiduczeks *Parzival* wurde gelobt als eine Bearbeitung, die historisches Beiwerk ablege und die Idee des humanistischen Helden, der die Welt des Feudalismus überschreite, ins Zentrum rücke. (C.D.)

154 WETZEL, René, "Erkennen und Verkennen. Schattenwurf und Spiegelbild in mittelalterlichen Tristandichtungen und -bildzeugnissen," *LiLi*, 180 (2015), 45–66.

Ausgehend von der bemerkenswerten Verteilung der *schate*-Belege (v. a. auf die Baumgartenszenen und die Minnegrotte) reflektiert der Beitrag die unterschiedlichen Dimensionen, die Schatten und Spiegelbild in Gottfrieds *Tristan* einnehmen, sowie deren unterschiedliche Funktionen. Hierfür wird auch die weltliche und geistliche Ikonographie in anderen künstlerischen Darstellungsformen herangezogen und schließlich auf die Reflexion von Möglichkeiten der Wahrnehmung und Erkenntnis eingegangen. (M.G.)

155 WICK, Maximilian, "Wahnsinn lesen. Parzival sieht rot," in *Literatur und Wahnsinn*, hg. von Helene von Bogen, Theresa Mayer, Shirin Meyer ZU SCHWABEDISSEN, Daniel SCHIERKE und Simon SCHNORR. Berlin: Frank & Timme, 2015, pp. 145–52.

Die Blutstropfenszene in Wolframs *Parzival* beruht auf einer Art von Wahnsinn, insofern die Zeichenstiftung nicht der Konvention entspricht. Indem Parzival, gezwungen durch die *triuwe*, in den Tropfen seine Geliebte sieht, widerspricht er den Gepflogenheiten der Zeichenstiftung. (N.B.)

156 WYSS, Ulrich, "Tristan/Tragik," in *Tragik vor der Moderne. Literaturwissenschaftliche Analysen*, hg. von Regina TOEPFER und Gyburg RADKE-UHLMANN. Heidelberg: Universitätsverlag Winter, 2015, pp. 343–54.

Nach Überlegungen zum Tragischen in der mittelalterlichen Literatur abseits der Heldenepik zeigt der Beitrag tragische Elemente in den Tristanromanen auf. Das durch die Elternvorgeschichte vererbte Leiden sowie die Liebestrank-Episode sind Indizien für authentische Tragik. Die Tristan-Erzählungen arbeiten sich sowohl "am Tragischen der Liebe ab" und führen vor Augen, "was die Tragik des Erzählens heißen müßte" (352). (L.Z.)

157 XUAN, Jing, "Vom Artushof nach King's Landing. Chrestien de Troyes und die Mediävisierung politischer Topographie," in *Handbuch Literatur & Raum*, hg. von Jörg DÜNNE und Andreas MAHLER. Berlin / Boston: De Gruyter, 2015, pp. 335–43.

Räume sind im Mittelalter nicht referentiell strukturiert, sondern konkretisieren kulturelle und soziale Erfahrung. Chrestien konstruiert in *Erec et Enide* einen politisch bedeutsamen Raum. Er markiert eine zentrifugale Dynamik vom dekadenten Herrschaftszentrum zum Abenteuerraum, die in der Inbesitznahme des eigenen Terrains mündet (Wiederaufnahme in J.R.R. Martins *A Song of Ice und Fire*). (N.B.)

158 ZIMMERMANN, Julia, "Narrative Lust am Betrug. Zur Nactânabus-Erzählung in Rudolfs von Ems *Alexander*," in *Verstellung und Betrug im Mittelalter und in der mittelalterlichen Literatur*, hg. von Matthias MEYER und Alexander SAGER. Göttingen: V&R unipress, 2015, pp. 261–79.

Ausgehend von Rainer Warnings *Tristan*-Analyse (BBSIA, LVI, 2004, 98), wird nach der narrativen Lust an List und Betrug im *Alexander* gefragt. Rudolf von Ems orientiert sich nicht nur im Prolog des *Alexander* an Gottfried, sondern auch in der höfischen Minnekasuistik und der Erzählstruktur seines Romans. (C.D.)

III Rezensionen

159 ANTUNES, Gabriela, *An der Schwelle des Menschlichen. Darstellung und Funktion des Monströsen in mittelhochdeutscher Literatur*. Trier: Wissenschaftlicher Verlag Trier, 2013, 308 p. (cf. *BIAS*, LXVII, 2015, 47).

Rez. von STANDKE, Matthias, *Arbitrium*, 33 (2015), 52–54.

160 BRANDT, Rüdiger, *Einführung in das Werk Gottfrieds von Straßburg*. Darmstadt: Wissenschaftliche Buchgesellschaft, 2012, 143 p. Einführungen Germanistik. (cf. *BIAS*, LXV, 2013, 17).

Rez. von FLECKEN-BÜTTNER, Susanne, *ZfdA*, 144 (2015), 91–94.

161 CHABR, Sabine, *Botenkommunikation und metonymisches Erzählen. Der "Parzival" Wolframs von Eschenbach*. Zürich: Chronos, 2013, 280 p. Medienwandel – Medienwechsel – Medienwissen, 23. (cf. *BIAS*, LXVII, 2015, 67).

Rez. von LINDEN, Sandra, *Germanistik*, 55 (2014), 618.

162 CHEN, Yen-Chun, *Ritter, Minne und der Gral. Komplementarität und Kohärenzprobleme im "Rappoltsteiner Parzifal"*. Heidelberg: Winter, 2015, 370 p. Studien zur Historischen Poetik, 18.

Rez. von SIETZ, Fabian, *ZfdA*, 144 (2015), 514–21.

163 *Chess in the Middle Ages und Early Modern Age. A Fundamental Thought Paradigm of the Premodern World*, hg. von Daniel O'SULLIVAN. Berlin / Boston: De Gruyter, 2012, 255 p.

Rez. von LUCHITSKAYA, Svetlana, *Mediaevistik*, 28 (2015), 387–90.

164 Der Stricker, *Daniel von dem blühenden Tal*, hg. von Michael RESLER. 3. Aufl., Berlin / Boston: De Gruyter, 2015, 322 p. Altdeutsche Textbibliothek, 92.

Rez. von CLASSEN, Albrecht, *Mediaevistik*, 28 (2015), 565–66.

165 DIMPEL, Friedrich Michael, *Freiräume des Anderserzählen im "Lanzelet"*. Heidelberg: Universitätsverlag Winter, 2013, 125 p. Beihefte zum Euphorion, 73. (cf. *BIAS*, LXVII, 2015, 74).

Rez. von DIETL, Cora, *Germanistik*, 55 (2015), 166.

166 EILERS, Helge, *Studien zu Sprache und Stil in alt- und mittelhochdeutscher Literatur*. Frankfurt a.M. u.a.: Verlag Peter Lang, 2015, 240 p.

Rez. von PIERCE, Marc, *Mediaevistik*, 28 (2015), 513–14.

167 *Freundschaftszeichen. Gesten, Gaben und Symbole von Freundschaft im Mittelalter*, hg. von Marina MÜNKLER, Antje SABLOTNY und Matthias STANDKE. Heidelberg: Winter, 2015, 355 p.

Rez. von CLASSEN, Albrecht, *Mediaevistik*, 28 (2015), 396–99.

168 *Handbuch der Sentenzen und Sprichwörter im höfischen Roman des 12. und 13. Jahrhunderts. Bd. 1: Einleitung und Artusromane bis 1230. Bd. 2: Artusromane nach 1230, Gralromane, Tristanromane*, hg. von Manfred EIKELMANN und Tomas TOMASEK. Berlin / Boston: De Gruyter, 2012. (cf. *BIAS*, LXV, 2013, 30).

Rez. von MIEDER, Wolfgang, *Arbitrium*, 33 (2015), 150–58.

169 HARTMANN, Heiko, *Einführung in das Werk Wolframs von Eschenbach*. Darmstadt: WBG, 2015, 134 p. Einführung Germanistik.

Rez. von CLASSEN, Albrecht, *Mediaevistik*, 28 (2015), 515–16.

170 HINTON, Thomas, *The "Conte du Graal" Cycle. Chretien de Troyes's "Perceval," the Continuations und French Arthurian Romance*. Cambridge: D. S. Brewer, 2012, 277 p. Gallica, 23. (cf. *BIAS*, LXV, 2013, 295).

Rez. von BURROWS, Darren, *ZrP*, 131 (2015), 549–53.

171 LEMBKE, Valeska, *Minnekommunikation. Sprechen über Minne als Sprechen über Dichtung in Epik und Minnesang um 1200*. Heidelberg: Universitätsverlag Winter, 2013, 469 p. Studien zur historischen Poetik, 14.

Rez. von PHILIPOWSKI, Katharina, *Germanistik*, 55 (2014), 606.

172 MALORY, Sir Thomas, *Morte Darthur*, hg. von P. J. C. FIELD. Cambridge: D. S. Brewer, 2013, 984 p. (cf. *BIAS*, LXVI, 2014, 292).

Rez. von DIETZ, Klaus, *Angl*, 133.3 (2015), 551–60.

173 MARTSCHINI, Elisabeth, *Schrift und Schriftlichkeit in höfischen Erzähltexten des 13. Jahrhunderts*. Kiel: Solivagus-Verlag, 2014, 664 p. (cf. *BIAS*, LXVII, 2015, 115).

Rez. von FASBENDER, Christoph, *ZfdA*, 144 (2015), 539–43.

174 *Mittelenglische Artusromanzen. Sir Percyvell of Gales, The Awntyrs off Arthure, The Weddynge of Sir Gawein und Dame Ragnell*, hg. von Jörg O. FICHTE. Stuttgart: S. Hirzel Verlag, 2014, 276 p. (cf. *BIAS*, LXVII, 2015, 41).

Rez. von FASBENDER, Christoph, *ZfG*, 25 (2015), 655–57.

175 *Monster. Fantastische Bilderwelten zwischen Grauen und Komik*, hg. von Peggy GROSSE, Ulrich G. GROSSMANN und Johannes POMMERANTZ. Nürnberg: Verlag des Germanischen Nationalmuseums, 2015, 511 p.

Rez. von CLASSEN, Albrecht, *Mediaevistik*, 28 (2015), 423–28.

176 MÜHLEMANN, Joanna, *Artus in Gold. Der "Erec"-Zyklus auf dem Krakauer Kronenkreuz*. Petersberg: Michael Imhof Verlag, 2013, 367 p. Studien zur internationalen Architektur- und Kunstgeschichte, 104. (cf. *BIAS*, LXVI, 2014, 81).

Rez. von SCHIROK, Bernd, *ZfdPh*, 134 (2015), 473–79.

177 *Perceforest. Sixième partie, Tomes I et II*, éd. critique par Gilles ROUSSINEAU. Bern: Droz, 2015, 1428 p. Textes littéraires du Moyen Âge, 631.

Rez. von CLASSEN, Albrecht, *Mediaevistik*, 28 (2015), 610–11.

178 PICKENS, Rupert T., *Perceval und Gawain in Dark Mirrors. Reflection und Reflexivity in Chrétien de Troyes's Conte del Graal*. Jefferson, NC: McFarland, 2015, 216 p.

Rez. von CLASSEN, Albrecht, *Mediaevistik*, 28 (2015), 525–26.

179 *Projektion – Reflexion – Ferne. Räumliche Vorstellungen und Denkfiguren im Mittelalter*, hg. von Sonja GLAUCH, Susanne KÖBELE und Uta STÖRMER-CAYSA. Berlin / Boston: De Gruyter, 2011, 477 p.

Rez. von SCHNEIDER, Christian, *Arbitrium*, 33 (2015), 282–86.

180 PUTTER, Ad, und Myra STOKES, *The Works of the Gawain Poet. Sir Gawain und the Green Knight, Pearl, Cleanness, Patience.* London: Penguin Classics, 2014, 1040 p. (cf. *BIAS*, LXVII, 2015, 420).

Rez. von BREEZE Andrew, *Mediaevistik*, 28 (2015), 613–15.

181 *Reading Skin in Medieval Literature und Culture*, hg. von Katie L. WALTER. New York: Palgrave Macmillan, 2013, 225 p.

Rez. von BARR, Jessica, *Mediaevistik*, 28 (2015), 451–53.

182 REBSCHLOE, Timo, *Der Drache in der mittelalterlichen Literatur Europas.* Heidelberg: Universitätsverlag Winter, 2014, 430 p. Beiträge zur älteren Literaturgeschichte (cf. *BIAS*, LXVII, 2015, 132).

Rez. von CLASSEN, Albrecht, *Mediaevistik*, 27 (2014), 267–68.
Rez. von MCCONNELL, Winder, *ZfdA*, 144 (2015), 127–32.

183 *Schreiborte des deutschen Mittelalters. Skriptorien – Werke – Mäzene*, hg. von Martin SCHUBERT. Berlin / Boston: De Gruyter, 2013, 777 p.

Rez. von GOERLITZ, Uta, *Germanistik*, 55 (2014), 607–08.
Rez. von JEEP, John M., *Mediaevistik*, 27 (2014), 257–60.

184 SCHULER-LANG, Larissa, *Wildes Erzählen – Erzählen vom Wilden. "Parzival", "Busant" und "Wolfdietrich D".* Berlin / Boston: De Gruyter, 2014, 370 p. Literatur – Theorie – Geschichte, 7. (cf. *BIAS*, LXVII, 2015, 147).

Rez. von CLASSEN, Albrecht, *Mediaevistik*, 28 (2015), 530–31.

185 SEEBER, Stefan, *Poetik des Lachens. Untersuchungen zum mittelhochdeutschen Roman um 1200.* Berlin / New York: De Gruyter, 2010, 326 p. Münchener Texte und Untersuchungen zur deutschen Literatur des Mittelalters, 140.

Rez. von SCHUMANN, Anica, *Arbitrium*, 32 (2014), 157–59.

186 SEELBACH, Sabine, *Labiler Wegweiser. Studien zur Kontingenzsemantik in der erzählenden Literatur des Hochmittelalters.* Heidelberg: Winter, 2011, 212 p. Beihefte zum Euphorion, 85. (cf. *BIAS*, LXIV, 2012, 53).

Rez. von GEISTHARDT, Constanze, *Arbitrium*, 33 (2015), 166–71.

187 SEIDEL, Katharina, *Textvarianz und Textstabilität. Studien zur Transmission der "Ívens saga", "Erex saga" und "Percevals saga"*. Tübingen: A. Francke Verlag, 2014, 248 p. Beiträge zur nordischen Philologie, 56.

Rez. von POPPE, Erich, *ZfdA*, 144 (2015), 545–49.

188 SPANGENBERGER, Nina, *Liebe und Ehe in den erzählenden Werken Hartmanns von Aue*. Frankfurt am Main u.a: Lang, 2012, 350 p. Kultur, Wissenschaft, Literatur, 26. (cf. *BIAS*, LXV, 2013, 59).

Rez. von WITTMANN, Viola, *Germanistik*, 55 (2014), 610–11.

189 STONES, Alison, *Gothic manuscripts 1260–1320. Part I, Vol. 1: Text & illustrations, Vol. 2: Catalogue*. London / Turnhout: Harvey Miller Publishers, 2013, 153 + 598 p. *Part II, Vol. 1: Catalogue & Illustrations, Vol. 2: Comparative Tables & Illustrations*. London / Turnhout: Harvey Miller Publishers, 2014, 287 + 581 p. A Survey of Manuscripts illuminated in France.

Rez. von WOLF, Jürgen, *ZfdA*, 144 (2015), 549–53.

190 STRITTMATTER, Ellen, *Poetik des Phantasmas. Eine imaginationstheoretische Lektüre der Werke Hartmanns von Aue*. Heidelberg: Universitätsverlag Winter, 2013, 422 p. Studien zur historischen Poetik, 15. (cf. *BIAS*, LXVII, 2015, 151).

Rez. von LINDEN, Sandra, *Germanistik*, 55 (2015), 163.

191 STROHSCHNEIDER, Peter, *Höfische Textgeschichten. Über Selbstentwürfe vormoderner Literatur*. Heidelberg: Universitätsverlag Winter, 2014, 370 p. GRM Beiheft, 55. (cf. *BIAS*, LXVII, 2015, 152).

Rez. von RAUMANN, Rachel, *Germanistik*, 56 (2015), 161.

192 TETHER, Leah, *The Continuations of Chrétien's "Perceval". Content und Construction, Extension und Ending*. Cambridge: D. S. Brewer, 2012, 241 p. Arthurian Studies, 79. (cf. *BIAS*, LXV, 2013, 318).

Rez. von WOLFZETTEL, Friedrich, *ZrP*, 131 (2015), 549–53.

193 *The Medieval Chronicle IX*, hg. von Erik KOOPER und Sjoerd LEVELT. Amsterdam / New York: Editions Rodopi, 2014, 324 p.

Rez. von CLASSEN, Albrecht, *Mediaevistik*, 28 (2015), 445–46.

194 *The Romance of Tristran by Beroul und Beroul II. A Diplomatic Edition und a Critical Edition*, hg. von und trans. Barbara SARGENT-BAUR. Toronto, ON: University of Toronto Press, 2015, 208 p.

Rez. von CLASSEN, Albrecht, *Mediaevistik*, 28 (2015), 529–30.

195 *The Romance of Tristran by Beroul und Beroul II. Student Edition und English Translation*, hg. von und trans. Barbara SARGENT-BAUR. Toronto, ON: University of Toronto Press, 2015, 208 p.

Rez. von CLASSEN, Albrecht, *Mediaevistik*, 28 (2015), 529–30.

196 TOEPFER, Regina, *Höfische Tragik. Motivierungsformen des Unglücks in mittelalterlichen Erzählungen*, Berlin / Boston: De Gruyter, 2013, 510 p. Untersuchungen zur deutschen Literaturgeschichte, 144.

Rez. von LAUFER, Esther, *Arbitrium*, 33 (2015), 147–49.

197 *Vergessene Texte des Mittelalters*, hg. von Nathanael BUSCH und Björn REICH. Stuttgart: Hirzel, 2014, 304 p.

Rez. von HUBER, Christoph, *Arbitrium*, 33 (2015), 143–47.

198 VOLLMANN, Justin, *Das Ideal des irrenden Lesers. Ein Wegweiser durch die "Krone" Heinrichs von dem Türlin*. Tübingen / Basel: Francke, 2008, 272 p. Bibliotheca Germanica, 53.

Rez. von KRAGL, Florian, *ZfdPh*, 134 (2015), 114–27.

199 *Wigamur*, hg. von Joseph M. SULLIVAN. Cambridge: D. S. Brewer, 2015, xxvi + 350 p. German Romance, 6.

Rez. von CLASSEN, Albrecht, *Mediaevistik*, 28 (2015), 542–43.

200 *Wolfram von Eschenbach. Ein Handbuch. Bd. 1: Autor, Werk, Wirkung. Bd. 2: Figuren-Lexikon, beschreibendes Verzeichnis der Handschriften, Bibliographien, Register, Abbildungen*, hg. von Joachim HEINZLE. Berlin / Boston: De Gruyter, 2011, 1445 p. (cf. *BIAS*, LXIV, 2012, 62).

Rez. von RÜTHER, Hanno, *Arbitrium*, 33 (2015), 43–48.

201 *Zwischen Herrschaft und Kunst. Fürstliche und adlige Frauen im Zeitalter Elisabeths von Nassau-Saarbrücken (14.-16. Jh.)*, hg. von Wolfgang HAUBRICHS und Patricia OSTER. Saarbrücken: Kommission für Saarländische Landesgeschichte und Volksforschung, 2013, 383 p.

Rez. von KELLER, Katrin, *RhVjbl*, 79 (2015), 315–16.

Spain, Portugal and Latin America

Bibliography for 2015 compiled by Ana Sofia Laranjinha

I Editions and Translations

202 CORREIA, Isabel, and José Carlos RIBEIRO MIRANDA, "Os Fragmentos A 19 da Biblioteca Geral da Universidade de Coimbra e a tradição textual do Lancelot," in *Seminário Medieval 2009–2011*, ed. Maria do ROSÁRIO FERREIRA, Ana Sofia LARANJINHA, and José Carlos MIRANDA. Porto: Estratégias Criativas, 2011, pp. 13–48.

Les auteurs éditent et analysent les courts fragments du "Lancelot en Prose" récemment découverts à Coimbra, qui semblent dater de la fin du XIIIe-début du XIVe siècle. D'une comparaison avec les versions manuscrites connues, ils déduisent la proximité des fragments A19 avec le ms. BNF fr. 751 et le ms. 9611 BNE.

II Critical and Historical Studies

203 AGUILAR I MONTERO, Miquel, "Motius folklòrics al Tristany i Iseut," *Tirant*, 16 (2013), online.

L'article rassemble et analyse les principaux motifs folkloriques présents dans les plus anciennes versions françaises de Tristan et Iseut et les classe selon l'index du folkloriste Stith Thompson.

204 AMOR, Lidia, "Escritura y metamorfosis en "Erec et Enide". La creación de un artificio poético," *Revista de Literatura Medieval*, 23 (2011), 29–42.

Chrétien de Troyes, par son développement du motif de la chasse au cerf blanc, semble avoir signalé l'existence d'un lien entre "Erec et Enide", le récit gallois et les "Métamorphoses" d'Ovide en utilisant le concept de

https://doi.org/10.1515/9783110467499-076

métamorphose, compris comme un moyen de révéler la véritable identité et les similitudes entre les êtres, les objets et les mythes.

205 Correia, Isabel, *Do Lancelot ao Lançarote de Lago. Tradição Textual e Difusão ibérica do ms. 9611 BNM.* Porto: Estratégias Criativas, 2015, 456 p.

Cette étude, résultat d'une thèse de doctorat soutenue en 2010, analyse la version castillane du "Lancelot en Prose" contenue dans le ms. 9611BNE et sa diffusion dans la Péninsule Ibérique. Les principales conclusions de cette étude sont que la traduction ibérique est très conservatrice, révèle des liens profonds, jusqu'à présent peu connus, avec la version française du "Lancelot" représentée par le ms.751BNF, et établit avec le cycle arthurien du Pseudo-Boron des rapports très intéressants qui vont au-delà de ceux que l'on avait identifié auparavant.

206 Correia, Isabel, "Supress or underline? "Lançarote de Lago" and the Image of Chivalry," in *Seminário Medieval 2009–2011*, ed. Maria do Rosário Ferreira, Ana Sofia Laranjinha, and José Carlos Miranda. Porto: Estratégias Criativas, 2011, pp. 49–59.

Isabel Correia analyse les modifications que le personnage de Gauvain subit dans la version castillane du "Lancelot en Prose" contenue dans le ms. 9611 BNE et en déduit la proximité de cette version par rapport au cycle du Pseudo-Boron, compte tenu de la déchéance du neveu d'Arthur.

207 Delpy, María Silvia, "La literatura artúrica en lengua latina. El caso de "De ortu Walwanii nepotis Arturi"" in *Estudios de literatura medieval en la Península Ibérica*, ed. Carlos Alvar. San Millán de la Cogolla (La Rioja): Cilengua, 2015, pp. 501–12.

"De Ortu Walwanii", le roman en prose latine préservé dans un seul manuscrit de la British Library, raconte les "enfances Gauvain", ses faits d'armes juvéniles. A. Delpy commente le style de l'œuvre et observe l'évolution du personnage.

208 Ferrer Gimeno, María Rosario, "Presencia del ciclo artúrico en las bibliotecas bajomedievales de la ciudad de Valencia (1416–1474)," *Revista de literatura medieval*, 23 (2011), 137–152.

Après un compte-rendu des témoins de la littérature arthurienne en Péninsule ibérique et des hypothèses quant aux voies de pénétration qu'elle aurait empruntées, Maria Rosario Ferrer étudie sa présence en 1416–1474, à Valence, à travers les titres du cycle arthurien qui surgissent dans les inventaires de notaires.

209 GARCEZ, Maria Helena Nery, "Sobrevivência da "Matéria de Bretanha" na "Mensagem" de Fernando Pessoa," in *De cavaleiros e cavalarias. Por terras de Europa e América*, ed. Lênia Márcia MONGELLI. São Paulo: Humanitas, 2012, pp. 455–62.

Nery Garcez soutient que "Mensagem" de Fernando Pessoa (1934), bien que construit sur le modèle des "Lusíadas" de Camões, est tout imbu de l'esprit de quête spirituelle de la "Demanda do Santo Graal".

210 GUTIÉRREZ GARCÍA, Santiago, "Las alusiones carolingias en la búsqueda del Grial y las concepciones cíclicas de los relatos artúricos en prosa," in *Estudios de literatura medieval en la Península Ibérica*, ed. Carlos ALVAR. San Millán de la Cogolla (La Rioja, Spain): Cilengua / Instituto de Historia del Libro y de la Lectura, 2015, pp. 637–58.

Les allusions à Charlemagne dans les Demandas ibériques permettent d'interroger les rapports entre les matières, mais aussi de mieux comprendre la construction d'un macrotexte qui intègre des éléments issus du discours historiographique et qui ordonne les périodes historiques – biblique, classique, chrétienne – d'après le point de vue chevaleresque.

211 GUTIÉRREZ TRÁPAGA, Daniel, "El "Ars moriendi" y la caballería en el "Tristán de Leonís" y el "Lisuarte de Grecia" de Juan Díaz," in *Estudios de literatura medieval en la Península Ibérica*, ed. Carlos Alvar. San Millán de la Cogolla (Rioja, Spain): Cilengua, 2015, pp. 673–94.

Cet article analyse l'influence de l'"Ars Moriendi" castillan dans les épisodes de la mort d'Amadís de Gaula et de Tristán, d'après le "Tristán de Leonís" (1501) et le "Lisuarte de Grecia" de Juan Díaz (1526). Ces morts exemplaires, modèles de la bonne mort chrétienne et chevaleresque, suivent les prescriptions de l'"Ars" et reflètent les coutumes funéraires de la haute noblesse.

212 Gutiérrez Trápaga, Daniel, "El regreso de Merlín en el "Belianís de Grecia" (III y IV) de Jerónimo Fernández," *Tirant*, 15 (2012), 99–112.

L'auteur s'intéresse au personnage de Merlin dans le "Belianis de Grecia" (III et IV) de Jerónimo Fernández. Pour comprendre sa caractérisation et sa fonction, il tient compte des sources de ce roman de chevalerie et aussi de la longue tradition médiévale de Merlin et distingue les traits traditionnels et les traits innovateurs que lui emprunte Fernández.

213 Gutiérrez Trápaga, Daniel, "'Fazme aver mala fin'. La muerte de Merlín en el "Baladro del sabio Merlín" a la luz del "Ars moriendi"," *Lingüística y Literatura*, 67 (2015), 23–38.

L'auteur analyse l'influence de l'"Ars moriendi" castillan dans l'épisode de la mort de Merlin selon la version du "Baladro del Sabio Merlin" (Burgos, 1498). Pour étayer la mauvaise mort de Merlin et son profil démoniaque, le "Baladro" utilise, entre autres éléments, les comportements identifiés comme funestes dans l'"Ars".

214 Laranjinha, Ana Sofia, "D. Dinis e o amor tristaniano," in *Cantigas trovadorescas: da Idade Média aos nossos dias*, ed. Graça Videira Lopes and Manuele Masini. Lisboa: Instituto de Estudos Medievais / Universidade Nova de Lisboa, 2014, pp. 55–64.

Etude de la présence de l'intertexte tristanien dans la chanson de D. Dinis "Meu amigo, nom poss'eu guarecer" (B 581 / V 184).

215 Laranjinha, Ana Sofia, "Galaaz escarnecido. Sobre a construção da Demanda do Santo Graal," in *O Riso. Teorias. Leituras. Realizações*, ed. Isabel Barros Dias, Elisa Nunes Esteves, and Margarida Reffóios. Casal de Cambra (Portugal): Caleidoscópio, 2015, pp. 85–94.

Dans la "Demanda", une traduction de la "Queste" du Pseudo-Boron, on peut déceler, grâce à des inconsistances dans le développement de l'intrigue et des personnages, plusieurs niveaux d'écriture. Outre le niveau qui remonte à une première rédaction du roman et celui qui résulte des transformations opérées par le Pseudo-Boron, on peut encore identifier, dans les scènes où Galaad et la victime de railleries, un troisième niveau de rédaction.

216 LARANJINHA, Ana Sofia, "La "Suite du Merlin", Gauvain et la naissance du thème de la haine entre les lignages de Lot et Pelinor," in *Seminário Medieval 2009–2011*, ed. Maria do Rosário FERREIRA, Ana Sofia LARANJINHA, and José Carlos MIRANDA. Porto: Estratégias Criativas, 2011, pp. 61–70.

L'auteur soutient que le motif de la haine entre les lignages de Lot et Pellinor, identifié par Bogdanow comme un des leitmotivs du cycle de la Post-Vulgate, aurait surgit pour la première fois dans la "Suite du Merlin", qui ne connaît pourtant pas encore la déchéance que ce personnage subira dans le "Tristan en Prose" et la "Queste". Laranjinha propose donc une nouvelle interprétation des rythmes d'écriture du cycle de la Post-Vulgate ou plutôt du Pseudo-Boron.

217 LARANJINHA, Ana Sofia, "Le motif de la traversée maritime dans la tradition tristanienne. Des poèmes à la première rédaction du "Tristan en Prose"," in *Actes du Colloque International "Lores te metras en la voie..." Mobilité et littérature au Moyen Âge. Formes, enjeux et signification*, ed. Carlos F. CLAMOTE CARRETO. Lisboa: Universidade Aberta, 2011, pp. 59–68.

Après un rappel de sa thèse sur la construction du "Tristan en Prose", A S Laranjinha se concentre sur les deux premières phases de rédaction de ce roman. A travers l'analyse du motif de la traversée maritime, elle montre que le premier rédacteur a une conception du monde très différente de son successeur. Le premier rédacteur (responsable de la préhistoire tristanienne, de la plupart des premières aventures de Tristan et de quelques autres épisodes au long du roman) est plus pessimiste en amour et construit un espace semé d'écueils. Il a aussi un tout autre rapport au temps, puisque les domaines où se niche le mal sont très souvent des îles où s'est figé le passé païen.

218 LARANJINHA, Ana Sofia, "Linhagens arturianas na Península Ibérica. O tempo das origens," in *Legitimação e linhagem na Idade Média peninsular*, ed. José Carlos RIBEIRO MIRANDA and Georges MARTIN. Porto: Estratégias Criativas, 2011, pp. 205–31.

Dans le cycle arthurien, l'"Estoire del Saint Graal" et le "Tristan en prose" dans sa partie initiale (la pré-histoire tristanienne) remontent à l'origine des lignages de leurs protagonistes. Alors que l'"Estoire del Saint Graal" place au premier plan le seul lignage chevaleresque et rigoureusement agnatique, dans la pré-histoire tristanienne, les aventures des ancêtres de

Tristan inaugurent un “anti-lignage” qui viole les principes de linéarité et de progression temporelle et bâtit sur le désordre les origines de l’amant d’Iseut. L’ESG est étudiée à partir de sa traduction portugaise.

219 LARANJINHA, Ana Sofia, “Palamedes. Sol negro da melancolia,” in *Arte da Cultura. Homenagem a Yvette Centeno*, ed. A. CORREIA, G. FRAGOSO, F. RIBEIRO, and M. CANAVEIRA. Lisboa: Colibri, 2011, pp. 339–51.

L’auteur montre comment Palamède, l’obscur alter ego de Tristan dans le “Tristan en Prose” et la “Queste” attribuée au Pseudo-Boron, hérite les traits mélancoliques de l’amant d’Iseut, ce qui explique qu’il ait entrepris la chasse de la Beste Diverse ou Glatissant, véritable réification de l’humeur mélancolique.

220 LENDO FUENTES, Rosalba, ““Ca sin falla en aquella sazón se començaron las justas e las batallas de los cavalleros, que duró luengos tiempos”. El inicio del universo artúrico en el “Baladro del sabio Merlin”,” in *Estudios de literatura medieval en la Península Ibérica*, ed. Carlos ALVAR. San Millán de la Cogolla: Cilengua, 2015, pp. 809–20.

La “Suite du Merlin” a été conçue comme une préparation aux aventures du Graal et à la destruction du royaume d’Arthur. Histoire de l’origine et de la faute originale, ce roman raconte les premières années du règne d’Arthur et explicite l’inceste du roi, rapporte les premières aventures des chevaliers arthuriens et le Coup Douloureux. Rosalba Lendo analyse ces aspects du roman en se penchant sur les innovations des deux versions du “Baladro del Sabio Merlín”: Burgos 1498 et Sevilha 1535.

221 MARQUES, Maria do Carmo, *No reino aventuroso de Artur. Um olhar sobre a mulher medieval a partir de uma leitura de A Demanda do Santo Graal*, Lisboa: Chiado, 2014, 278 p.

Ce livre est le résultat d’une thèse de maîtrise (Universidade da Madeira, 2013) qui se penche sur les personnages féminins de la “Demanda do Santo Graal” et met en rapport les modèles présentés par cet ouvrage et la société où se s’intègre son public.

222 MARTINS, Ana Rita, “Merlim: Druida, Profeta e Feiticeiro,” in *O Imaginário Medieval*, ed. Carlos Guardado DA SILVA. Torres Vedras: Edições Colibri –

Câmara Municipal de Torres Vedras – Instituto Alexandre Herculano, 2014, pp. 47–60.

Après quelques observations sur la notion de magie, l'auteure présente deux figures druidiques qui auraient pu inspirer la création du personnage de Merlin: Myrddin (cf. The Book of Taliesin) et Lailoken (cf. The Life of St. Kentigern). Ensuite, elle s'occupe d'ouvrages où Merlin surgit sous différents aspects: la "Vita Merlini" de Geoffrey of Monmouth, la "Morte d'Arthur" de Thomas Malory et le "Livre du Graal" de Robert de Boron.

223 MIRANDA, José Carlos Ribeiro, Ana Sofia LARANJINHA, and Isabel CORREIA, "O ciclo do Pseudo-Boron à luz da mais recente investigação em Portugal," in *E fizerom taes maravilhas... Histórias de Cavaleiros e de Cavalarias*, ed. Lênia Márcia Mongelli. São Paulo: Ateliê, 2012, pp. 233–64.

Dans cet article signé par trois chercheurs de l'Université de Porto qui présentent quelques conclusions du projet "Inventário Arturiano do Ocidente Ibérico Medieval", Miranda soutient que la partie cyclique du "Lancelot en Prose" a connu des variations bien plus profondes que ne l'admet en général la critique. Ainsi, le ms. BNF fr. 751 donne d'Arthur une image très négative et idéalise par contraste Galehot, qui est frappé par la "mescheance". Ces traits rapprochent cette version du "Lancelot" contenu dans le ms. 9611 BNE et les textes du cycle du Pseudo-Boron. Isabel Correia, de son côté, présente de façon plus détaillée les passages qui rapprochent la version du "Lancelot" de Madrid du cycle du Pseudo Boron. Finalement, A. S. Laranjinha, s'appuyant sur la construction du thème de la haine entre les lignages de Lot et Pelinor et sur l'évolution du personnage de Gauvain, soutient que la "Suite du Merlin" précède toutes les versions du "Tristan en Prose" parvenues jusqu'à nous et montre aussi, en s'appuyant sur des passages problématiques, que toutes les versions connues du "Tristan en Prose" intègrent plusieurs phases de rédaction qu'elles harmonisent tant bien que mal.

224 RIQUER, Alexandre de, *Escalibor. Un cant modernista artúric conquereix el món / Un canto modernista artúrico conquista el mundo*, María Angela CERDÀ I SURROCA, Montserrat PRAT SERRA, and Juan Miguel ZARANDONA. Madrid: Sial, 2014, Colección Trivium. Biblioteca de Textos y Ensayo, 27.

La publication d'un volume d'hommage à Alexandre de Riquer (1856–1920), écrivain et artiste du modernisme catalan, a fourni l'occasion d'une nouvelle publication du chant VII ("Escalibor") du "Poema del Bosch" (publié en 1910) et de nombreux paratextes: introductions, essais, articles de recherche, bibliographie, chronologie, illustrations originales de l'artiste-poète lui-même (car son oeuvre graphique traite les thèmes arthuriens), etc., le tout, en espagnol, catalan et français. Cet ouvrage comprend le chant original rédigé en catalan prénormatif et une collection de versions en prose, aussi bien en catalan contemporain qu'en toutes sortes de langues majoritaires ou minoritaires du monde.

225 SILVA, Carlos Guardado da, "A floresta e os medos na Idade Média: uma leitura possível de Chrétien de Troye," in *O Imaginário Medieval*, ed. Carlos Guardado DA SILVA. Torres Vedras: Edições Colibri – Câmara Municipal de Torres Vedras – Instituto Alexandre Herculano, 2014, pp. 73–79.

Etude sur la forêt comme un espace inconnu et effrayant dans la période médiévale, et sa représentation dans les romans de Chrétien de Troyes, où cet espace constitue soit une force d'attraction, soit de répulsion. La forêt est l'espace du voyage à différents niveaux : physique, psychologique, symbolique, initiatique.

226 SILVA, Rafaela Simões da, "Lancelot na Contra-Luz do Rei David," in *Seminário Medieval 2009–2011*, ed. Maria do Rosário FERREIRA, Ana Sofia LARANJINHA, and José Carlos MIRANDA. Porto: Estratégias Criativas, 2011, pp. 71–94.

Dans le "Lancelot en Prose", le roi David est présent non seulement comme ancêtre du héros éponyme, mais aussi par l'identification entre le roi biblique et l'amant de Guenièvre, dans un processus semblable à celui de la typologie. Les références bibliques ajoutent à la crédibilité du personnage et à la consistance de l'intrigue.

227 TATO FONTAIÑA, Laura, "Sobrevivência da "Matéria de Bretanha" na literatura galega do século XX. "Na noite estrelecida", de Ramón Cabanillas, e "Amor de Artur", de X. L. Méndez Ferrín," in *De cavaleiros e cavalarias. Por terras de Europa e Américas*, ed. Lênia Márcia MONGELLI. São Paulo: Humanitas, 2012, pp. 333–40.

Laura Tato observe la présence de la matière de Bretagne dans la littérature galicienne du vingtième siècle, en particulier chez Ramón Cabanillas et Méndez Ferrín. Alors que Cabanillas, l'un des défricheurs du nationalisme galicien à la fin du XIXe siècle, a des intentions surtout politiques, les romanciers du XXème siècle privilégient les éléments littéraires et Mendez Ferrín est un des initiateurs de la “narration arthurienne”.

228 Trujillo, José Ramón, “El espacio de la proeza y sus motivos narrativos. Justas, torneos y batallas en la materia artúrica hispânica,” *Revista de poética medieval*, 26 (2012), 325–56.

Trujillo analyse l’espace de l’exploit à travers les motifs narratifs des joutes et des tournois dans les “Demandas” ibériques, leur structure et leur variation, la relation avec le système de valeurs sous-jacent et leur rôle comme moteurs de l’histoire. Les joutes et les tournois reflètent la valeur individuelle et permettent une hiérarchisation des chevaliers, avec des conséquences significatives dans la structure narrative

229 Varandas, Angélica, “A perseguição do javali encantado nos contos mitológicos celtas galeses,” in *O Imaginário Medieval*, ed. Carlos Guardado da Silva. Torres Vedras: Edições Colibri – Câmara Municipal de Torres Vedras – Instituto Alexandre Herculano, 2014, pp. 73–79.

Etude sur la présence du sanglier dans la mythologie (gréco-latine, scandinave, hindoue et celtique) et la littérature, dans ses différentes dimensions: psychopompe, symbole de guerre ou encore animal très récurrent dans les “histoires de lieux”. L’auteur se concentre principalement sur la culture celtique et le thème de la persécution du sanglier enchanté et son association avec la figure du roi Arthur, à savoir dans “Culhwch et Olwen”, dans l’“Historia Brittonum” du Pseudo-Nennius et dans l’“Historia Regum Britanniae” de Geoffroy de Monmouth, point de départ des traditions arthuriennes.

230 Zarandona, Juan Miguel, “From Pondal to Cabanillas. Ossian and Arthur in the Making of a Celtic Galicia,” *Liburna. Revista Internacional de Humanidades*, 6 (2013) 135–158.

Zarandona se penche sur le “Rexurdimento”, mouvement romantique galicien qui défend la langue et la culture galicienne en s’appuyant sur la théorie de la Galice celtique. Il examine les fondements scientifiques discutables de cette théorie et fait un compte rendu des oeuvres littéraires qui se nourissent de légendes celtiques et mythologie arthurienne.

231 Zarandona, Juan Miguel, “La ópera “Artus”, de Sebastià Trullol i Plana y Amadeu Vives: la recuperación de un libreto perdido,” in *Miscel•lània in memoriam Alfons Serra-Baldó (1909–1993) en el centenari del seu naixement*, ed. Lidia Anoll and Lluna Llecha Llop. Barcelona: Publicacions de l’Abadia de Montserrat – Editorial Barcino, 2011, pp. 255–79.

Après une courte présentation de la réception de l’oeuvre de Walter Scott en Catalogne et en particulier de “The Bridal of Triermain”, son seul poème de thème arthurien, qui inspira l’opéra disparu de Sebastià Trullol et Amadeu Vives, Zarandona plaide pour la transcription du libretto manuscrit et fragmentaire conservé dans la Bibliothèque de Catalogne.

France

Bibliographie pour 2015 établie par Annie Combes, Damien De Carné, Sébastien Douchet, Christine Ferlampin-Acher, Alban Gautier, Adeline Latimier, Yannick Mosset, Catherine Nicolas, Joanna Pavlevski-Malingre, Fabienne Pomel et Michelle Szkilnik

I Éditions

232 *Le Roi Leïr, Version des XIIe et des XIIIe siècles*, éd. François ZUFFEREY, Gilberte NUSSBAUMER, Alain CORBELLARI et Valérie CANGEMI. Paris: Champion Classiques, 2015, 284 p.

Il s'agit d'une édition bilingue présentant six variations sur le thème du roi Lear. En annexe, des tableaux chronologique, synoptique et généalogique ainsi qu'un index des noms propres facilitent la navigation entre les différentes versions.

233 *Le Roman de Torec. Roman van Torec,* éd. Baukje FINET-VAN DER SCHAAF. Grenoble: ELLUG, 2015, 255 p.

Roman van Torec fait partie de la *Lancelotcompilatie*, qui donne la version la plus étendue du *Lancelot* en moyen néerlandais, conservée dans un seul ms. (Bibliothèque royale de la Haye K. B. hs. 129 A 10). Après une introduction qui résume le texte, en présente les sources et l'originalité, une notice évoque la tradition arthurienne médiévale en moyen néerlandais, ainsi que la tradition manuscrite et les éditions de ce texte, qui est le remaniement d'une version perdue, attribuée à Jacob van Maerlant. Le texte édité, celui de l'édition D. F. Johnson et G. H. M. Claassens (Cambridge, D. S. Berwer, 2003), est présenté face à la traduction en français. Suivent un index des noms propres et des éléments de bibliographie.

https://doi.org/10.1515/9783110467499-086

II Études Critiques et Historiques

234 Albert, Sophie, "L'Enlumineur de toute chevalerie. Relire et réécrire le renom de Febus, ancêtre de Guiron, dans les manuscrits de Paris, BnF, fr. 358–363 (fin du XVe siècle)," in *Sens, Rhétorique et Musique. Études réunies en hommage à Jacqueline Cerquiglini-Toulet*, éd. Sophie Albert, Mireille Demaules, Estelle Doudet, Sylvie Lefèvre, Christopher Lucken et Agathe Sultan. Paris: Champion, 2015, pp. 473–84.

L'article relève les références mythologiques dans une compilation tardive de *Guiron le courtois* en montrant comment Febus, ancêtre de Guiron, est magnifié au XIIIe siècle par des comparaisons avec des héros bibliques (Adam, Samson, Absalon), puis avec Hercule au XVe siècle. De même la princesse de Northumberland, qui a éconduit Febus et causé sa mort, est comparée à Ève, mais aussi à la cruelle Albine, fondatrice d'Albion.

235 Alibert, Laurent, *Le Roman de Jaufré et les Narty Kaddžytæ. Modalités du merveilleux et structures indo-européennes*. Paris: Honoré Champion, 2015, 450 p. Nouvelle Bibliothèque du Moyen Âge, 116.

Comparaison dans le sillage de Dumézil et à partir d'une double compétence linguistique en occitan et en ossète, entre *Jaufré* et les légendes des Nartes, en trois parties, portant sur les motifs (la terre *gaste* et la pénurie alimentaire, les "mythes" de décapitation, les présents et talismans, le traitement de l'hostilité entre les représentants des deuxième et troisième fonctions), les personnages (Jaufré/Girflet, Syrdon, Queu et l'enchanteur du roman occitan, les héros solaires, Batradz et Arthur, la fée et le monde aquatique), les "aspects culturels dans le traitement du merveilleux" (l'aventure et l'expédition, les bestiaires, les symboliques des couleurs, l'hyperbole, la place du christianisme, "l'au-delà, le chant sacré et le cheval", les relations de l'amour et de la merveille).

236 *Artus de Bretagne. Du manuscrit à l'imprimé*, éd. Christine Ferlampin-Acher. Rennes: Presses Universitaires de Rennes, 2015, 363 p.

Ce volume, consacré à ce roman en prose du XIVe siècle encore inédit, s'attache à la représentation originale de la chevalerie, au renouvellement de la matière arthurienne, aux insertions lyriques et à la complexe tradition manuscrite, parfois illustrée, mais aussi à sa diffusion: suites du XVe siècle, éditions du XVIe, versions abrégées du XVIIIe ou de la Bibliothèque bleue au XIXe. Il aborde donc les mutations de ce texte sur six siècles en croisant les points de vue de la littérature, de l'histoire du livre, de la codicologie et de l'iconographie. Outre les quinze articles, C. Ferlampin-Acher propose une introduction, des perspectives et une bibliographie.

237 BAUDRY, Robert, *A la conquête des graals des temps modernes.* Lyon: Edition du Cosmogone, 2015, 187 p.

Auteur d'un essai sur *Graal et Littératures d'aujourd'hui* (1998), Robert Baudry poursuit ici son enquête en s'attachant à un corpus culturel contemporain. Il étudie ainsi les modalités d'inscription du Graal dans les romans de Stephen Lawhead (graal chrétien), de Bernard Cornwell (quête du Saint Vessel), d'Italo Calvino (satire du graal), d'Umberto Echo ("réduction du graal"), de Michel Rio (négativité de la quête) mais aussi dans la série *Kaamelott* d'Alexandre Astier ("ridicule du graal"). Il montre également que la quête du graal a pu faire l'objet de dérives ésotériques criminelles (Otto Rahn) ou d'amalgames douteux (romans de Dan Brown, de Kate Moss ou de Peter Berling). Le volume s'achève sur une composition poétique de l'auteur, "Vers le Graal", contribution à cette conquête inachevée.

238 BAUDRY, Robert, "Le mythe du Graal et son Élucidation. Nouvelle lecture vers le sens premier du *Conte du Graal*," *Bien dire et bien aprandre*, 31 (2015), 153–68.

Grâce à l'Élucidation, R.B. entend retrouver le sens premier du mythe du Graal, modifié par Chrétien : la guérison du roi blessé de l'Autre Monde est analysée comme la restauration du pouvoir des divinités païennes.

239 BERTHELOT, Anne, "La dame du lac et l'automate. Quand la technologie remplace la magie," in *Engins et machines. L'imaginaire mécanique dans les textes médiévaux*, éd. Fabienne POMEL. Rennes: Presses Universitaires de Rennes, 2015, pp. 193–206.

En se basant sur une sélection de séquences qui jouent sur l'ambiguïté entre magie et technologie dans *Cleomadès*, *Perceforest* et *les Prophesies de Merlin*, cet article analyse le fonctionnement de ces deux concepts et leur interaction pour arriver à la conclusion qu'il n'y a pas nécessairement incompatibilité entre magie et technique : dans une certaine mesure, la technologie peut se mettre au service de la magie, à moins que les triomphes de la technique ne soient malgré tout redevables à l'art de *nigremance*.

240 Besson, Anne, *Constellations. Des mondes fictionnels dans l'imaginaire contemporain*, Paris: CNRS Editions, 2015, 559 p.

L'auteure s'attache à souligner une évolution du rapport aux fictions dans l'occident postmoderne. Au centre de ces nouvelles pratiques et de sa réflexion se trouve la notion d'univers fictionnel dont il s'agit d'étudier les "déclinaisons multimédiatiques et collaboratives". Les fictions sont désormais perçues comme des mondes imaginaires sujets à un développement participatif, et pouvant aboutir à un univers partagé interrogeant les statuts de l'artiste et de l'art. Face à la diversité des objets et des phénomènes culturels considérés, résultant d'une veille culturelle menée entre 2008 et 2012, Anne Besson adopte une démarche résolument interdisciplinaire, associant les théories de la fiction et les *cultural studies*. Elle consacre quelques pages aux relectures diverses de la geste arthurienne, dans les différents médias envisagés.

241 Blaise, Marie, "L'angle et la branche. Autorité et déliaison dans le *Haut Livre du Graal*," *RLR*, 119 (2015), 85–112.

Sous le regard de la psychanalyse et à la lumière de la mélancolie, les morceaux de chair dispersés dans le roman, le découpage en branches, la dispersion des figures d'autorité, et l'éclatement de l'identité du héros mettent au jour les ruines d'une conjointure perdue et révèlent un graal transformé en fétiche ou en "moule à avatars".

242 Bouget, Hélène, "Merveilles, machines et automates dans les romans de *Perlesvaus*," in *Engins et machines. L'imaginaire mécanique dans les textes médiévaux*, éd. Fabienne Pomel. Rennes: Presses Universitaires de Rennes, 2015, pp. 175–92.

Liées au merveilleux, des machines ou des automates véhiculent dans ce texte les tensions idéologiques et esthétiques propres au roman et à la manière hétérogène dont la matière de Bretagne y est travaillée. Les adaptations et remaniements ultérieurs, notamment la traduction galloise du XIVe siècle et les imprimés français de 1516 et 1523 lissent en revanche ces disparités de façon différente, révélant certaines modalités de réception du roman arthurien et de la matière de Bretagne en général, et soulignant par comparaison le caractère atypique du *Perlesvaus* du XIIIe siècle.

243 BOUGET, Hélène, “Repenser le Perlesvaus. Le sens de l’équivoque,” *RLR*, 119 (2015), 23–41.

Relecture du *Haut Livre du Graal* selon le point de vue rhétorique et herméneutique de l’énigme pour montrer que si l’obscurcissement du sens auquel s’applique le roman ne relève jamais de l’énigme à proprement parler, il met face à face le sens chrétien qui préexiste à l’écriture et qu’elle doit intégrer, et le merveilleux profane de la matière bretonne qu’elle ne parvient pas à rationaliser et à intégrer à une conjointure.

244 BROWNLEE, Marina, “Des usages politiques d’un prequel arthurien: Rustichello, Palamède et Byzance,” in *Sens, Rhétorique et Musique. Études réunies en hommage à Jacqueline Cerquiglini-Toulet*, éd. Sophie ALBERT, Mireille DEMAULES, Estelle DOUDET, Sylvie LEFÈVRE, Christopher LUCKEN et Agathe SULTAN. Paris: Champion, 2015, pp. 77–98.

Comparaison du *conte du Vieil Chevalier* qui ouvre la compilation de Rusticien de Pise avec la version byzantine postérieure. Jugés à l’aune des valeurs homériques, la cour d’Arthur et l’idéal chevaleresque sont encore davantage dégradés dans la traduction grecque. Seul Palamède, rapproché de son homologue antique injustement tué, demeure un parangon de courtoisie et d’esprit chevaleresque, malgré son paganisme.

245 CHASE, Carol, “Swordplay and wordplay. Tournaments in the Burgundian prose *Erec*,” *CRM*, 30 (2015), 373–90.

Le tournoi-mêlée recule au XVe siècle au bénéfice des joutes individuelles. Mais le prosateur bourguignon d’Érec a adopté la forme ancienne pour le tournoi qu'il ajoute à la fin de son récit. C'est probablement que la valeur chevaleresque est pour lui la pierre de touche de la qualité royale.

246 CIONE, Cornelia, François DEQUESNE et Noëlle-Christine REBICHON, “Les Neuf Preux de Belvès (Dordogne),” *Bien dire et bien aprandre*, 31 (2015), 139–50.

Étude du programme peint des *Neuf Preux* (sans doute fin XVe-début XVIe siècle) dans l'Hôtel de Commarques (Belvès, Dordogne) ; de manière originale, le blason d'Arthur y est une Vierge noire à l'Enfant.

247 COMBES, Annie, "Entre prose et vers : affleurements et interférences. La *Deuxième Continuation* du *Conte du Graal*," in *Wauchier de Denain, polygraphe du XIIIe siècle*, éd. Sébastien DOUCHET. Aix-en-Provence: Presses universitaires de Provence, 2015, pp. 113–33.

Étude de l'influence de la forme prose sur l'écriture romanesque en vers de Wauchier, et plus particulièrement du *Lancelot en prose* auquel le récit en vers emprunte nombre de procédés et motifs narratifs, sans toutefois les faire aboutir, créant ainsi un texte marqué par une "esthétique de l'indécision".

248 CORBELLARI, Alain, "Onirisme et pulsion de mort dans le *Perlesvaus*," *RLR*, 119 (2015), 113–32.

Dans le songe de Cahus qui montre au lecteur le monde arthurien *in aenigmate*, le *Perlesvaus* se montre comme un roman insaisissable où les frontières sont poreuses et où les enchâssements s'inversent dans d'infinis renversements, quitte à faire du roman le champion de la mise en échec des systèmes.

249 DEBERNARDI, Léa, "Le cycle des fresques du Château de la Manta. Quelques considérations sur l'interprétation iconographique," *Bien dire et bien aprandre*, 31 (2015), 115–38.

Étude du cycle de fresques de la *Sala baronale* du Château de la Manta (ca. 1420), contenant entre autres une représentation d'Arthur parmi les Neuf Preux ; l'interprétation minore notamment l'influence du *Livre du Chevalier Errant* de Thomas III de Saluces sur le cycle de la Manta.

250 DI CARPEGNA FALCONIERI, Tommaso, *Médiéval et militant. Penser le contemporain à travers le Moyen Âge*. Paris: Publications de la Sorbonne, 2015, 318 p.

L'auteur invite, à travers cette étude d'ampleur, à interroger le sens et le place du médiévalisme dans nos sociétés et nos systèmes politiques contemporains en montrant combien ce Moyen Âge constamment invoqué – conçu comme un âge barbare, temps des extrémistes religieux et des maladies ou comme un temps magnifié des origines, du merveilleux – se détache radicalement de l'histoire médiévale et repose sur des stéréotypes dont l'auteur parvient parfois à retracer la genèse. La référence arthurienne, notamment la chevalerie et la quête du Graal, a ainsi pu être mobilisée pour légitimer des constructions identitaires, politiques et nationalistes, de contrecultures diverses ou encore faire l'objet d'interprétations ésotériques et métaphoriques qui servent une critique du monde moderne, une conception particulière de l'art ou une enquête existentielle.

251 DUCOS, Joëlle, "*Cuer de cire, cuer d'aïmant*. La matière comme métaphore," in *Savoirs et fiction au Moyen Âge et à la Renaissance*, éd. Dominique BOUTET et Joëlle DUCOS. Paris: Presses de l'université Paris-Sorbonne, 2015, pp. 201–220.

L'article explicite les différents sens de la double métaphore "cuer de cire" / "cuer d'aïmant" présente dans le *Lancelot* (discours de la Dame du Lac sur la chevalerie) en la mettant en relation avec divers textes issus de la littérature, de la théologie, de la science et de la magie.

252 FERLAMPIN-ACHER, Christine, "De la geste au geste. Jeux de main et caresses dans *Artus de Bretagne*", *CRM*, 30 (2015), 297–313.

Mise en valeur de la force suggestive des notations gestuelles dans *Artus de Bretagne* (notamment dans la représentation de l'intimité). C.F.-A. démontre l'originalité de ce traitement par rapport aux proses antérieures tout en soulignant que l'entrain et la vivacité qui se manifestent ainsi rappellent plus le *Lancelot* et le *Tristan* qu'ils n'annoncent les proses tardives.

253 FERLAMPIN-ACHER, Christine, "Icare, Dédale, Phaéton et Elie. Les ailes volantes dans *L'Historia Regum Britaniae* de Geoffroy de Monmouth, *Le Roman de Brut* de Wace et *Perceforest*," in *Engins et machines. L'imaginaire mécanique dans les textes médiévaux*, éd. Fabienne POMEL. Rennes: Presses Universitaires de Rennes, 2015, pp. 229–42.

Bladud tient de Dédale, Icare, Phaéton et Elie. Dans la version donnée par David Aubert, la poix et le ciment qui servent à faire tenir les ailes tirent le modèle du côté des arts mécaniques. L'anecdote du "vol" du bénédictin Eilmer de Malmesbury a pu influencer la constitution du personnage. Bladud n'est donc pas que l'avatar littéraire d'une figure mythologique ;

en résonance avec les représentations contemporaines du savoir des arts mécaniques, il manifeste leur ambition et leur dévalorisation. C'est pourquoi il ne trouve pas place dans une mythologie bourguignonne par ailleurs accueillante à Thésée et à la Toison d'Or.

254 FERLAMPIN-ACHER, Christine, "L'arbalète de Passelion dans *Perceforest*. L'objet, entre tension idéologique et jeu," in *Engins et machines. L'imaginaire mécanique dans les textes médiévaux*, éd. Fabienne POMEL. Rennes: Presses Universitaires de Rennes, 2015, pp. 65–85.

La dévalorisation attendue de l'arbalète semble remplacée par la confrontation entre plusieurs représentations de l'armement du chevalier, entre tradition et renouveau, non sans ambiguïtés. L'enfance du héros et la dimension ludique de la scène, portée par un jeu verbal, du berceau enfantin au *bersault* qui désigne la cible en ancien français, et par une réécriture décalée du motif du Cœur Mangé, invitent à lire dans cet épisode une étape essentielle dans l'évolution sexuelle du héros Passelion, un moment clef dans son apprentissage du langage et une métaphore.

255 FERLAMPIN-ACHER, Christine, "Le clerc, la Beste et le Lucidaire. Merveilleux et savoir dans quelques romans féeriques en prose des XIVe et XVe siècles," in *Savoirs et fiction au Moyen Âge et à la Renaissance*, éd. Dominique BOUTET et Joëlle DUCOS. Paris: Presses de l'Université Paris-Sorbonne, 2015, pp. 43–58.

L'article montre que le savoir clérical n'est pas étranger aux fictions arthuriennes des XIVe et XVe siècles (essentiellement *Artus de Bretagne*, *Perceforest* et *Ysaïe le Triste*). Dans cette perspective, sont envisagées les insertions savantes, les inventions romanesques inspirées de la culture savante et les procédés de mise à distance du savoir.

256 FERLAMPIN-ACHER, Christine, "Le maître et la marguerite. Les dialogues dans *Artus de Bretagne*," in *Les états du dialogue à l'âge de l'humanisme*, éd. Emmanuel BURON, Philippe GUÉRIN et Claire LESAGE. Rennes-Tours: Presses Universitaires de Rennes – Presses Universitaires François Rabelais, 2015, pp. 243–53.

Comparant le manuscrit et l'imprimé du XVIe siècle, CFA observe l'élimination du dialogue de séduction par le clerc sous la forme d'un exposé encyclopédique : la matrice du débat du clerc et du chevalier est ainsi mise à mal alors qu'elle soutenait la version du XIVe siècle avec deux héroïnes aux noms de fleurs comme juges et un clerc qui fonctionnait comme doublure cléricale l'emportant implicitement sur Artus.

257 FERLAMPIN-ACHER, Christine, "Se promène-t-on dans les romans médiévaux avant 1450?" *Travaux de littérature*, 28 (2015), 11–25.

Après une étude lexicologique posant le problème de la rareté du vocabulaire de la promenade de plaisance en ancien français, l'auteur montre la discrétion du motif dans les romans, avant de mettre en évidence, surtout pour la fin du Moyen Âge, quelques figures de princes poètes et de clercs chevaliers se promenant et l'émergence dans les textes de pratiques sociales ritualisées.

258 FOEHR-JANSSENS, Yasmina, "Le genre du désir dans le *Lancelot en prose*," in *Sens, Rhétorique et Musique. Etudes réunies en hommage à Jacqueline Cerquiglini-Toulet*, éd. Sophie ALBERT, Mireille DEMAULES, Estelle DOUDET, Sylvie LEFÈVRE, Christopher LUCKEN et Agathe SULTAN. Paris: Champion, 2015, pp. 587–601.

En analysant l'épisode de l'amie d'Hector et celui d'Hélène sans Per, l'article montre que dès le *Lancelot en prose* se manifeste une mise en question discrète de l'éthique de la *fin'amor*. Des failles apparaissent dans le discours amoureux et les personnages principaux, tout en souscrivant à la fable courtoise, n'en sont peut-être pas dupes.

259 FORÊT, Jean-Claude, "Robert Lafont, le médiéviste et son désir," in *Les Troubadours dans le texte occitan du XXe siècle*, éd. Marie-Jeanne VERNY. Paris: Classiques Garnier, 2015, pp. 293–315.

Robert Lafont a élaboré une théorie particulière du Moyen Âge, opérant la synthèse de l'épopée et de la lyrique et construisant une réflexion sur le désir. Son œuvre littéraire reflète ces recherches. *Lo Tèrç Morir*, à la fois roman chevaleresque et roman courtois, illustre les thèses développées dans *Le Chevalier et son Désir*, et réécrit le roman de Perceval en en inversant les données.

260 GAGGERO, Massimiliano, "La place de la *Deuxième Continuation* dans le cycle en vers du *Conte du Graal* et dans l'œuvre de Wauchier de Denain,"

in *Wauchier de Denain, polygraphe du XIIIe siècle*, éd. Sébastien DOUCHET. Aix-en-Provence: Presses Universitaires de Provence, 2015, pp. 135–53.

Reprenant les travaux de Corin Corley, l'auteur réévalue à partir d'analyses codicologiques et textuelles les bornes de la *Deuxième Continuation*. La validité de cette hypothèse aurait pour conséquence de redéfinir les contours de l'œuvre romanesque de Wauchier et d'attribuer à la *Première Continuation* une septième branche.

261 GAMBINO, Francesca, "Su alcuni nodi testuali del *Tristan* di Thomas," *Rom*, 133 (2015), 283–52.

Grâce à son expérience de traductrice, l'auteure examine des passages restés obscurs dans les fragments du roman de Thomas.

262 GIOVÉNAL, Carine, *Le Chevalier et le Pèlerin. Idéal, rire et réalité chez Raoul de Houdenc, XIIIe siècle*, Aix-en-Provence: Presses Universitaires de Provence, 2015, 256 p. Senefiance, 62.

Cet essai est consacré à la construction des personnages du chevalier et du pèlerin dans l'œuvre de Raoul de Houdenc (la *Vengeance Raguidel* ayant été écartée). On y trouvera notamment des analyses de *Méraugis de Portlesguez* en tant que roman comique et parodique (chap. 2) et une étude littéraire du personnage principal (chap. 3).

263 GRIMBERT, Joan Tasker, "Refashioning combat in Chrétien's *Cligés* for the Burgundian court," *CRM*, 30 (2015), 359–72.

Une comparaison des grandes scènes de combat du *Cligès* de Chrétien et de sa réfection bourguignonne montre que cette dernière attache beaucoup plus d'importance aux duels, tournois et batailles. Elle reste plus proche de Chrétien dans le cas des tournois ; soit nostalgie, soit effet de l'idéalisation que Chrétien avait déjà imposée au thème et que suivit la réalité.

264 HALARY, Marie-Pascale, "Le *Perlesvaus* et l'ornementation," *RLR*, 119 (2015), 43–65.

Les décors et les objets qui garnissent l'espace du *Perlesvaus* en se parant de toutes les séductions du roman d'Antiquité restent déceptifs car, du point de vue stylistique, la haute *escriture* du roman n'est pas une écriture ornée. Adossée à la figure du Christ, elle se fait *sermo humilis*.

265 *Histoires des Bretagnes 5. En marge*, éd. Hélène BOUGET et Magali COUMERT. Brest: CRBC, 2015, 349 p.

Ce volume rassemble les communications de trois journée d'études et les travaux d'archéologues, historiens, littéraires, historiens de l'art, linguistes sur les espaces d'entre-deux, de contact ou de conflits, investis par des figures de marginaux. Organisé en quatre parties dotées chacune d'une introduction, il rassemble dix-huit articles. Dans "Zone frontalière, limite spatiale", C. Brett, R. Flechner, P. Kernevez, M. P. Baudry et P. Victorin étudient respectivement les marches bretonnes, le pape Grégoire et les missions, les marges de la Bretagne médiévale, les forteresses poitevines des marches de Bretagne et la reconstruction légendaire du combat des Trente de Froissart à la La Villemarqué. Dans "Individus en marge", A. Gautier, J. C. Meuret, A. Queillé et M. Poilvez s'intéressent à Aethelfrith de Northumbrie, au mouvement érémitique à l'est de la Bretagne, à Perceval et aux éléments tristaniens des hors-la-loi des sagas norroises. "Frontières symboliques et culturelles" aborde avec B. F. Roberts, B. Lewis, C. Ferlampin-Acher et H. Tristram le bilinguisme, les poètes gallois du bas Moyen Âge, *Artus de Bretagne* et une prose épique irlandaise, *The Cattle raid of Cuailnge*. Enfin, "Marges du parchemin" envisage les marges des manuscrits avec V. Launay, C. Lloyd-Morgan, M. Tanabé et S. Cassagnes-Brouquet autour des Chabot, sires de Rais, des *marginalia* des manuscrits gallois, des livres d'heures bretons et d'un missel breton.

266 IMPERIALI, Christophe, "Le voir et le voir : savoir et point de vue dans le *Perlesvaus*. Une approche narratologique," *RLR*, 119 (2015), 3–21.

Retour sur l'épisode du Château de l'Enquête et des commentaires de l'ermite destinés à Gauvain envisagé comme une métalepse.

267 IMPERIALI, Christophe, *Perceval en question. Eloge de la curiosité*. Paris: Classiques Garnier, 2015, 279 p.

L'auteur étudie l'évolution du mythe de Perceval du XIIe siècle à nos jours, à travers deux axes d'analyse : les structures relationnelles familiales et le sens métapoétique du mythe. Le premier axe le conduit à envisager la relation du mythe de Perceval avec le mythe d'Oedipe, et à étudier l'œuvre de Julien Gracq comme déploiement d'une "structure percevalienne" profonde; le second axe envisage la quête du Graal comme quête d'un sens ou quête poétique, à travers les œuvres de Wagner, Proust, Bonnefoy, Handke ou encore Perec, lues comme les véritables "arts poétiques percevaliens".

268 *L'Historia regum Britannie et les "Bruts" en Europe*, éd. Hélène Tétrel et Géraldine Veysseyre. Paris: Classiques Garnier, 2015, 368 p.

L'ouvrage se compose de six parties, chacune consacrée à une aire linguistique. Sont d'abord étudiées les premières réécritures latines de Geoffroy de Monmouth, ses versions galloises, le *Roman de Brut* de Wace et les autres "Bruts" insulaires, la place de l'*Historia regum Britannie* dans les compilations en prose, les "Bruts" islandais, puis enfin une adaptation castillane des *Prophéties de Merlin*. Une introduction des éditrices, une bibliographie, des résumés, un index des noms et un index des manuscrits et des imprimés anciens complètent l'étude.

269 La Bretèque (de), François Amy, "Quand les chevaliers de la table ronde se mettent [pour de bon] à table. Nourriture et manières de table dans Kaamelott," in *Chaire, Chair et bonne Chère*, éd. Françoise Mignon et Michel Adroher. Perpignan: Presses Universitaires de Perpignan, 2014, pp. 213–29.

L'auteur étudie dans *Kaamelott* les différentes fonctions du repas, qui apparaît comme un véritable moteur du comique : moment privilégié des conflits familiaux, de relations diplomatiques parodiques ou encore prétexte à la satire sociale, le repas est également au centre de jeux de langage qui le déplacent vers les champs du combat ou de la sexualité.

270 Lacy, Norris J., "'Coda'. *Chinon of England* (1597), or the limits of romance," *CRM*, 30 (2015), 441–50.

Présentation d'un roman du XVIe siècle rempli d'allusions et de références arthuriennes. L'auteur évalue la distance ("ironique") avec laquelle sont reprises ces données relatives à Arthur et à la Table Ronde.

271 *Le Moyen Âge par le Moyen Âge, même. Réception, relectures et réécritures des textes médiévaux dans la littérature française des XIVe et XVe siècle*, éd. Laurent Brun, Silvère Menegaldo, Anne Bengtsson et Dominique Boutet. Paris: Champion, 2015, 325 p.

Le livre interroge la façon dont la littérature française de la fin du Moyen Âge a reçu, relu et réécrit les textes médiévaux antérieurs. La troisième partie de l'ouvrage, consacrée à la matière arthurienne, comporte quatre contributions portant sur l'héritage des formes versifiées dans les mises en prose romanesques, les "jeux" du narrateur dans *Melyador*, la définition du *Cycle Vulgate* dans les manuscritts et les imprimés du XIVe siècle en tant que "cycle" ou "roman-somme", la traduction et l'adaptation de Chrétien de Troyes dans les pays nordiques. En marge de ce chapitre, deux articles traitent du *Roman de la Dame a la Lycorne et du Biau Chevalier au Lyon* et de la réécriture des traditions arthuriennes et mérovingiennes chez Jean d'Outremeuse.

272 LEGRAND, Sandrine ET Marie-Madeleine CASTELLANI, "Introduction," *Bien dire et bien aprandre*, 31 (2015), 5–15.

Étude générale de la tradition littéraire et iconographique des Neuf Preux.

273 LOISON, Marc, *Les Jeux littéraires de Raoul de Houdenc. Ecritures, allégories, et réécritures*. Paris: Honoré Champion, 2015, 456 p.

L'ouvrage propose d'abord une étude de la figure de l'auteur élaborée à partir de sa culture littéraire. L'analyse se concentre ensuite sur l'hétérogénéité des formes et des discours représentés dans l'oeuvre de Raoul de Houdenc en général et au sein de chacun de ses textes. Est ainsi défini un art de la variété commun aux différentes productions de l'auteur. Un intérêt particulier est porté au traitement de l'allégorie par Raoul de Houdenc, ainsi qu'aux modalités de l'intertextualité et de la parodie dans son œuvre. Une dernière partie est consacrée à sa réception et étudie ses différentes réécritures.

274 NICOLAS, Catherine, "*Perlesvaus*. Bibliographie récente," *RLR*, 119 (2015), 133–48.

Bibliographie qui recense les ouvrages et éditions parus dans les vingt dernières années.

275 NICOLAS, Catherine, "*Perlesvaus*. Le sacrement de l'écriture?" *RLR*, 119 (2015), 67–84.

Révélant des mystères du Graal *tot apertement*, sous une forme à la fois horrible et *esperitele*, le *Perlesvaus* associe des montagnes de chair à des flots de sang, laissant ouverte la question d'une sacrement de l'écriture qui pourrait ouvrir une voie de charité.

276 PAVLEVSKI, Joanna, "Les chars dans *Táin bó Cuailnge*. Entre histoire et imagerie symbolique," in *Engins et machines. L'imaginaire mécanique dans les textes médiévaux*, éd. Fabienne POMEL. Rennes: Presses Univsersitaires de Rennes, 2015, pp. 29–63.

Machines extraordinaires, les chars constituent des témoignages précieux de l'âge du fer et du haut Moyen Âge irlandais, dont les traces archéologiques sont presque inexistantes en Irlande. Ils permettent également d'éclairer les principes de composition d'un récit épique qui reste, sur certains points, énigmatique, et de comprendre le fonctionnement symbolique de l'objet dans l'histoire et dans la diégèse. Instrument de valorisation du héros, le char fonctionne comme un signal métonymique traduisant l'identité de son possesseur. Son usage permet d'établir des distinctions taxinomiques et axiologiques entre les personnages.

277 REBICHON, Noëlle-Christine, "Diffusion et réception de la galerie des Neuf Preux en Italie. Étude des peintures murales du Palais Trinci (Ombrie)," *Bien dire et bien aprandre*, 31 (2015), 85–114.

Étude iconographique de la fresque des Neuf Preux du Palais Trinci (1411–1412), contenant aussi une brève étude de la diffusion littéraire du motif des Neuf Preux en Italie.

278 *Repenser le Perlesvaus*, éd. Catherine NICOLAS, Armand STRUBEL et Jean-René VALETTE. Montpellier: Bureau de la Société pour l'étude des langues romanes, 2015, 281 p.

La partie thématique de ce numéro de la *RLR* s'applique à "Repenser le *Perlesvaus*" en multipliant les points de vue sur ce grand roman énigmatique. Le second volet de cette enquête s'attache aux formes pour expérimenter à nouveaux frais le potentiel de mise en œuvre du sens du *Haut Livre du Graal*.

279 *Sens, Rhétorique et Musique. Etudes réunies en hommage à Jacqueline Cerquiglini-Toulet*, éd. Sophie ALBERT, Mireille DEMAULES, Estelle DOUDET,

Sylvie LEFÈVRE, Christopher LUCKEN et Agathe SULTAN. Paris: Honoré Champion, 2015, 1020 p.

5 des 60 articles offerts à Jacqueline Cerquiglini-Toulet sont consacrés à la littérature arthurienne et recensés au nom de leur auteur.

280 TAYLOR, Jane H. M., "Experiments in fiction. Framing and reframing romance at the end of the Middle Ages, and beyond. Introduction," *CRM*, 30 (2015), 287–95.

Introduction à un dossier consacré à plusieurs romans de la seconde moitié du Moyen Âge littéraire ; l'auteur rappelle l'ampleur du chantier de réhabilitation en cours.

281 UELTSCHI, Karin, *Petite histoire de la langue française. Le chagrin du cancre.* Paris: Imago, 2015, 269 p.

Retraçant l'histoire de la langue française en vue de sa vulgarisation, l'auteur consacre quelques pages à la relation que le vers et la prose entretiennent avec la véracité dans la mentalité médiévale et illustre son propos en s'appuyant en partie sur la littérature du graal. Les connexions avec la cour anglaise et leur répercutions sur la langue française sont aussi évoquées.

282 VALETTE, Jean-René, "Fiction arthurienne et "authenticité théologique". La *Queste del Saint Graal*," in *Savoirs et fiction au Moyen Âge et à la Renaissance*, éd. Dominique BOUTET et Joëlle DUCOS. Paris: Presses de l'université Paris-Sorbonne, 2015, 123–42.

L'article s'attache à expliciter la formule de Marie-Dominique Chenu reconnaissant à la *Queste del Saint Graal* une "authenticité théologique". Il examine la conformité du texte à la culture chrétienne (patristique, liturgie, corpus biblique) ("authenticité de la référence") et sa réceptivité aux enjeux sociaux et idéologiques de son temps relatifs à la chevalerie ("authenticité du sens").

283 VALETTE, Jean-René, "Le Graal et le silence de l'Église," *Revue d'histoire de l'Eglise de France*, 101.2 (2015), pp. 262–76.

Pourquoi l'institution ecclésiastique est-elle restée très largement indifférente à l'égard du Graal ? Les prises de positions dogmatiques ou disciplinaires autour du Graal sont de fait extrêmement rares, que ce soit pour valider le matériau ou pour le condamner. Ce silence vaut tout autant pour l'objet Graal lui-même que pour les récits qui l'entouraient (Joseph d'Arimathie, etc.) ou pour l'idéologie qu'il véhiculait (chevalerie "célestielle", etc.). La réponse réside peut-être dans le fait que "pour l'Église, le silence constituait sans doute la seule possibilité. L'authenticité théologique dont le mythe du Graal était porteur ne lui permettait pas de le condamner. L'orientation idéologique dont il était le vecteur ne l'autorisait pas non plus à le faire sien." (p. 275)

284 *Wauchier de Denain, polygraphe du XIIIe siècle*, éd. Sébastien Douchet. Aix-en-Provence: Presses Universitaires de Provence, 2015, 166 p.

Ce volume consacré au caractère polygraphique de l'oeuvre de Wauchier de Denain réunit huit études dont les deux dernières se penchent sur la *Deuxième Continuation* du *Conte du Graal*, en particulier sur la contamination de l'écriture en vers par la forme prose (Annie Combes) et sur les frontières et la cohérence textuelle de ce roman arthurien tel qu'il apparaît dans les manuscrits cycliques en vers de Graal (Massimiliano Gaggero).

III Comptes Rendus

285 *Le Roman de Merlin en prose*, Corinne Füg-Pierreville. Paris: Champion Classiques, 2014, 496 p. (cf. *BIAS*, LXVII, 2015, 315).

C.R. par Berthelot, Anne, *Perspectives médiévales*, 36 (2015), online.

286 *L'Historia regum Britannie et les "Bruts" en Europe*, éd. Hélène Tétrel et Géraldine Veysseyre. Paris: Classiques Garnier, 2015, 368 p.

C.R. par Laurent, Françoise, *CRM*, 2015 (2015), online.

287 Mela, Charles, *Variations sur l'Amour et le Graal*. Geneva: Droz, 2012, 203 p. (cf. *BIAS*, LXV, 2013, 185).

C.R. par Valette, Jean-René, *Rom*, 133 (2015), 507–12.

288 Obry, Vanessa, *Et pour ce fu ainsi nommee. Linguistique de la désignation et écriture du personnage dans les romans français en vers des XIIe et XIIIe siècles*. Genève: Droz, 2013, 466 p.

C.R. par Bouget, Hélène, *Perspectives médiévales*, 36 (2015), online.
C.R. par James-Raoul, Danièle, *Rom*, 133 (2015), 246–52.

Great Britain and Ireland

Bibliography for 2015 compiled by Kit Kapphahn

I Editions and Transcriptions

289 CHRÉTIEN DE TROYES, *The Complete Story of the Grail. Chrétien de Troyes' Perceval and its continuations*, ed. and trans. by Nigel BRYANT. Woodbridge: Boydell & Brewer, 2015, 634 p. Arthurian Studies.

The mysterious and haunting Grail makes its first appearance in literature in Chrétien de Troyes' Perceval at the end of the twelfth century. But Chrétien never finished his poem, leaving an unresolved story and an incomplete picture of the Grail. Not only did it inspire quite separate works; his own unfinished poem was continued and finally completed by no fewer than four other writers. The Complete Story of the Grail is the first ever translation of the whole of the rich and compelling body of tales contained in Chrétien's poem and its four Continuations.

290 *Il Tristano Corsiniano*, ed. by Gloria ALLAIRE. Woodbridge: Boydell & Brewer, 2015, 228 p. Italian Literature, 3.

The Tristano Corsiniano is preserved in a unique manuscript of the Biblioteca Corsiniana housed at the Accademia Nazionale dei Lincei in Rome (MS 55.K.5; formerly Rossi 2593). Written in a mixture of northeastern Italian dialects, the manuscript was probably copied in the third quarter of the fourteenth century. The contents are a much abbreviated descendent of the noted French prose Roman de Tristan; opening with Dinadan's amusing discourses and misadventures, the majority of the story concerns the famous three-day Tournament at Loverzep, and concludes with King Arthur and Lancelot visiting Tristan, Yseut and their companions.

https://doi.org/10.1515/9783110467499-103

II Critical and Historical Studies

291 ALVAR, Carlos, "The Matter of Britain in Spanish Society and Literature from Cluny to Cervantes," in *The Arthur of the Iberians. The Arthurian Legends in the Spanish and Portuguese Worlds*, ed. David HOOK. Cardiff: University of Wales Press, 2015, pp. 187–270.

Alvar highlights the shift from Visigothic to Carolingian culture in medieval Iberia to show how Arthurian material entered the peninsula and overviews the earliest visual presentations of peninsular Arthurian material and considers the medieval Hispanic fashion for Arthurian personal names.

292 ARCHIBALD, Elizabeth, "Ruodlieb and Romance in Latin. Audience and Authorship," in *Telling the Story in the Middle Ages: Essays in Honour of Evelyn Birge Vitz*, ed. Kathryn A. DUYS, Elizabeth EMERY, and Laurie POSTLEWATE. Woodbridge: Boydell & Brewer, 2015, pp. 171–86.

Examines storytelling by clerics, focusing on fragments of the *Ruodlieb*, an eleventh-century Latin verse narrative that combines elements from various traditions. Archibald compares it to *Apollonius of Tyre* and later Arthurian Latin romances, speculating about the hybrid nature of Latin romance.

293 *Arthurian Literature XXXII*, ed. Elizabeth ARCHIBALD and David JOHNSON. Woodbridge: Boydell & Brewer, 2015, 218 p.

The essays collected here put considerable emphasis on Arthurian narratives in material culture and historical context, as well as on purely literary analysis, a reminder of the enormous range of interests in Arthurian narratives in the Middle Ages, in a number of different contexts.

294 BADEN-DAINTREE, Anne, "Kingship and the Intimacy of Grief in the Alliterative Morte Arthure," in *Emotions in Medieval Arthurian Literature*, ed. Frank BRANDSMA, Carolyne LARRINGTON, and Corinne SAUNDERS. Woodbridge: Boydell & Brewer, 2015, pp. 87–104.

Argues that the king's grief occupies a liminal space which, while normally private, can sometimes occur publicly with a high level of intimacy.

295 Brandsma, Frank, "Emotion and Voice. 'Ay' in Middle Dutch Arthurian Romances," in *Emotions in Medieval Arthurian Literature. Body, Mind, Voice*, ed. Frank Brandsma, Carolyne Larrington, and Corinne Saunders. Woodbridge: Boydell & Brewer, 2015, pp. 143–60.

Focuses on a single exclamation that can express fear, admiration, curiosity, and sadness, providing the audience with direct access to the characters' minds.

296 Breeze, Andrew, "The Historical Arthur and Sixth-Century Scotland," *Northern History*, 52.2 (2015), 158–81.

The twelve battles of Arthur listed by the ninth-century Historia Brittonum have been a intractable problem. This paper gives an outline of discussion past and present, before offering some conclusions on where the conflicts were and what they imply for the historical Arthur and Northern history in the sixth century.

297 Cartlidge, Neil, "The Werewolf of Wicklow. Shapeshifting and Colonial Identity in the Lai de Melion," in *Medieval Romance and Material Culture*, ed. Nicholas Perkins. Woodbridge: Boydell & Brewer, 2015, pp. 75–90.

This essay is an analysis of the implied cultural geography of the Lai de Melion, an anonymous Old French narrative lay now extant only in a thirteenth-century manuscript in the Bibliothèque d'Arsenal in Paris.

298 Chapman, James, *Swashbucklers. The costume adventure series*. Manchester: University of Manchester Press, 2015, 296 p.

Swashbucklers is the first study of one of the most popular and enduring genres in television history – the costume adventure series. It maps the history of swashbuckling television from its origins in the 1950s to the present. It places the various series in their historical and institutional contexts and also analyses how the form and style of the genre has changed over time. And it includes case studies of major swashbuckling series including The Adventures of Robin Hood, The Buccaneers, Ivanhoe, William Tell, Zorro, Arthur of the Britons, Dick Turpin, Robin of Sherwood, and others.

299 Clark, David Eugene, "Scribal modifications to concluding formulae in the Winchester Manuscript," in *Arthurian Literature XXXII*, ed. Elizabeth Archibald and David Johnson. Woodbridge: Boydell & Brewer, 2015, pp. 123–54.

Analyses concluding formulae in the Winchester manuscript version of Malory's Morte Darthur, compared with Caxton's printed version. Argues that scribes made numerous and significant changes to the structure and division of Malory's text.

300 Cooper, Helen, "Arthur in Transition. Malory's *Morte Darthur*," in *Romance and History: Imagining time from the medieval to the early modern period*, ed. Jon Whitman. Cambridge: Cambridge University Press, 2015, pp. 120–36.

Cooper argues that Malory's Morte Darthur became the source text for later writers presenting Arthurian material in English. By the twentieth century, Arthur had developed enough cultural prominence that writers indirectly drew upon Malory as their source, often without attribution or knowledge of the medieval original.

301 Cooper, Helen, "Malory's Enigmatic Smiles," in *Emotions in Medieval Arthurian Literature. Body, Mind, Voice*, ed. Frank Brandsma, Carolyne Larrington, and Corinne Saunders. Woodbridge: Boydell & Brewer, 2015, pp. 181–88.

Cooper argues that smiles in the Morte Darthur mostly signify joy, and that Malory appears to carry meanings close to the surface, but can require detailed attention.

302 Day, Jenny, "Weapons and fighting in "Y Gododdin"," *Studia Celtica*, 49 (2015), 121–47.

The paper presents a quantitative survey of weapon-related terminology and imagery in Y Gododdin, discussing the kinds of weapons mentioned, how they are used, and by whom. Comparisons are drawn with other Welsh poetry and with archaeological and historical evidence.

303 DICKSON, Morgan, "The Image of the Knightly Harper. Symbolism and Resonance," in *Medieval Romance and Material Culture*, ed. Nicholas PERKINS. Woodbridge: Boydell & Brewer, 2015, pp. 199–214.

This essay explores the symbolism and material contexts of a number of knightly figures who play the harp in twelfth-century Insular texts. Tristan is perhaps the best known of the harpers, and Horn is close at his heels, followed by the more problematic Hereward.

304 *Emotions in Medieval Arthurian Literature. Body, Mind, Voice*, ed. Frank BRANDSMA, Carolyne LARRINGTON, and Corrine SAUNDERS. Woodbridge: Boydell & Brewer, 2015, 221 p.

Literary texts complicate our understanding of medieval emotions; they not only represent characters experiencing emotion and reaction emotionally to the behaviour of others within the text, but also evoke and play upon emotion in the audiences which heard these texts performed or read. The presentation and depiction of emotion in the Arthurian legend is the subject of this volume. The essays presented here explore notions of embodiment, the affective quality of the construction of mind, and the intermediary role of the voice as both an embodied and consciously articulating emotion.

305 FUKSAS, Anatole, "Ire, Peor and their Somatic Correlates in Chrétien's Chevalier de la Charrette," in *Emotions in Medieval Arthurian Literature. Body, Mind, Voice*, ed. Frank BRANDSMA, Carolyne LARRINGTON, and Corinne SAUNDERS. Woodbridge: Boydell & Brewer, 2015, pp. 67–86.

Uses evidence from neuroscience to discuss the range of meanings in two Old French works.

306 FULTON, Helen, "Translating Europe in Medieval Wales," in *Writing Europe, 500–1450. Texts and Contexts*, ed. Aiden CONTI, Orietta DA ROLD, and Philip SHAW. Woodbridge: Boydell & Brewer, 2015, pp. 159–74.

Explores the European influences on vernacular Welsh medieval literary culture.

307 GARCÍA, Santiago Gutiérrez, "Arthurian Literature in Portugal," in *The Arthur of the Iberians. The Arthurian Legends in the Spanish and Portu-*

guese Worlds, ed. David Hook. Cardiff: University of Wales Press, 2015, pp. 58–117.

García argues that Arthurian literature was influential in medieval Portugal before the mid-thirteenth century and offers detailed summaries of Portuguese Arthurian texts. He suggests a need to reconsider the scholarly association of the entrance of Arthurian material into Portugal with Alfonso III. He also discusses post-medieval Portuguese Arthurian chivalric romances.

308 Gilbert, Jane, "Being-in-the-Arthurian-World: Emotion, Affect and Magic in the Prose Lancelot, Sartre and Jay," in *Emotions in Medieval Arthurian Literature*, ed. Frank Brandsma, Carolyne Larrington, and Corrine Saunders. Woodbridge: Boydell & Brewer, 2015, pp. 13–30.

Jean-Paul Sartre's 1939 Esquisse d'une théorie des émotions emerges from his engagement with Edmund Husserl's phenomenology, which studies consciousness from the point of view of the first-person subject interrelating with objects. The Sketch outlines what a phenomenological theory of the emotions might look like.

309 Gillingham, John, "Richard of Devizes and a 'rising tide of nonsense'. How Cerdic Met King Arthur," in *The Long Twelfth-Century View of the Anglo-Saxon Past*, ed. Martin Brett and David A. Goodman. Farnham: Ashgate, 2015, pp. 141–58.

Gillingham discusses the influence of Geoffrey of Monmouth on Richard of Devizes, a late twelfth-century Benedictine who belonged to Winchester Cathedral priory. He highlights the points at which Richard diverges from his Galfridian source, especially Richard's invention of a decisive battle between King Arthur and Cerdic of Wessex, his presentation of Wessex as land that Arthur and Modred granted to Cerdic, and his presentation of the Anglo-Saxons as descended from Britons who went to Germany.

310 Gracia, Paloma, "Arthurian Material in Iberia," in *The Arthur of the Iberians. The Arthurian Legends in the Spanish and Portuguese Worlds*, ed. David Hook. Cardiff: University of Wales Press, 2015, pp. 11–32.

Gracia examines the medieval reception of Arthurian material in the Iberian Peninsula. She argues that Arthurian texts penetrated into Peninsular culture. She also overviews some of the main Catalan translations and recreations of Arthurian narratives and stresses Catalan interest in narratives involving Lancelot, Tristan, and the Holy Grail.

311 Gracia, Paloma, "The Post-Vulgate Cycle in the Iberian Peninsula," in *The Arthur of the Iberians. The Arthurian Legends in the Spanish and Portuguese Worlds*, ed. David Hook. Cardiff: University of Wales Press, 2015, pp. 271–88.

Gracia introduces the Spanish and Portuguese textual witnesses of the Post-Vulgate cycle, describing codicological features as well as narrative content. Reminding readers that it is uncertain into which Peninsular language the original French narrative cycle was translated, Gracia offers an overview of the scholarly positions attached to the debate.

312 Gradín, Pilar Lorenzo, "The Matière de Bretagne in Galicia from the XIIth to the XVth Century," in *The Arthur of the Iberians. The Arthurian Legends in the Spanish and Portuguese Worlds*, ed. David Hook. Cardiff: University of Wales Press, 2015, pp. 118–61.

Gradín argues that the Occitan troubadours played an intermediary role in the transmission of the Arthurian tradition to the Iberian peninsula. She also points out the divergences between Peninsular and French versions of Arthurian narratives.

313 Griffin, Miranda, *Transforming Tales. Rewriting Metamorphosis in Medieval French Literature*. Oxford: Oxford University Press, 2015, 270 p.

Transforming Tales argues that the study of transformation is crucial for understanding a wide range of canonical work in medieval French literature. From the lais and Arthurian romances of the twelfth and thirteenth centuries, through the Roman de la Rose and its widespread influence, to the fourteenth-century Ovide moralisé and the vast prose cycles of the late Middle Ages, metamorphosis is a recurrent theme, resulting in some of the best-known and most powerful literature of the era.

314 Hanning, Robert W., "Inescapable History. Geoffrey of Monmouth's History of the Kings of Britain and Arthurian romances of the twelfth and thirteenth centuries," in *Romance and History. Imagining time from the*

medieval to the early modern period, ed. Jon WHITMAN. Cambridge: Cambridge University Press, 2015, pp. 55–73.

Hanning uses Geoffrey of Monmouth's presentation of King Leir's tomb as a metaphor for the ways in which Geoffrey's text created a monument for Britain's fictive history that also propelled that history forward to generate the new vernacular literary genre of chivalric romance.

315 HATT, Cecilia, *God and the Gawain-Poet. Theology and Genre in Pearl, Cleanness, Patience and Sir Gawain and the Green Knight*. Cambridge: D.S. Brewer, 2015, 249 p.

Hatt argues that the Gawain-poet presents a coherent artistic vision in the four poems that are collected together in the manuscript. She examines Pearl as a dream-vision, Cleanness as a sermon, Patience as a fable, and Sir Gawain and the Green Knight as an Arthurian quest-romance, ultimately arguing that, in each of these works, the poet stresses complete dependance on God. Hatt also posits that Sir Gawain and the Green Knight is intended to provoke the narrative's audience to debate about the social and moral effects of romance.

316 HOOK, David, "Arthur Goes Global. Arthurian Material in Hispanic and Portuguese America and Asia," in *The Arthur of the Iberians. The Arthurian Legends in the Spanish and Portuguese Worlds*, ed. David HOOK. Cardiff: University of Wales Press, 2015, pp. 382–407.

Hook argues that the Iberian Peninsula was important to the diffusion of Arthurian literature. He discusses Arthurian allusions in Conquistador narratives, copies of Arthurian texts that were brought into the New World, and the prevalence of Arthurian personal names among sixteenth-century Hispanic immigrants in America and Asia.

317 KENDALL, Elliot, "The Evolution of Cooperation in The Avowyng of Arthur," in *Medieval Romance and Material Culture*, ed. Nicholas PERKINS. Woodbridge: Boydell & Brewer, 2015, pp. 111–28.

Discusses materiality and the body in The Avowyng of Arthur.

318 KENNEDY, Edward D., "The prose Brut, Hardyng's Chronicle, and the alliterative Morte Arthure. The end of the story," in *Romance and History. Imag-*

ining time from the medieval to the early modern period, ed. Jon WHITMAN. Cambridge: Cambridge University Press, 2015, pp. 105–19.

Kennedy examines how the prose Brut, Hardyng's Chronicle, and the alliterative Morte Arthure present the ending of King Arthur's story. He argues that, although the alliterative text is the most popular of these narratives today, medieval audiences would have been more familiar with the prose Brut and Hardyng's Chronicle.

319 LABBIE, Erin Felicia, "Pop Medievalism," in *Studies in Medievalism XXIV: Medievalism on the Margins*, ed. Karl FUGELSO, Vincent FERRÉ, and Alicia C. MONTOYA. Woodbridge: Boydell & Brewer, 2015, pp. 21–30.

Considers modern interpretations of medieval material, including Arthurian, in contemporary culture.

320 LANGESLAG, Paul S., *Seasons in the Literatures of the Medieval North*. Woodbridge: Boydell & Brewer, 2015, 258 p.

This book analyses the narrative and psychological functions of seasonal settings in the literatures of medieval England and Iceland from the eighth to the fourteenth century, from Beowulf to Sir Gawain and the Green Knight. Dealing with both the material realities and the figurative functions of the seasonal cycle, it interprets seasonal spaces in myth and literature as conventionalised environments, where society deals with outside threats and powers which manifest themselves in marginal landscapes.

321 LARRINGTON, Carolyne, "Mourning Gawein. Cognition and Affect in Diu Crône and Some French Gauvain-Texts," in *Emotions in Medieval Arthurian Literature. Body, Mind, Voice*, ed. Frank BRANDSMA, Carolyne LARRINGTON, and Corinne SAUNDERS. Woodbridge: Boydell & Brewer, 2015, pp. 123–42.

Analyses the emotional affect on readers and characters in the scene in an episode in which the audience has information about an emotional display the characters do not.

322 LARRINGTON, Carolyne, *The Land of the Green Man. A Journey Through the Supernatural Landscapes of the British Isles*. London: I.B. Tauris & Co, 2015, 256 p.

How have the remarkably persistent folkloric traditions of the British Isles formed and been formed by the psyches of those who inhabit them? Larrington explores the diverse ways in which a myriad of fantastical beings has moulded the nation's cultural history, including references to Arthurian traditions.

323 LEITCH, Megan, *Romancing Treason. The Literature of the Wars of the Roses*. Oxford: Oxford University Press, 2015, 218 p.

Romancing Treason addresses the scope and significance of the secular literary culture of the Wars of the Roses, and especially of the Middle English romances that were distinctively written in prose during this period. Megan Leitch argues that the pervasive textual presence of treason during the decades c.1437–c.1497 suggests a way of conceptualising the understudied space between the Lancastrian literary culture of the early fifteenth century and the Tudor literary cultures of the early and mid-sixteenth century.

324 LYNCH, Andrew, "What cheer? Emotion and Action in the Arthurian World," in *Emotions in Medieval Arthurian Literature. Body, Mind, Voice*, ed. Frank BRANDSMA, Carolyne LARRINGTON, and Corinne SAUNDERS. Woodbridge: Boydell & Brewer, 2015, pp. 47–64.

Analyses and contrasts public moments of emotional expression for Arthurian characters.

325 MANUWALD, Henrike, "Carving the Folie Tristan. Ivory Caskets as Material Evidence of Textual History," in *Medieval Romance and Material Culture*, ed. Nicholas PERKINS. Woodbridge: Boydell & Brewer, 2015, pp. 215–32.

Examines the relationship between word and image, manuscript and ivory, with regard to the Folie Tristan.

326 MARTÍN, Antonio Contreras, "The Hispanic Versions of the Lancelot en prose. Lanzarote del Lago and Lançalot," in *The Arthur of the Iberians. The Arthurian Legends in the Spanish and Portuguese Worlds*, ed. David HOOK. Cardiff: University of Wales Press, 2015, pp. 289–308.

Despite the prolific diffusion of the Vulgate's Lancelot en prose in Iberia, only two textual witnesses survive. Martín describes each of these manuscripts in detail, considering codicological and narrative features and potential textual sources. He also examines textual evidence from the later medieval period that attests to the narrative's popularity.

327 McKinstry, Jamie, *Middle English Romance and the Craft of Memory*. Woodbridge: Boydell & Brewer, 2015, 289 p. Studies in Medieval Romance.

In Middle English romances many memories are created, stored, forgotten, and rediscovered by both the characters and audience; such memory work is not, however, either simple or obvious. This study examines the ways in which recollection is achieved and sustained through physical, cognitive, and interpretative challenges. It uses examples such as Sir Gawain and the Green Knight, Sir Orfeo, and Emaré, alongside romances by Chaucer and Malory, to investigate the genre's reliance on individual and collective memorial processes.

328 *Medieval Romance and Material Culture*, ed. Nicholas Perkins. Woodbridge: Boydell & Brewer, 2015, 311 p.

Medieval romance narratives glitter with the material objects that were valued and exchanged in late-medieval society: lovers' rings and warriors' swords, holy relics and desirable or corrupted bodies. Romance, however, is also a genre in which such objects make meaning on numerous levels, and not always in predictable ways. These new essays examine from diverse perspectives how romances respond to material culture, but also show how romance as a genre helps to constitute and transmit that culture.

329 Megías, José Manuel Lucía, "The Surviving Peninsular Arthurian Witnesses. A Description and an Analysis," in *The Arthur of the Iberians. The Arthurian Legends in the Spanish and Portuguese Worlds*, ed. David Hook. Cardiff: University of Wales Press, 2015, pp. 33–57.

Megías points out that we only have evidence of eighteen manuscripts and nine printed witnesses of Hispanic Arthurian texts that circulated in medieval Iberia. He describes each of the known witnesses and hypothesises that the paucity in surviving material might result from manuscripts being fragmented and reused.

330 NIEVERGELT, Marco, "The Place of Emotion. Space, silence and interiority in the Stanzaic Morte Arthur," in *Arthurian Literature XXXII*, ed. Elizabeth ARCHIBALD and David JOHNSON. Woodbridge: Boydell & Brewer, 2015, pp. 31–58.

Discusses emotion in relation to space in the Stanzaic Morte, indicating a subtle attitude to subjectivity and interiority.

331 NORRIS, Ralph, "Another source for Malory's 'Tale of Sir Gareth'," in *Arthurian Literature XXXII*, ed. Elizabeth ARCHIBALD and David JOHNSON. Woodbridge: Boydell & Brewer, 2015, pp. 59–74.

Sheds new light on Malory's posible source(s) for 'The Tale of Sir Gareth' and also on the popular Fair Unknown theme.

332 PERKINS, Nicholas, "Introduction. The Materiality of Medieval Romance and The Erle of Tolous," in *Medieval Romance and Material Culture*, ed. Nicholas PERKINS. Woodbridge: Boydell & Brewer, 2015, pp. 1–22.

Explores how medieval romances respond to material culture, but also how romance itself helps to constitute and transmit that culture. Includes discussion of Chrétien's romances.

333 RADULESCU, Raluca, "Tears and Lies. Emotions and the Ideals of Malory's Arthurian World," in *Emotions in Medieval Arthurian Literature. Body, Mind, Voice*, ed. Frank BRANDSMA, Carolyne LARRINGTON, and Corinne SAUNDERS. Woodbridge: Boydell & Brewer, 2015, pp. 105–22.

Argues that extreme emotions expressed both at the individual and the collective level in the Morte Darthur bring out an essential tool in the interpretation of Malory's politically astute rewriting of the Arthurian story.

334 RAMOS, Rafael, "Amadís de Gaula," in *The Arthur of the Iberians. The Arthurian Legends in the Spanish and Portuguese Worlds*, ed. David HOOK. Cardiff: University of Wales Press, 2015, pp. 364–81.

Ramos argues for the originality and impact of Amadís de Gaula, a Castilian text that imitates the adventures of Lancelot and Tristan. He studies the text's adherence to and modifications of the Arthurian tradition and asserts the narrative's influence on chivalric literature.

335 Randles, Sarah, "Heraldic imagery in the embroidered Tristan narratives," in *Arthurian Literature XXXII*, ed. Elizabeth Archibald and David Johnson. Woodbridge: Boydell & Brewer, 2015, pp. Arthurian Literature XXXII.

Examines fragments of needlework and heraldic devices in the later Tristan legends. These devices emphasise aspects of the plot, but also link patrons to prestigious legendary figures.

336 Rikhardsdottir, Sif, "Translating Emotion. Vocalisation and Embodiment in Yvain and Ívens saga," in *Emotions in Medieval Arthurian Literature. Body, Mind, Voice*, ed. Frank Brandsma, Carolyne Larrington, and Corinne Saunders. Woodbridge: Boydell & Brewer, 2015, pp. 161–80.

Analyses scene of grief in Chrétien and its Norse translations, demonstrating that the French version has a more emotive vocabulary while the Norse ues more interiority of emotion.

337 Robeson, Lisa, "Warre and Worshyppe'. Depictions of Battle in Malory's Le Morte Darthur," in *Arthurian Literature XXXII*, ed. Elizabeth Archibald and David Johnson. Woodbridge: Boydell & Brewer, 2015, pp. 75–104.

Argues that battle scenes in Malory's Morte Darthur offer lessons in chivalric kingship as well as chivalry itself, and that chivary must be embodied in the person of the king.

338 Robles, Lourdes Soriano, "The Matière de Bretagne in the Corona de Aragón," in *The Arthur of the Iberians. The Arthurian Legends in the Spanish and Portuguese Worlds*, ed. David Hook. Cardiff: University of Wales Press, 2015, pp. 182–86.

Robles examines the reception of Arthurian material in the Crown of Aragòn in the twelfth and thirteenth centuries. She considers the circulation and translation into Catalan of Arthurian texts and offers an overview of the first native Arthurian texts, which were composed in the fourteenth century. She also discusses the influence of French Arthurian texts on Catalan chivalric romances.

339 Saunders, Corinne, "Mind, Body and Affect in Medieval English Arthurian Romance," in *Emotions in Medieval Arthurian Literature*, ed. Frank

BRANDSMA, Carolyne LARRINGTON, and Corinne SAUNDERS. Woodbridge: Boydell & Brewer, 2015, pp. 31–46.

Discusses the medieval roots of a shift toward 'affect' in literary studies.

340 SÉVÈRE, Richard, "Malory's 'Chivalric Cliques'. Public and private felyshyp in the Arthurian community," in *Arthurian Literature XXXII*, ed. Elizabeth ARCHIBALD and David JOHNSON. Woodbridge: Boydell & Brewer, 2015, pp. 105–22.

Considers Arthurian fellowship in Malory through the lens of Cicero's comments on friendship in *De amicitia*, and emphasises the comfort of fellowship as well as its dangers in the Arthurian world.

341 *Studies in Medievalism XXIV. Medievalism on the Margins*, ed. Karl FUGELSO, Vincent FERRÉ, and Alicia C. MONTOYA. Woodbridge: Boydell & Brewer, 2015, 258 p.

This volume not only defines medievalism's margins, as well as its role in marginalizing other fields, ideas, people, places, and events, but also provides tools and models for exploring those issues and indicates new subjects to which they might apply. Contains material on modern interpretations of Arthuriana.

342 TAHKOKALLIO, Jaako, "Update to the list of manuscripts of Geoffrey of Monmouth's Historia Regun Britanniae," in *Arthurian Literature XXXII*, ed. Elizabeth ARCHIBALD and David JOHNSON. Woodbridge: Boydell & Brewer, 2015, pp. 187–204.

Adds recent discoveries to list of manuscripts of Geoffrey of Monmouth's *Historia regum Britanniae*.

343 *Telling the Story in the Middle Ages. Essays in Honour of Evelyn Birge Vitz*, ed. Kathryn A. DUYS, Elizabeth EMERY, and Laurie POSTLEWATE. Woodbridge: Boydell & Brewer, 2015, 282 p.

The storyteller stands at the crossroads of orality and performance, surrounded by a circle of rapt listeners. Evelyn Birge Vitz has challenged a generation of scholars to join the circle, listen as they read, and exchange pen for performance. A tribute to her work, the fifteen essays in this volume attend to the qualities of voice, their registers and dynamics, whether practiced or impromptu, falsified, overlapping, interrupted or whispered. Includes some Arthurian material and the theoretical framework may be of interest to Arthurians.

344 *The Arthur of the Iberians. The Arthurian Legends in the Spanish and Portuguese Worlds*, ed. David HOOK. Cardiff: University of Wales Press, 2015, 531 p.

This volume fills a gap in Arthurian studies. The collection of twelve essays offers an overview of Arthurian materials in the languages and cultures of the Iberian Peninsula, which include Spanish, Portuguese, Catalan, and Galician. It also examines Arthurian narratives in places that were colonised by the Spanish and Portuguese, bringing in indigenous American, Latin American, and Philippine Arthurian stories. The collection highlights medieval Arthurian texts that have significantly impacted the development of Spanish literature, particularly the Post-Vulgate cycle, narratives about Tristan, and narratives about Lancelot.

345 TORRE, María Luzdivina Cuesta, "The Iberian Tristan Texts of the Middle Ages and Renaissance," in *The Arthur of the Iberians. The Arthurian Legends in the Spanish and Portuguese Worlds*, ed. David HOOK. Cardiff: University of Wales Press, 2015, pp. 309–63.

Torre studies the legend of Tristan's medieval Castilian textual witnesses and relates two different versions of the narrative. Examines Castilian Tristan texts in light of the broader European Tristan legends, the relationships between the Iberian Peninsula's various Tristan manuscripts, and the reworking of these sources by late medieval printed editions.

346 TRACY, Larissa, "Wounded Bodies. Kingship, National Identity and Illegitimate Torture in the English Arthurian Tradition," in *Arthurian Literature XXXII*, ed. Elizabeth ARCHIBALD and David JOHNSON. Woodbridge: Boydell & Brewer, 2015, pp. 1–30.

Argues that the inclusion or omission of torture in English texts reflects particular attitudes to the use of torture in English law and society.

347 WINGFIELD, Emily, "Lancelot of the Laik and the Literary Manuscript Miscellany in 15th- and 16th-century Scotland," in *Insular Books: Vernacular manuscript miscellanies in late medieval Britain*, ed. Margaret CONNOLLY and Raluca RADULESCU. Oxford: Oxford University Press, 2015, pp. 209–30.

Wingfield overviews the main features of Scottish literary manuscript miscellanies and uses CUL MS Kk.1.5, which contains a unique witness of the Older Scots romance Lancelot of the Laik as a case study. She suggests that analysing Lancelot within its wider manuscript context supports established scholarly perspectives of the romance as a text that promotes good governance.

348 WOOD, Lucas, "Of werewolves and wicked women. Melion's misogyny reconsidered," *Medium Aevum*, 84.1 (2015), 60–88.

Discusses the motif of the werewolf in Old French romance and its particular concerns with masculinity.

349 *Writing Europe, 500–1450. Texts and Contexts*, ed. Aiden CONTI, Orietta DA ROLD, and Philip SHAW. Woodbridge: Boydell & Brewer, 2015, 216 p.

Medieval Europe was characterized by a sophisticated market for the production, exchange and sale of written texts. This volume brings together papers on a range of topics, centred on manuscript studies and textual criticism, which explore these issues from a pan-European perspective. They examine the prolonged and varied processes through which Europe's different parts entered into modern reading, writing and communicative practices, drawing on a range of approaches and perspectives; they consider material culture, multilingualism in texts and books, book history, readers, audience and scribes across the Middle Ages. At least one chapter is of Arthurian interest.

350 ZARANDONA, Juan Miguel, "The Contemporary Return of the Matter of Britain to Iberian Letters (XIXth to XXIst Centuries)," in *The Arthur of the Iberians. The Arthurian Legends in the Spanish and Portuguese Worlds*, ed. David HOOK. Cardiff: University of Wales Press, 2015, pp. 408–45.

Surveys Iberian Arthurian literature from the nineteenth to the twenty-first centuries, argues that nineteenth-century texts renewed peninsular interest in Arthurian literature, highlights peninsular texts that were inspired by Tennyson and Wagner, and considers narratives that imagine a Celtic past for Galicia. Also overviews neo-medieval texts, films, comics, and children's literature.

Italie

Bibliographie pour 2015 établie par Beatrice Barbiellini Amidei, Matteo Cambi, Fabrizio Cigni, Maria Colombo Timelli, Martina Crosio, Barbara Ferrari, Pierre Anatole Fuksas, Massimiliano Gaggero, Gioia Paradisi, Arianna Punzi, Stefano Resconi, Roberto Tagliani

I Éditions et Traductions

351 Beltrami, Pietro, "Una traduzione di Maria di Francia. Il *Lai del Caprifoglio*," *Studi di Filologia Italiana*, 72 (2014), 5–10.

P.B. offre ici une belle traduction italienne, en vers, du *Chèvrefeuille* de Marie de France, basée sur l'édition Rychner (1966), sauf pour les v. 62 et 109, pour lesquels – en suivant l'opinion de R. Trachsler – Beltrami adopte le texte du manuscrit *S*, et donc l'édition de Mireille Demaules (1995). (M.C.T.)

352 de Carné, Damien et Yan Greub, "Fragments des Continuations du *Conte du Graal* aux Archives Départementales de Nancy. 1. La Première Continuation," *MR*, 39.2 (2015), 293–320.

Après avoir décrit les sept fragments d'un manuscrit (*n*) qui conservent des passages de la *Première* et de la *Troisième Continuation*, les Auteurs étudient et éditent ceux de la *Première Continuation*, qui peuvent être assignés à la rédaction brève (*ASPU*); la proximité *n / A* permet en particulier de reconnaître les innovations introduites par Guiot par rapport au modèle commun. (M.G.)

353 *La Struzione della Tavola Ritonda (I Cantari di Lancillotto),* a cura di Maria Bendinelli Predelli. Firenze: Società Editrice Fiorentina, 2015, 208 p. Studi, 17.

Version revue et mise à jour de l'édition publiée par M.B.P. en 2012 (cf. *BIAS*, LXV, 2013, 391). Le volume est enrichi d'une étude introductive qui

https://doi.org/10.1515/9783110467499-120

analyse le rapport des *cantari* transmis par le ms. Firenze, BML, Plut. LXXVIII 23 avec leur source directe: une version perdue (vraisemblablement en vulgaire italien) de la *Mort le roi Artu*. (B.F.)

354 Lagomarsini, Claudio, "Due giunte inedite (Febusso e Lancillotto) alla corona di sonetti sugli affreschi giotteschi di Castel Nuovo," *SM*, 56 (2015), 195–223.

L'auteur identifie un nouveau témoin (*FL*[4]) de la série de sonnets sur les héros du passé attribuée à Giovanni da Firenze / Malizia Barattone, qui se serait inspiré des fresques perdues de la Sala Maior de Castelnuovo. *FL*[4] est seul (sur dix témoins) à présenter deux sonnets consacrés à Lancelot et Fébus. L'auteur en donne une édition et une étude détaillée, et les attribue à la série originale. (M.G.)

355 *Lais di Guingamor, Tydorel, Tyolet*, a cura di Margherita Lecco. Alessandria: Edizioni dell'Orso, 2015, 133 p. Studi e Ricerche, 135.

Édition annotée de trois lais anonymes, sur la base du ms. Paris, BnF, fr. 1104, accompagnée d'une traduction italienne en regard. L'introduction fait le point sur le parcours de ce genre narratif: de Marie de France à la 'nouvellisation' de la fin du moyen âge. La "Nota al testo" comprend la description des manuscrits, la datation et la localisation des poèmes, quelques observations sur la langue et la métrique. L'édition proprement dite est suivie de trois "Complementi" (étymologie du mot *lai*, définition, établissement du corpus), d'un petit Glossaire et de la Bibliographie. (B.F.)

II Études Critiques et Historiques

356 Belletti, Gian Carlo e Margherita Lecco, *Romanzi, racconti, "Lais". Saggi di letteratura medievale*. Alessandria: Edizioni dell'Orso, 2014, 243 p.

Il s'agit d'un recueil de sept articles, dont deux de sujet arthurien: l'un, de G.B. ("Per una lettura ideologica del *Guillaume d'Angleterre*," pp. 1–65), avait déjà paru dans *L'Immagine Riflessa*, 11, 1988 (cf. *BBSIA*, XLII, 1990, 113); l'autre, de M.L. ("Onomastica arturiana in lingua d'oc e d'oïl," pp. 181–209), étudie deux noms dont le sens et l'origine n'ont pas encore été complètement élucidés: le nom du chevalier Jaufre dans le roman homonyme et celui de l'animal monstrueux contre lequel se bat le roi Artus: le Chapalu. (B.F.)

357 Bertolucci Pizzorusso, Valeria, "Strategie dantesche. Francesca e il *Roman de Lancelot*," in Bertolucci Pizzorusso, Valeria, *Cinque interpretazioni dantesche*. Pisa: Pacini Fazzi, 2015, pp. 55–76.

Article déjà paru dans *Saggi danteschi per Alfredo Stussi a cinquant'anni dalla sua laurea, Nuova Rivista di Letteratura Italiana*, 13.1–2 (2010), 135–50 (cf. *BIAS*, LXV, 2013, 395). (B.F.)

358 Branca, Vittore, *Studi sui Cantari*. Introduzione di Daniela Delcorno Branca. Firenze: Olschki, 2014, 132 p.

À cent ans de la naissance de V. Branca, ce volume réunit deux études publiées respectivement en 1936 ("Il cantare trecentesco e il Boccaccio del *Filostrato* e del *Teseida*") et en 1963 ("Nostalgie tardogotiche e gusto del fiabesco nella tradizione narrativa dei cantari"). L'Introduction de D.D.B. souligne la précocité de certaines intuitions qui sont à la base du renouvellement des études sur la littérature 'canterina'. (B.F.)

359 Cigni, Fabrizio, "Dante, Boccaccio e i significati della Corte. Qualche osservazione a margine," in *Boccaccio e la Romagna*, a cura di Gabriella Albanese e Paolo Pontari. Ravenna: Longo Editore, 2015, pp. 201–05.

Les manuscrits du *Tristan* et du *Lancelot* en prose offrent un témoignage direct des différences entre les milieux courtois de l'Italie du Nord, où la lecture des romans en langue originale était une pratique courante, et l'Italie des Comuni, où ces mêmes textes étaient traduits et adaptés à des contextes non courtois. (B.F.)

360 Cigni, Fabrizio, "La *Francesca da Rimini* e il dibattito sul Canto V dell'*Inferno*," in *Io ho quel che ho donato. Convegno di studi su Gabriele d'Annunzio nel 150° della nascita*, a cura di Cecilia Gibellini. Bologna: CLUEB, 2015, pp. 65–79.

L'A. illustre savamment la tragédie *Francesca da Rimini* (1901) de Gabriele D'Annunzio, mise en scène de l'épisode dantesque de Paolo et Francesca, par rapport à son intertexte littéraire et son noyau arthurien et aux motifs du *Roman de Tristan* en prose. (B.B.A.)

361 DELCORNO BRANCA, Daniela, "Alcina e Melissa: le fate del *Furioso* o la rilettura di un *topos*," in *L'"Orlando Furioso". L'arte contemporanea legge l'Ariosto. Incantamenti, passioni e follie*, a cura di Sandro PARMIGGIANI. Cinisello Balsamo (Milano): Silvana Editoriale, 2014, pp. 225–31.

L'A. réfléchit sur le thème des fées dans l'œuvre d'Ariosto: avec Alcina, Melissa, Logistilla, Manto, au-delà de l'archétype traditionnel, le poète réalise une humanisation des personnages, et valorise, par sa lecture allégorique, la nature ambivalente de la fée, miroir de la complexité du réel. (B.B.A.)

362 DELCORNO BRANCA, Daniela, "La linea cortese di Boccaccio e dei suoi lettori tra Romagna ed Emilia," in *Boccaccio e la Romagna*, a cura di Gabriella ALBANESE e Paolo PONTARI. Ravenna: Longo Editore, 2015, pp. 47–65.

Analyse de la réception par Boccace de la Romagne représentée dans la *Commedia*. Même si l'intitulé *prencipe Galeotto* donné au *Decameron* révèle l'impact de l'épisode de Francesca da Rimini (*Inf.* V) sur le recueil de Boccace, celui-ci privilégie surtout le cadre de l'ancienne Romagne courtoise, dont l'éloge est prononcé par Guido del Duca dans *Purg.* XIV. (B.F.)

363 FUKSAS, Anatole Pierre, "Hierarchical Segmentation of Chrétien's *Chevalier au Lion* in MS. Montpellier, Bibliothèque Interuniversitaire, Section Médecine, H 252 (FF. 1R-12V)," in *Nel segno del testo. Edizioni, materiali e studi per Oronzo Pecere*, a cura di Lucio DEL CORSO, Franco DE VIVO e Antonio STRAMAGLIA. Firenze: Gonnelli, 2015, pp. 307–16.

A.P.F. analyse les fragments du *Chevalier au Lion* dans le manuscrit de Montpellier: *tituli* et lettrines de dimensions différentes traduisent visuellement une hiérarchisation en épisodes et en sous-épisodes. La prise en compte de ces éléments pourrait rentrer à plein titre dans l'élaboration d'un stemma. (M.C.T.)

364 FUKSAS, Anatole Pierre, "Prosopopea, allegoria e forze tematiche nei romanzi di Chrétien de Troyes," *Rhesis, International Journal of Linguistics, Philology and Literature, Literature*, 4.2 (2013), 147–74.

L'A. analyse et discute la fonction de quelques personnifications dans le *Chevalier au Lion* et le *Chevalier de la Charrette*: plutôt que constituer un cadre véritablement allégorique, celles-ci répondent à une visée didactique qui correspond à la cohérence entre matiere et sen. (M.C.T.)

365 Galbiati, Roberto, "Morgana e la dimora di Fortuna: un personaggio e un luogo dell'*Inamoramento de Orlando*," *Giornale Storico della Letteratura Italiana*, 192 (2015), 3–48.

L'A. réfléchit sur la présentation de la fée Morgane par Boiardo, son règne, le rapprochement avec Fortune. (B.B.A.)

366 Grange, Huw, "The Versions of the *Prose Tristan*, with Particular Reference to ms. 164 of the Fondation Martin Bodmer," *MR*, 39 (2015), 321–49.

H.G. propose une analyse codicologique et linguistique du manuscrit 164 de la Fondation Bodmer (Genève) afin d'essayer de le classer à l'intérieur de la tradition manuscrite – particulièrement embrouillée – du *Tristan* en prose; acéphale, cette copie aurait été composée et assemblée non pas en Italie, comme on l'a souvent affirmé, mais en Bourgogne (provenance confirmée par deux signatures de possesseurs de la seconde moitié du 15e siècle). (M.C.T.)

367 Guglielmetti, Rossana, "Come (non) costruire un *curach*. L'edizione della *Navigatio sancti Brendani*," *Ecdotica*, 10 (2013), 223–51.

Cet article s'ouvre en rappelant le voyage *ad imitationem Brendani* de Tim Severin (1977) sur un *curach* construit selon les indications (inexactes) fournies par l'édition Selmer (1959) de la *Navigatio sancti Brendani*. Cela permet d'analyser en détail quelques limites de cette édition, en démontrant l'utilité d'une approche lachmannienne au texte, inaugurée par Orlandi et menée à terme par R.G. elle-même (cf. *BIAS*, LXVII, 2015, 441). (R.T.)

368 Guglielmetti, Rossana, "Navigando con Brandano. Le mille rotte di una tradizione contaminata," *Cdt*, 17.3 (2013), 161–86.

Travail préparatoire pour une nouvelle édition critique de la *Navigatio sancti Brendani* (cf. *BIAS*, LXVII, 2015, 441), cet essai explore le problème de la contamination, phénomène marquant la tradition de la *Navigatio* ainsi que de nombreux autres textes latins du Moyen Âge, résultat des méthodes de copie adoptées dans les anciens *scriptoria*. (R.T.)

369 HEIJKANT, Marie-José, "Sulla nuova edizione critica del 'Tristano Corsiniano'," *MR*, 38 (2014), 427–37.

Cet examen détaillé du *Tristano Corsiniano* récemment publié par R. Tagliani (cf. *BBSIA*, LXIV, 2011, 480) met en relief l'apport scientifique de cette nouvelle édition, signale les particularités du texte par rapport au *Tristan* en prose et au *Tristano Panciatichiano*, et discute quelques traductions proposées dans le glossaire. (B.F.)

370 LAGOMARSINI, Claudio, "*Je laisse la prose pour vers*. Sulla genesi dei testi in versi nei romanzi arturiani in prosa del XIII secolo," *Cdt*, 18.3 (2015), 297–314.

Article intéressant, visant à éclaircir la question délicate de la genèse des pièces en vers – lyriques et narratives – dans le *Tristan* en prose et dans *Guiron le Courtois*. L'analyse des traditions manuscrites permet à C.L. d'appuyer avec prudence la thèse selon laquelle la composition de ces pièces reviendrait aux auteurs mêmes des romans en prose. (M.C.T.)

371 MANTOVANI, Dario, "Un''officina' di genere, tra cantare e poema in ottava rima," *Cdt*, 17.3 (2014), 45–73.

Cet article analyse les *Cantari di Lancillotto*, *Piramo* e *Tisbe*, l'*Istoria di Alessandro Magno* de Domenico Scolari et les *Eroidi* de Domenico da Monticchiello. Contrairement aux cantari les plus caractéristiques, ces textes exploitent des sources écrites et montrent un emploi limité du style formulaire en offrant un exemple de réécriture du genre *canterino* à un niveau plus soutenu. (G.P.)

372 MATERNI, Marta, "*Le chavelier Guiron* in Italia. Un portolano bibliografico per le coste pisano-genovesi," *Francigena*, 1 (2015), 109–64.

Mise au point critique sur l'édition de *Guiron le Courtois* et sur les manuscrits produits entre Gênes et Pise. Plutôt que pour la méthode lachmanienne adoptée par l'équipe *Guiron*, l'A. opte pour une démarche sensible à l'existence de rédactions propres aux différentes régions de diffusion du texte, et propose l'analyse du manuscrit italien V1. (M.G.)

373 Meneghetti, Maria Luisa, *Storie al muro. Temi e personaggi della letteratura profana nell'arte medievale*. Torino: Einaudi, 2015, 488 p.

Richement illustré, ce livre est consacré à l'étude des représentations artistiques de sujets profanes de la littérature romane médiévale. Un premier chapitre théorique est suivi de quatre autres chapitres répartis par genres, qui illustrent tous les épisodes significatifs pour l'étude de ce domaine. Le sens à attribuer à chaque épisode est recherché en l'analysant dans le contexte particulier de sa réalisation artistique, par rapport à sa fonction, à ses commanditaires, à ses liens avec l'histoire de la tradition du/des texte/s impliqué/s. Lancelot est le héros romanesque le plus représenté dans les témoignages artistiques, suivi de Tristan et Yvain. (S.R.)

374 Murgia, Giulia, "Allegorie scritturali nell'*Historia de Merlino*. Le profezie di Blasio," in *In altre parole. Forme dell'allegoria nei testi medioevali*, a cura di Patrizia Serra. Milano: Franco Angeli, 2015, pp. 188–96.

Le ms. Parma, Biblioteca Palatina, Pal. 39 de l'*Historia de Merlino* se caractérise par des ajouts qui insistent sur la figure du protagoniste et sur la symbolique et les parallélismes bibliques et christiques. Le prophète devient ainsi le médiateur entre le monde arthurien et les données de la *Genèse*, selon une allégorie qui reflète la production didactique du Moyen Âge italien. (M.C.T.)

375 Murgia, Giulia, "Il tema della tomba degli amanti nella *Tavola Ritonda* a confronto con la tradizione tristaniana francese e castigliana," *Cdt*, 18.2 (2015), 9–50.

The author explores the theme of the tomb in some of the texts which present the *clôture visuelle* of Tristan and Iseut's death. Special attention is given to the *Tavola Ritonda*, which introduces some interesting hagiographic overtones, such as the eucharistic mystery associated to the pilgrimage to Tristan's sepulcher. (P.A.F.)

376 Murgia, Giulia, "L'allegoria della Bianca Serpente nell'*Historia de Merlino*," in *In altre parole. Forme dell'allegoria nei testi medioevali*, a cura di Patrizia Serra. Milano: Franco Angeli, 2015, pp. 177–87.

Réécriture italienne des *Prophecies*, l'*Historia de Merlino* (seconde moitié du XVe siècle) est transmise par deux manuscrits et de nombreux imprimés anciens: G.M. étudie en particulier la réception des personnages de Merlin, dont est soulignée la duplicité foncière, et de la Dame du Lac, qui assume une fonction métanarrative. (M.C.T.)

377 Murgia, Giulia, "L'allegoria della Bianca Serpente nelle *Prophecies de Merlin*. Una lettura dell'*enserrement* di Merlino alla luce di *Genesi* (1–3)," in *In altre parole. Forme dell'allegoria nei testi medioevali*, a cura di Patrizia Serra. Milano: Franco Angeli, 2015, pp. 153–76.

G.M. relit l'épisode de l'*enserrement* de Merlin par la Dame du Lac à la lumière de la *Genèse*: Merlin figure d'Adam, la Dame figure d'Ève-serpent. L'allégorie biblique permettrait aussi d'interpréter certains passages des *Prophecies*, œuvre complexe qui associe une réflexion sur la nature de la femme à une réinterprétation de la figure de Merlin, devenu le porte-parole de la doctrine chrétienne. (M.C.T.)

378 Murgia, Giulia, *La Tavola Ritonda tra intrattenimento ed enciclopedismo*. Roma: Sapienza Università Editrice, 2015, 458 p. Collana Studi e Ricerche, 29.

Dans ce riche volume l'A. essaie d'interpréter la *Tavola Ritonda*, anonyme et atypique compilation arthuro-tristanienne de la Toscane du XIVe s., à la lumière de l'encyclopédisme et de la culture scientifique italienne. Le mélange d'érudition littéraire et de matière chevaleresque de ce texte, qui connaît aussi d'autres rédactions (ombriennes et padanes), se détache ainsi de la tradition des volgarizzamenti et des adaptations régionales des *Tristans* italiens. Parmi les mérites de cette monographie, la complétude des approches et la prise en compte des recherches les plus récentes. (F.C.)

379 Paradisi, Gioia, "Codificazione e formularità nella rappresentazione letteraria degli affetti. Note sul *Tristano Riccardiano*," *Rhesis, International Journal of Linguistics, Philology and Literature, Literature*, 5.2 (2015), 102–23.

G.P. étudie les expressions de l'affectivité dans le *Tristan* du ms Firenze, Bibl. Riccardiana 2543. Les dynamiques de l'émotivité s'avèrent être en rapport avec l'aventure, qui structure le rythme narratif et permet en même temps d'exalter la psychologie des personnages: si leurs comportements sont parfois stéréotypés, leur affection n'en est pour autant pas limitée. (M.Ca.)

380 Ponceau, Jean-Pierre, "L'*Estoire del Saint Graal* et la *Queste del Saint Graal*. Un problème de chronologie relative," *MR*, 38 (2014), 251–86.

L'A. argumente en faveur de l'antériorité de l'*Estoire del saint Graal* par rapport à la *Queste*, en analysant les passages où celle-ci se réfère à l'*Estoire* et les épisodes communs aux deux textes, qui présentent aussi des passages formellement identiques. Le récit de la *Queste* résume l'*Estoire*, qui permet parfois d'en combler les lacunes textuelles. (M.G.)

381 Punzi, Arianna, "L'allegoria nel *Lancelot* en prose," *Rhesis, International Journal of Linguistics, Philology and Literature, Literature*, 4.2 (2013), 71–97.

Dans cet article, qui vise à montrer la présence et l'importance de l'allégorie dans le *Lancelot* en prose, A.P. analyse les passages du roman dans lesquels, grâce à un jeu de révélations du passé et de préfigurations, la lettre du texte s'enrichit d'un sens symbolique qui oriente l'interprétation du récit. (M.Ca.)

382 Rabboni, Renzo, "Il *Libro de Galvano* di Evangelista Fossa," in *Generi e contaminazioni. Studi sui cantari, l'egloga volgare e la prima imitazione petrarchesca*, a cura di Renzo Rabboni. Roma: Aracne, 2013, pp. 181–211.

Après avoir précisé les rapports de filiation entre les témoins imprimés du *Cantare de Galvano*, toujours inédit, l'A. analyse les influences multiples des genres italiens contemporains, qui éloignent la composante féérique du poème de Fossa du merveilleux breton de ses sources: *Ponzela Gaia* et *Astore e Morgana*. (B.F.)

383 Rabboni, Renzo, "Per il testo (e la datazione) dei *Cantari di Lancelotto*," in *Generi e contaminazioni. Studi sui cantari, l'egloga volgare e la prima imitazione petrarchesca*, a cura di Renzo Rabboni. Roma: Aracne, 2013, pp. 137–80.

La section du ms. Firenze, BML, Plut. LXXVIII 23, contenant les *Cantari di Lancelotto* remonterait à la fin du XIVe siècle. R.R. discute plusieurs passages du texte en proposant des corrections aux éditions précédentes (il ignore toutefois celle de M. Bendinelli Predelli parue en 2012: cf. *BIAS*, LXV, 2013, 391). (B.F.)

384 SERRA, Patrizia, "Percorsi allegorici nella *Mule sans frein*," in *In altre parole. Forme dell'allegoria nei testi medioevali*, a cura di Patrizia SERRA. Milano: Franco Angeli, 2015, pp. 70–81.

La *Mule sans frein* propose, sous forme allégorique, le récit du chemin de l'âme vers la rédemption; le parcours de Gauvain, parti à la recherche du frein, objet hautement symbolique, sur la demande d'une *damoisele* qui incarne sans doute la Vérité, s'oppose à celui de Keu, incapable de dépasser le sens littéral de la *queste*. (M.C.T.)

385 SERRA, Patrizia, "Rivisitazioni allegoriche della tradizione arturiana: il *Tornoiemenz Antecrist* di Huon de Méry," in *In altre parole. Forme dell'allegoria nei testi medioevali*, a cura di Patrizia SERRA. Milano: Franco Angeli, 2015, pp. 82–93.

Article déjà paru dans Patrizia Serra, "Il viaggio allegorico tra visioni dell'Aldilà e romanzo arturiano nella letteratura medievale francese," in *La parola utile. Saggi sul discorso morale nel Medioevo*, dir. Duilio Caocci, Rita Fresu, Patrizia Serra, Lorenzo Tanzini. Roma: Carocci, 2012, pp. 68–82 (cf. *BIAS*, LXV, 2013, 415). (M.C.T.)

386 SPADINI, Elena, "'En autre penser'. Il ms. Hamilton 49 nella tradizione del *Lancelot* in prosa," *Cdt*, 17.1 (2014), 141–75.

The Manuscript Hamilton 49, which belong to the group of manuscripts produced in Genoa at the end of the 13th century, preserves a portion of the prose *Lancelot*. The A. studies its material features and the peculiarities of this copy and places Hamilton 49 in the manuscript tradition. (A.P.)

387 SPETIA, Lucilla, "L'Aldilà tra meraviglioso e fantastico nella narrazione romanza e mediolatina alla fine del XII secolo (e inizi del XIII): *Guigemar* e *Partenopeus de Blois*, *De Nugis Curialium* (e *Otia Imperialia*)," *Rhesis, International Journal of Linguistics, Philology and Literature, Literature*, 5.2 (2015), 148–201.

Après la création du Purgatoire, les voyages dans l'Au-delà (Owein, Saint Brendan) exercent leur influence sur *Partenopeu de Blois* et *Guigemar* (insertion de *mirabilia* dans la description des aventures); d'autre part, dans les histoires de revenants, tels le *De Nugis Curialium* et les *Otia impe-*

rialia, Walter Map et Gervais de Tilbury diabolisent les comportements chevaleresques et courtois, condamnés dans l'au-delà. (M.Ca.)

388 VIRDIS, Maurizio, "L'*Atre périlleux. Membra disjecta* ricomposte in allegoria," in *In altre parole. Forme dell'allegoria nei testi medioevali*, a cura di Patrizia SERRA. Milano: Franco Angeli, 2015, pp. 127–35.

Roman centré sur Gauvain, l'*Atre périlleux* peut être interprété selon une clé de lecture allégorique; le dédoublement du héros, la quête destinée à récupérer son *renon* et son *non*, conjuguent néanmoins une dimension spéculative et sacrée avec le registre humoristique qui imprègne le texte tout entier. (M.C.T.)

389 VIRDIS, Maurizio, "Marie de France. L'allegoria sottotraccia," in *In altre parole. Forme dell'allegoria nei testi medioevali*, a cura di Patrizia SERRA. Milano: Franco Angeli, 2015, pp. 101–26.

M.V. propose une lecture allégorique de deux lais: *Guigemar*, où le lecteur est appelé à interpréter le rapport entre rêve et réalité à l'aune de l'allégorie; et *Lanval*, où l'allégorie s'impose comme le sens du texte lui-même. (M.C.T.)

390 ZAGNI, Giovanni, "La fortuna dei romanzi arturiani francesi in Italia," *Humanistica*, 8.1 (2013), 151–66.

Examen approfondi des études sur la production et la circulation de la littérature arthurienne en Italie au Moyen Âge, tant pour les textes en langue d'oïl que pour leurs traductions italiennes. Organisé par matières, cet article constitue une contribution précieuse pour l'approche de la production scientifique arthurienne des années 1998–2012. (R.T.)

391 ZINELLI, Fabio, "I codici francesi di Genova e Pisa. Elementi per la definizione di una scripta," *MR*, 39 (2015), 82–127.

Les manuscrits copiés à Gênes par des scribes pisans (1284–1299) présentent des traits des dialectes toscans occidentaux, auxquels s'ajoutent des éléments génois, occitans voire des formes du français d'outremer. La tradition manuscrite de ce corpus, qui comprend de nombreux textes arthuriens, témoigne d'une part de la pratique des copistes, d'autre part de la présence / circulation à Gênes de modèles textuels différents. (M.G.)

III Comptes Rendus

392 *The Arthur of the Italians. The Arthurian Legend in Medieval Italian Literature and Culture*, a cura di Gloria ALLAIRE e F. Regina PSAKI. Cardiff: University of Wales Press, 2014, 352 p. (cf. *BIAS*, LXVII, 2015, 376).

C.R. par INFURNA, Marco, *Lettere italiane*, 67 (2015), 192–95.

393 *Les Aventures des Bruns. Compilazione guironiana del secolo XIII attribuibile a Rustichello da Pisa*, ed. critica a cura di Claudio LAGOMARSINI. Firenze: Sismel. Edizioni del Galluzzo, 2014, 620 p. (cf. *BIAS*, LXVII, 2015, 436).

C.R. par CIGNI, Fabrizio, *Lettere italiane*, 67 (2015), 415–18.
C.R. par RÉDACTION DE MR, *MR*, 39 (2015), 201–02.

394 BARBER, Richard, "Edward III's Arthurian Enthusiasm Revisited: *Perceforest* in the Context of Philippa of Hainaut and the Round Table Feast of 1344," *AL*, 30 (2013), 55–74 (cf. *BIAS*, LXVI, 2014, 301).

C.R. par COLOMBO TIMELLI, Maria, *SF*, 58.174 (2014), 571.

395 BÉDIER, Joseph, *Le Roman de Tristan et Iseut*, éd. critique par ALAIN CORBELLARI. Genève: Droz, 2012, 384 p. (cf. *BIAS*, LXVI, 2014, 742).

C.R. par MELIGA, Walter, *SF*, 59.177 (2015), 563.

396 BÉROUL, *Tristano e Isotta*, a cura di GIOIA PARADISI. Alessandria: Edizioni dell'Orso, 2013, 420 p. (cf. *BIAS*, LXVI, 2014, 449).

C.R. par HESS, Dominik, *RCPhR*, 15 (2014), 36–39.
C.R. par NOTO, Giuseppe, *SF*, 59.175 (2015), 122.

397 BOTERO GARCÍA, Mario, *Les Rois dans le Tristan en prose. (Ré)écritures du personnage arthurien*. Paris: Honoré Champion, 2011, 436 p. (cf. *BIAS*, LXIV, 2012, 138).

C.R. par ROCCATI, Matteo G., *SF*, 58.172 (2014), 118.

398 Bouget, Hélène, *Écritures de l'énigme et fiction romanesque. Poétiques arthuriennes (XIIe–XIIIe siècles).* Paris: Honoré Champion, 2011, 536 p. (cf. *BIAS*, LXIV, 2012, 139).

C.R. par Roccati, Matteo G., *SF*, 59.177 (2015), 563–64.

399 Bryant, Nigel, "Pagan Gods and the Coming of Christianity in *Perceforest*," *AL*, 30 (2013), 75–85 (cf. *BIAS*, LXVI, 2014, 310).

C.R. par Colombo Timelli, Maria, *SF*, 58.174 (2014), 571.

400 Buschinger, Danielle, *Tristan allemand*. Paris: Honoré Champion, 2013, 360 p. (cf. *BIAS*, LXVI, 2014, 195).

C.R. par Biancardi, Simone, *MR*, 39 (2015), 219–21.

401 *Il Cavaliere del Pappagallo*, Introduzione traduzione e note di Eliana Creazzo. Soveria Mannelli: Rubbettino, 2011, 216 p. (cf. *BIAS*, LXIV, 2012, 478).

C.R. par Meliga, Walter, *SF*, 58.174 (2014), 567.

402 Chalumeau, Chloé, "L'Île Tournoyante, lieu de la difficile coexistence des savoirs dans l'*Estoire del Saint Graal*," *Bien dire et bien aprandre*, 30 (2014), 25–38 (cf. *BIAS*, LXVII, 2015, 242).

C.R. par Crosio, Martina, *SF*, 59.177 (2015), 560.

403 Chardonnens, Noémie, "Entre interpolation et emprunt. Réflexions autour de *Perceforest*," in *Le texte dans le texte. L'interpolation médiévale*, a cura di Annie Combes e Michelle Szkilnik. Paris: Classiques Garnier, 2013, pp. 105–21 (cf. *BIAS*, LXVI, 2014, 199).

C.R. par Colombo Timelli, Maria, *SF*, 58.174 (2014), 562.

404 Chase, Carol J., "Le scribe-éditeur du Paris, BnF, fr. 2455. Le créateur d'une version particulière de l'*Estoire del Saint Graal*," in *Le texte dans le texte. L'interpolation médiévale*, a cura di Annie Combes e Michelle Szkilnik. Paris: Classiques Garnier, 2013, pp. 197–213 (cf. *BIAS*, LXVI, 2014, 200).

C.R. par COLOMBO TIMELLI, Maria, *SF*, 58.174 (2014), 562.

405 CHASE, Carol J., "Transmuer de rime en prose: The Transformation of Chrétien de Troyes' *Joie de la Cour* Episode in the Burgundian Prose *Erec* (1450–1460)," *AL*, 30 (2013), 101–15 (cf. *BIAS*, LXVI, 2014, 317).

C.R. par COLOMBO TIMELLI, Maria, *SF*, 58.174 (2014), 571.

406 *Le Chevalier aux deux épées. Roman arthurien du XIIIe siècle*, texte présenté et traduit par Damien DE CARNÉ. Paris: Classiques Garnier, 2012 (cf. *BIAS*, LXV, 2013, 145).

C.R. par TRACHSLER, Richard, *SF*, 59.177 (2015), 564.

407 *Chrétien de Troyes et la tradition du roman arthurien en vers*, a cura di Annie COMBES, Patrizia SERRA, Richard TRACHSLER e Maurizio VIRDIS. Paris: Classiques Garnier, 2013, 353 p. (cf. *BIAS*, LXVII, 2015, 246).

C.R. par COLOMBO TIMELLI, Maria, *SF*, 58.174 (2014), 564–65.

408 COLOMBO TIMELLI, Maria, "Le *Livre de Caradoc* dans la version en prose de 1530. Une 'école des femmes'?" *Bien dire et bien aprandre*, 30 (2014), 165–78 (cf. *BIAS*, LXVII, 2015, 247).

C.R. par CROSIO, Martina, *SF*, 59.177 (2015), 561.

409 COLOMBO TIMELLI, Maria, "Sur le lexique de la *Troisième Continuation de Perceval* en prose," *MF*, 72 (2013), 19–45.

C.R. par CIFARELLI, Paola, *SF*, 59.175 (2015), 127.

410 *A Companion to Marie de France*, a cura di Logan E. WHALEN. Leiden / Boston: Brill, 2011, 335 p. (cf. *BIAS*, LXV, 2013, 626).

C.R. par MELIGA, Walter, *SF*, 59.175 (2015), 121–22.

411 ELEY, Penny, '*Partonopeus de Blois*'. *Romance in the Making*. Woolbridge: Brewer, 2011, 260 p. (cf. *BIAS*, LXVII, 2015, 488).

C.R. par LECCO, Margherita, *RCPhR*, 15 (2014), 98–101.

412 GAGGERO, Massimiliano, "L'épée brisée dans le *Conte du Graal* et ses Continuations," in *Dai pochi ai molti. Studi in onore di Roberto Antonelli*, a cura di Paolo CANETTIERI e Arianna PUNZI. Roma: Viella, 2014, pp. 855–83 (cf. *BIAS*, LXVII, 2015, 459).

C.R. par COLOMBO TIMELLI, Maria, *SF*, 59.176 (2015), 341.

413 GUYÉNOT, Laurent, *La mort féerique. Anthropologie du merveilleux XIIe–XVe siècle*. Paris: Classiques Garnier, 2011, 400 p.

C.R. par ROCCATI, Matteo G., *SF*, 58.174 (2014), 564.

414 HÉRICHÉ-PRADEAU, Sandrine, "Inscriptions et images dans quelques romans en prose (XIIIe-XVe siècles)," *MA*, 119 (2013), 375–401.

C.R. par COLOMBO TIMELLI, Maria, *SF*, 58.173 (2014), 341.

415 HINTON, Thomas, *The "Conte du Graal" Cycle. Chretien de Troyes's "Perceval," the Continuations, and French Arthurian Romance*. Cambridge: D. S. Brewer, 2012, 277 p. Gallica, 23 (cf. *BIAS*, LXV, 2013, 295).

C.R. par MORATO, Nicola, *MR*, 38 (2014), 446–48.

416 KINOSHITA, Sharon, e Peggy MCCRACKEN, *Marie de France: A Critical Companion*. Cambridge: D. S. Brewer, 2012, 228 p. (cf. *BIAS*, LXV, 2013, 296).

C.R. par CLASSEN, Albrecht, *SM*, 56 (2015), 982–84.

417 KOBLE, Nathalie, "Pour un nouveau tombeau de Merlin. L'interpolation à l'œuvre dans un manuscrit cyclique du *Lancelot-Graal* (Paris, BnF, fr. 98)," in *Le texte dans le texte. L'interpolation médiévale*, a cura di Annie COMBES e Michelle SZKILNIK. Paris: Classiques Garnier, 2013, pp. 215–34.

C.R. par COLOMBO TIMELLI, Maria, *SF*, 58.174 (2014), 562.

418 *Lais, épîtres et épigraphes en vers dans le cycle de 'Guiron le Courtois'*, a cura di Claudio LAGOMARSINI. Paris: Classiques Garnier, 2015, 213 p. Textes littéraires du Moyen Âge, 36.

C.R. par RÉDACTION DE MR, *MR*, 39 (2015), 450–51.

419 *Libro d'amore attribuibile a Giovanni Boccaccio. Volgarizzamento del De Amore di Andrea Cappellano. Testi in prosa e in versi*, edizione critica a cura di Beatrice BARBIELLINI AMIDEI. Firenze: Accademia della Crusca, 2013, 459 p. (cf. *BIAS*, LXVI, 2014, 450).

C.R. par DECARIA, Alessio, *MR*, 38 (2014), 461–63.

420 MARZANO, Stefania, "Une mise en prose inédite du XVIe siècle. Le *Compte du mantheau maltaillé* (BnF, fr. 2153)," in *Pour un nouveau répertoire des mises en prose. Roman, chanson de geste, autres genres*, a cura di Maria COLOMBO TIMELLI, Barbara FERRARI e Anne SCHOYSMAN. Paris: Classiques Garnier, 2014, pp. 213–27 (cf. *BIAS*, LXVII, 2015, 295).

C.R. par RICCI, Mariagrazia, *SF*, 59.177 (2015), 568.

421 *Mémoires arthuriennes*, a cura di Danielle QUÉRUEL. Troyes: Médiathèque du Grand Troyes, 2012, 368 p. (cf. *BIAS*, LXV, 2013, 213).

C.R. par FERRARI, Barbara, *SF*, 59.176 (2015), 340–41.

422 *Le Meraviglie di Rigomer (Les Merveilles de Rigomer). Tradizione manoscritta e tradizione narrativa*, a cura di MARGHERITA LECCO. Alessandria: Edizioni dell'Orso, 2013, 198 p. (cf. *BIAS*, LXVI, 2014, 451).

C.R. par CARAPEZZA, Francesco, *MR*, 39 (2015), 204–05.

423 MILLAND-BOVE, Bénédicte, "Bible et romans. Quelques contacts à la faveur d'interpolations," in *Le texte dans le texte. L'interpolation médiévale*, a cura di Annie COMBES e Michelle SZKILNIK. Paris: Classiques Garnier, 2013, pp. 85–104 (cf. *BIAS*, LXVI, 2014, 241).

C.R. par COLOMBO TIMELLI, Maria, *SF*, 58.174 (2014), 561–62.

424 *Navigatio Sancti Brendani. Alla scoperta dei segreti meravigliosi del mondo*, edizione critica a cura di Giovanni ORLANDI e Rossana GUGLIELMETTI. Traduzione italiana e commento di Giovanni ORLANDI. Firenze: Edizioni del Galluzzo per la Fondazione Ezio Franceschini, 2014, 215 p. (cf. *BIAS*, LXVII, 2015, 441).

C.R. par FRAVVENTURA, Vera, *SM*, 56 (2015), 371–77.

425 *Perceforest. Un roman arthurien et sa réception*, a cura di Christine FER-LAMPIN-ACHER. Rennes: Presses Universitaires de Rennes, 2012, 463 p. (cf. *BIAS*, LXV, 2013, 226).

C.R. par FINOTTI, Irene, *SF*, 58.172 (2014), 124–25.

426 *Perceforest. Sixième partie, Tomes I et II*, éd. critique par Gilles ROUSS-INEAU. Bern: Droz, 2015, 1428 p. Textes littéraires du Moyen Âge, 631 (cf. *BIAS*, LXVII, 2015, 529).

C.R. par LAGOMARSINI, Claudio, *MR*, 39 (2015), 451–52.

427 PIOLETTI, Antonio, *La porta dei cronotopi. Tempo-spazio nella narrativa romanza*. Soveria Mannelli: Rubbettino, 2014, 292 p. (cf. *BIAS*, LXVII, 2015, 471).

C.R. par CADIOLI, Luca, *MR*, 39 (2015), 457–58.

428 *La Queste del Saint Graal (The Quest for the Holy Grail) from the Old French Lancelot of Yale 229 with Essays, Glossaries, and Notes to the Text*, a cura di Elizabeth MOORE WILLINGHAM. Turnhout: Brepols, 2012, 344 p.

C.R. par TRACHSLER, Richard, *SF*, 58.174 (2014), 565–67.

429 ROLLAND, Marc, *Re Artù*. Bologna: Il Mulino, 2011, 152 p. (cf. *BIAS*, LXIV, 2012, 506).

C.R. par MELIGA, Walter, *SF*, 58.172 (2014), 117–18.

430 *La Struzione della Tavola Ritonda (I Cantari di Lancillotto)*, Maria BENDI-NELLI PREDELLI. Firenze: Società Editrice Fiorentina, 2015, 208 p. Studi, 17 (cf. *BIAS*, LXVIII, 2016, 355).

C.R. par LEONARDI, Lino, *MR*, 39 (2015), 474–76.

431 TAYLOR, Jane H.M., *Rewriting Arthurian Romance in Renaissance France. From Manuscript to Printed Book*. Cambridge: Brewer, 2014. (cf. *BIAS*, LXVII, 2015, 414).

C.R. par BARALE, Elisabetta, *SF*, 59.175 (2015), 125–26.
C.R. par MONTORSI, Francesco, *RCPhR*, 15 (2014), 150–55.

432 TRACHSLER, Richard, "De la chimère au mirage. L'interpolation et la critique textuelle," in *Le texte dans le texte. L'interpolation médiévale*, a cura di Annie COMBES e Michelle SZKILNIK. Paris: Classiques Garnier, 2013, pp. 15–29 (cf. *BIAS*, LXVI, 2014, 264).

C.R. par COLOMBO TIMELLI, Maria, *SF*, 58.174 (2014), 561.

433 *Les versions en prose du Purgatoire de saint Patrice en ancien français*, édition critique, introduction et notes par Martina DI FEBO. Paris: Honoré Champion, 2013, 294 p. (cf. *BIAS*, LXVI, 2014, 177).

C.R. par COLOMBO TIMELLI, Maria, *SF*, 58.174 (2014), 567–68.

434 VICTORIN, Patricia, "La rétro-écriture ou l'écriture de la nostalgie dans le roman arthurien tardif: *Ysaïe le Triste*, *Le Conte du Papegau* et *Mélyador* de Froissart," *AL*, 30 (2013), 117–39 (cf. *BIAS*, LXVI, 2014, 382).

C.R. par COLOMBO TIMELLI, Maria, *SF*, 58.174 (2014), 571.

435 WAHLEN, Barbara, "Adjoindre, disjoindre, conjoindre. Le recyclage d'*Alixandre l'Orphelin* et de l'*Histoire d'Erec* dans *Guiron le Courtois* (Paris, BnF, fr. 358–363)," in *Le texte dans le texte. L'interpolation médiévale*, a cura di Annie COMBES e Michelle SZKILNIK. Paris: Classiques Garnier, 2013, pp. 235–47 (cf. *BIAS*, LXVI, 2014, 273).

C.R. par COLOMBO TIMELLI, Maria, *SF*, 58.174 (2014), 562.

436 WALTER, Philippe, *Gauvain le chevalier solaire*. Paris: Imago, 2013, 313 p. (cf. *BIAS*, LXVI, 2014, 271).

C.R. par BARILLARI, Sonia Maura, *MR*, 39 (2015), 210–12.

437 ZAMBON, Francesco, *Metamorfosi del Graal*. Roma: Carocci, 2012, 411 p. (cf. *BIAS*, LXV, 2013, 419).

C.R. par MELIGA, Walter, *SF*, 59.177 (2015), 564.

438 Zussa, Gaëlle, *Merlin. Un mythe médiéval recyclé dans la production culturelle contemporaine*. Genève: Slatkine, 2010, 488 p. (cf. *BIAS*, LXIV, 2011, 231).

C.R. par Roccati, Matteo G., *SF*, 58.173 (2014), 335.

Japon

Bibliographie pour 2015 établie par Yasufumi Takana, Akiko Nii et Noriaki Watanabe

I Éditions

439 Robert de Boron, *Merlin l'Enchanteur*, traduit par Ayumi Yokoyama. Tokyo: Kodansha, 2015, 283 p.

Traduction japonaise de *Merlin* de Robert de Boron d'après l'édition Micha avec les notes et le commentaire. (A.Y.)

II Études Critiques et Historiques

440 Fuwa, Yuri, "The Quest for 'a better text'. Editorial impulses in publishing Malory's *Morte Darthur*," in *Travel Books and Travelling Books*, éd. Takami Matsuda. Tokyo: Keio University Press, 2015, pp. 39–71.

The printing history of Malory's editions reveals intriguing interactions between the editors, printers, publishers, and readers. This paper examines the changing concept of "a better text" in relation to Sir Walter Scott and Joseph Haslewood, highlighting the competing publishing backgrounds of the 1816 and 1817 reprints of *Morte Darthur*. (Y. F.)

441 Komiya, Makiko, "'Here Sir Gawayne Slew Sir Vwayne His Cousyn Germayne'. Field's Alteration on Malory's *Morte Darthur*," *Poetica*, 83 (2015), 107–19.

Analyses Field's emendations on Malory's new edition. The editor omits the byname of "Uwayne les Avoutres," changing Gawayne's victim from a fellow knight of the Round Table into his own kinsman, Uwayne le Blaunche Maynes. Consequently, Field successfully foreshadows the Round Table's tragedy, concerning its split by kinship and fraternity. (M.K.)

https://doi.org/10.1515/9783110467499-139

442 Sasaki, Shigemi, "Morts/Plaies et Arts Médico-Magiques, Romans en prose des XIIIe et XIVe siècles (Essai de relecture)," in *Mythes, Symboles et Rites II*, éd. Chiwaki Shinoda. Chiba: Rakuro, 2015, pp. 31–46.

Signale l'alternance de "gesir" et d'"a genouz": gisent "andui" Arthur et Mordret (éd. Frappier, §190), veillée du premier, son meurtre de Lucan "gisant mort a terre". Les "enchantemenz" de Morgue (§50) éclairent ses départ et "retour" dans le tombeau: "Ci gist" le roi Arthur "voirement" (§194). (S.S.)

443 Takagi, Masako, "Retrograde Text. Manifestation of Authenticity?" *Studies in Medieval English Language and Literature*, 30 (2015), 59–69.

BL MS Additional 10099 was once considered a text more archaic than Caxton's edition. Its linguistic features, however, should be considered rather dialectal, as the scribe shows many traits characteristic of a Northerner, and it in fact seems to be mostly copied from Caxton's edition itself. (M.T.)

III Comptes Rendus

444 *Histoire d'Arthur et de Merlin. Roman moyen-anglais du XVIe siècle, traduit par Anne* Berthelot *à partir du manuscrit Auchinleck.* Grenoble: ELLUG, 2014, 169 p. (cf. *BIAS*, LXVI, 2014, 174).

C.R. par Watanabe, Kôji, *The Chuo Univ. Review*, 288 (2014), 214–17.

445 Walter, Philippe, *Gauvain le chevalier solaire*. Paris: Imago, 2013, 313 p. (cf. *BIAS*, LXVI, 2014, 271).

C.R. par Watanabe, Kôji, *Bulletin d'Études Françaises de l'Université Chuo*, 47 (2015), 223–54.

Roumanie

Bibliographie pour 2015 établie par Brindusa Grigoriu

II Études Critiques et Historiques

446 Gradu, Diana, Écrire et parler français au Moyen Âge. Cluj-Napoca: Casa Cărții de Știință, 2015, 220 p.

Le livre explore le monde linguistique médiéval français, en particulier, l'ancien français de l'Île de France. Il s'agit d'un regard descriptif et sélectif qui part du IXe siècle et se prolonge jusqu'au XIIIe siècle arthurien. Cette grammaire de l'ancien français s'adresse au public roumain et étranger, jeune et universitaire.

447 Grigoriu, Brîndușa, "Émotions linguistiques. L'amer / la mer dans le corpus tristanien," in *Actes du colloque international Le Français de la Francophonie: altérité intime, identité plurielle (28–29 martie 2014)*, éd. Felicia Dumas. Iași: Junimea, 2015, pp. 64–73.

The medieval romances of Tristan – especially Thomas's and Gottfried's – offer a relevant field for the study of emotional expressions. Tristan and Ysolt's identities are linguistically built, as their speech acts shape their erotic ethos. Talking about love – whether in French or in German – develops verbal as well as behavioral skills.

448 Grigoriu, Brindusa, "Le *lovendrins.* Un bouquet francophone du XIIe siècle," *Revue roumaine d'études francophones*, 7 (2015), 13–29.

The love potion of Tristan and Ysolt is a literary nexus of sensations; in Béroul's Norman romance, it fuses the powers of wine, of fire, but also of unnameable plants, in a magic proportion meant to last for three years. Our article aims at analysing this complex experience.

https://doi.org/10.1515/9783110467499-141

449 Grigoriu, Brîndușa, "Le Rocher de la Résurrection dans la littérature du XIIe siècle," *Anastasis. Research in Medieval Culture and Art*, 2 (2015), 217–25.

In twelfth-century French narratives, the rock is a sign of the divine : Tristan's leap into the other-world of Béroul, as well as Marie de France's depiction of Bisclavret's metamorphosis require an adequate scenery for an act in need of legitimization. Stone indicates a form of literary resurrection.

450 Ilina, Alexandra, "Dinadan, le couard chevalier hardi ou la revanche de la parole," *Alcinoé*, 6 (2015), 129–49.

Cet article examine la position de l'atypique chevalier Dinadan par rapport à trois types de problématiques qui se dégagent du *Tristan en prose* : la typologie, contestée par les nouvelles figures, la hiérarchie des matières littéraires, question qui se trouve au cœur du roman, et la conscience littéraire.

451 Ilina, Alexandra, "Rivalité mimétique dans le *Roman de Tristan en Prose*. Considérations sur Kahedin," *APS*, 60.3 (2015), 159–71.

Vestige des légendes tristaniennes versifiées, Kahedin est récupéré par la mise en prose du roman et devient un double du protagoniste. L'article s'intéresse à la modalité dont la rivalité mimétique organise le destin du personnage et aux échos de sa brève apparition sur l'organisation romanesque.

452 Ilina, Alexandra, "Un paradoxe littéraire médiéval. Le Sarrasin dans *Le roman de Tristan*," *Revista Cercurilor Studențești ale Departamentului de Limba și Literatura Franceză*, 4 (2015), 13–22.

À travers l'analyse de ce personnage central du roman, l'article tente à mettre en lumière la position de la hiérarchie dans le texte: objet constant du désir et de la réflexion, l'ascension hiérarchique s'avère impossible pour les personnages tels Palamèdes, figure contrastive et vecteur des contrariétés.

453 Oanca-Ruset, Monica, "Marie De France's *Eliduc.* An Example of Twelfth Century Transnational Literary Character?" *University of Bucharest Review. A Journal of Literary and Cultural Studies*, 4.2 (2014), 41–49.

Eliduc can be perceived as a transnational hero (or literary character), because he moves in an environment which is equally Christian and magic, in a blend which defines it as uniquely Celtic, but is translated and presented to an Anglo-Norman audience identified by a different mentality, and thus nationality.

454 Oanca-Ruset, Monica, "Predestination and Divine Foreknowledge in *The Quest of the Holy Grail*," *Anuarul Facultăţii de Teologie Ortodoxă a Universităţii Bucureşti*, 2015 (2015), 393–405.

The knowledge imparted through visions predicting the outcome of the Quest is moral and didactic, rather than prophetic. By explaining the divine visions and revelations to the questers, the clerics state that God's providence is a sign of God's love, Who wants to guide them towards fulfilling their divine calling.

455 Spremić Končar, Milica, "The Arthurian Legend in Wace's *Roman de Brut*," *Revue de Philologie*, 42.2 (2015), 33–53.

This paper analyses the Arthurian section of Wace's *Roman de Brut* and argues that in the character of Arthur and the dominant atmosphere at his court there emerge intimations of a knightly kind of life and courtly love, concepts entirely different from the belligerent civilization depicted by Geoffrey of Monmouth.

456 Spremić Končar, Milica, "The Beginnings of the Arthurian legend in Geoffrey of Monmouth's *Historia Regum Britanniae*," *Revue de Philologie*, 26.2 (2015), 203–19.

This paper discusses Geoffrey of Monmouth's biography and sources and provides a detailed storyline of the Arthurian section of his *Historia Regum Britanniae* (1136) in which the legend of King Arthur was recounted for the first time in English literature.

457 VOICU, Mihaela, "'A vorbi altfel' sau cum să respingi chipul hâd al disperării," *Caietele Institutului Catolic – Rațiunile speranței*, 22 (2014), 169–82.

L'article propose une lecture de l'épisode de la Demoiselle Hideuse du *Conte du Graal* de Chrétien de Troyes dans la perspective de l'espérance. Pour surmonter la tentation du désespoir il ne suffit pas de se résigner ; il faut se vider de soi-même pour faire place à une Réalité transcendante.

458 VOICU, Mihaela, "Espaces autres à prétention centripète dans le roman arthurien en vers," *Logiques de l'excentrique. Heterotopos*, 8 (2015), 15–34.

Pour le roman arthurien, la cour se constitue en centre de la narration aussi bien que centre d'un monde idéal. Toutefois, des espaces "excentriques" peuvent revendiquer une prétention "centripète". L'article identifie trois de ces espaces dans *L'Âtre périlleux*, *Les Merveilles de Rigomer* et *Le Bel Inconnu*.

Scandinavia

Bibliography for 2015 compiled by Sofia Lodén

I Editions and Transcriptions

459 *Elíss saga ok Rósamundar. Diplomatarisk, XML-koda tekstutgåve etter teksten i De la Gardie 4–7 4° (ca. 1270)*, ed. Ingvil BUDAL. Oslo: Medieval Nordic Text Archive, 2015.

Ingvil Brügger Budal here presents a diplomatic edition of the Old Norse text *Elíss saga ok Rósamundar*, publicly available at www.menota.org.

II Critical and Historical Studies

460 BAMPI, Massimiliano, "The Eufemiavisor and Konung Alexander. Diverging Ideologies?" in *The Eufemiavisor and Courtly Culture. Time, Texts and Cultural Transfer*, ed. Olle FERM, Ingela HEDSTRÖM, Sofia LODÉN, Jonatan PETTERSSON, and Mia ÅKESTAM. Stockholm: Kungl. Vitterhets Historie och Antikvitets Akademien, 2015, pp. 20–31.

Massimiliano Bampi discusses the connections between the *Eufemiavisor* and *Konung Alexander*, all texts in Old Swedish. He argues that these texts are linked to each other not only on a stylistic level but also when it comes to how they deal with the aristocratic ideology.

461 BANDLIEN, Bjørn, "Didactic Literature for Women and Romance in the Age of Queen Eufemia of Norway," in *The Eufemiavisor and Courtly Culture. Time, Texts and Cultural Transfer*, ed. Olle FERM, Ingela HEDSTRÖM, Sofia LODÉN, Jonatan PETTERSSON, and Mia ÅKESTAM. Stockholm: Kungl. Vitterhets Historie och Antikvitets Akademien, 2015, pp. 32–48.

In this article, Bandlien discusses different attitudes towards didactic literature for women and how the Norwegian Queen Eufemia, the commis-

https://doi.org/10.1515/9783110467499-145

sioner of the so-called *Eufemiavisor*, considered romances as a didactic tool.

462 Bergqvist, Kim, "Debating the Limitations of Kingship in Fourteenth-Century Sweden. Political Language and Norms in Romance and Chronicle," in *The Eufemiavisor and Courtly Culture. Time, Texts and Cultural Transfer*, ed. Olle Ferm, Ingela Hedström, Sofia Lodén, Jonatan Pettersson, and Mia Åkestam. Stockholm: Kungl. Vitterhets Historie och Antikvitets Akademien, 2015, pp. 67–85.

Kim Bergqvist analyses the Old Swedish *Eufemiavisor* in light of their historical context and relates them to the Old Swedish verse chronicle *Erikskrönikan*. He argues that the Swedish romances articulate the conflict between the aristocracy and the monarchy.

463 Budal, Ingvil, "Formulaic Violence of a Poor Quality? The Case of Elis saga ok Rósamundu and Elie de Saint Gille," in *Medieval Nordic Literature in its European Context*, ed. Else Mundal. Oslo: Dreyer Forlag, 2015, pp. 262–84.

Ingvil Brügger Budal discusses the Old Norse riddarasaga *Elis saga ok Rósamundu*, translated from the Old French chanson de geste *Elie de Saint Gille*. She examines the encyclopedic entries written about these texts and the various assessments of their good or bad literary quality.

464 Busby, Keith, "Generic Hybridity and Memory in Hertig Fredrik av Normandie," in *The Eufemiavisor and Courtly Culture. Time, Texts and Cultural Transfer*, ed. Olle Ferm, Ingela Hedström, Sofia Lodén, Jonatan Pettersson, and Mia Åkestam. Stockholm: Kungl. Vitterhets Historie och Antikvitets Akademien, 2015, pp. 98–108.

In this article, Keith Busby discusses the origins the Old Swedish *Hertig Fredrik av Normandie*, arguing that the text is securely rooted in the tradition of francophone literature. He also points out a connection between the Old Swedish text and events in Irish history.

465 Ferm, Olle, "The Emergence of Courtly Literature in Sweden. A Critical Discussion of Swedish Research," in *The Eufemiavisor and Courtly Culture. Time, Texts and Cultural Transfer*, ed. Olle Ferm, Ingela Hedström, Sofia Lodén, Jonatan Pettersson, and Mia Åkestam. Stockholm: Kungl. Vitterhets Historie och Antikvitets Akademien, 2015, pp. 109–20.

Olle Ferm discusses the previous research on the emergence of courtly literature in Sweden. He questions the idea that the Old Swedish *Eufemiavisor* were the first examples of courtly literature in the country and tones down the view of Swedish backwardness.

466 JOHANSSON, Karl G., "Queen Eufemia, The Norwegian Élite and the Background of the Eufemiavisor," in *The Eufemiavisor and Courtly Culture. Time, Texts and Cultural Transfer*, ed. Olle FERM, Ingela HEDSTRÖM, Sofia LODÉN, Jonatan PETTERSSON, and Mia ÅKESTAM. Stockholm: Kungl. Vitterhets Historie och Antikvitets Akademien, 2015, pp. 136–61.

Karl G. Johansson discusses the role of the Norwegian court and élite as an important background for the emergence of the Old Swedish *Eufemiavisor*. He argues that the *Eufemiavisor* represent the starting point of a move of literate court culture from Western to Eastern Scandinavia.

467 JUCKNIES, Regina, "Through an Old Danish Lens? Precious Stones in the Late Medieval Danish Reception of Courtly Literature," in *The Eufemiavisor and Courtly Culture. Time, Texts and Cultural Transfer*, ed. Olle FERM, Ingela HEDSTRÖM, Sofia LODÉN, Jonatan PETTERSSON, and Mia ÅKESTAM. Stockholm: Kungl. Vitterhets Historie och Antikvitets Akademien, 2015, pp. 162–75.

In this article, Regina Jucknies discusses the role of magical-medical stones in the Old Danish renderings of the *Eufemiavisor* and how the texts relate to other vernacular texts.

468 LAYHER, William, "Appendix: Manuscripts of the Eufemiavisor," in *The Eufemiavisor and Courtly Culture. Time, Texts and Cultural Transfer*, ed. Olle FERM, Ingela HEDSTRÖM, Sofia LODÉN, Jonatan PETTERSSON, and Mia ÅKESTAM. Stockholm: Kungl. Vitterhets Historie och Antikvitets Akademien, 2015, pp. 273–84.

William Layher here presents a list and description of the different Old Swedish and Old Danish manuscripts of the *Eufemiavisor*.

469 LODÉN, Sofia, "The Eufemiavisor. A Unified Whole," in *The Eufemiavisor and Courtly Culture. Time, Texts and Cultural Transfer*, ed. Olle FERM, Ingela HEDSTRÖM, Sofia LODÉN, Jonatan PETTERSSON, and Mia ÅKESTAM.

Stockholm: Kungl. Vitterhets Historie och Antikvitets Akademien, 2015, pp. 176–88.

Sofia Lodén discusses the links between the three Old Swedish *Eufemiavisor*. She argues that the texts form a unified whole, not only stylistically but also in their content and points out a number of literary themes that bind them together.

470 PENEAU, Corinne, "Pouvoir et distinction des Eufemiavisor à l'Erikskrönika," in *The Eufemiavisor and Courtly Culture. Time, Texts and Cultural Transfer*, ed. Olle FERM, Ingela HEDSTRÖM, Sofia LODÉN, Jonatan PETTERSSON, and Mia ÅKESTAM. Stockholm: Kungl. Vitterhets Historie och Antikvitets Akademien, 2015, pp. 189–220.

Corinne Péneau analyses the Old Swedish *Eufemiavisor* in relation to the chronicle *Erikskrönikan* and raises the question why the history of Sweden, as it is presented in the chronicle, is written as if it were an *Eufemiavisa*.

471 SULLIVAN, Joseph M., "Making the Woods More Negative and Praising Life at Court. Herr Ivan and the Hero's Descent into the Forest," in *The Eufemiavisor and Courtly Culture. Time, Texts and Cultural Transfer*, ed. Olle FERM, Ingela HEDSTRÖM, Sofia LODÉN, Jonatan PETTERSSON, and Mia ÅKESTAM. Stockholm: Kungl. Vitterhets Historie och Antikvitets Akademien, 2015, pp. 235–54.

The author analyses the Old Swedish *Herr Ivan* and its relation to Chrétien de Troyes' French source *Le Chevalier au lion*. He focuses on the descriptions that are given of the court and the woods and reveals how the attitudes to these spaces are modified in the Old Swedish translation.

472 *The Eufemiavisor and Courtly Culture. Time, Texts and Cultural Transfer*, ed. Olle FERM, Ingela HEDSTRÖM, Sofia LODÉN, Jonatan PETTERSSON, and Mia ÅKESTAM. Stockholm: Kungl. Vitterhets Historie och Antikvitets Akademien, 2015, 288 p.

The present volume contains proceedings from the symposium *The Eufemiavisor and Courtly Culture. Time, Texts and Cultural Transfer*, held in Stockholm in October 2012. The conference was attended by a wide international audience from the Nordic and European countries as well as the USA, and draw attention to the three Old Swedish chivalric verse narratives *Herr Ivan*, *Flores och Blanzeflor* and *Hertig Fredrik av Normandie*, commonly known as the *Eufemiavisor* – Songs of Eufemia – and their historical and cultural contexts.

473 WOLLIN, Lars, "Chivalry and the Scriptures," in *The Eufemiavisor and Courtly Culture. Time, Texts and Cultural Transfer*, ed. Olle FERM, Ingela HEDSTRÖM, Sofia LODÉN, Jonatan PETTERSSON, and Mia ÅKESTAM. Stockholm: Kungl. Vitterhets Historie och Antikvitets Akademien, 2015, pp. 255–72.

In this article, Lars Wollin relates the Old Swedish *Eufemiavisor* to biblical works, in particular the so-called *Pentateuch paraphrase*, which dates to around the turn of the fourteenth century.

Suisse

Bibliographie pour 2015 établie par Fanny Maillet

I Éditions

474 *Prophetie und Politik. Die Explanatio in Prophetia Merlini Ambrosii des Alanus Flandrensis,* Edition mit Übersetzung und Kommentar von Clara Wille. Bern: Peter Lang, 2015, 864 p. Lateinische Sprache und Literatur des Mittelalters, 49.

Édition et traduction du commentaire et du texte de la *Vita Merlini* de Geoffroy de Monmouth. Le travail minutieux de C.W. permet d'éclairer les conditions de production et le sens de cette *Explanatio*, attribuée de manière convaincante à Alain Flandrensis, abbé de Cîteaux et évêque d'Auxerre, et située autour de l'année 1170. Le premier volume contient les deux textes latins et un index des notions, le second leur traduction en allemand, un commentaire critique et des tables généalogiques.

II Études Critiques et Historiques

475 Chardonnens, Noémie, *L'autre du même: emprunts et répétitions dans le Roman de Perceforest*. Genève: Droz, 2015, 736 p. Publications romanes et françaises, 263.

Ce volume imposant par sa taille et l'ampleur de son sujet est le fruit d'une thèse lausannoise dans laquelle l'auteure étudie les phénomènes d'écho et de reprises inter- et intratextuelles qui animent le *Roman de Perceforest* et les rouages de cette "machine romanesque", confirmant la difficulté à classer l'œuvre dans un compartiment générique. D'utiles annexes facilitent la compréhension du langage des emprunts perceforestiens: un glossaire des notions prises à la théorie littéraire (689–96) et des arbres généalogiques (697–98).

https://doi.org/10.1515/9783110467499-150

III Comptes Rendus

476 *Le Roman de Merlin en prose*, éd. Corinne Füg-Pierreville. Paris: Champion Classiques, 2014, 496 p. (cf. *BIAS*, LXVII, 2015, 315).

C.R. par Wunderli, Peter, *VR*, 75 (2016), 294–302.

477 Moran, Patrick, *Lectures cycliques. Le réseau inter-romanesque dans les cycles du Graal du XIIIe siècle*. Paris: Champion, 2014, 714 p. (cf. *BIAS*, LXVII, 2015, 303).

C.R. par Larghi, Gerardo, *VR*, 74 (2015), 309–12.

478 *Perceforest. Sixième partie, Tomes I et II*, éd. critique par Gilles Roussineau. Bern: Droz, 2015, 1428 p. Textes littéraires du Moyen Âge, 631. (cf. *BIAS*, LXVII, 2015, 529).

C.R. par Chardonnens, Noémie, *VR*, 74 (2015), 328–31.

479 *Prophetie und Politik. Die Explanatio in Prophetia Merlini Ambrosii des Alanus Flandrensis*, Edition mit Übersetzung und Kommentar von Clara Wille. Bern: Peter Lang, 2015, 864 p. Lateinische Sprache und Literatur des Mittelalters, 49.

C.R. par Berthelot, Anne, *Perspectives médiévales*, 36 (2015), online.

North America (USA and Canada)

Bibliography for 2015 compiled by Anne Berthelot

I Editions and Transcriptions

480 MALORY, Sir Thomas, *Le Morte D'Arthur. Condensed and Modernized, with an Introduction*, ed. Trans. and adapt. by Joseph GLASER. Indianapolis / Cambridge, MA: Hackett Publishing Company, 2015, 368 p.

Based on Caxton's edition, offers a very much condensed and modernized version of Malory's text, that "selectively prun[es] over-elaborate passages that can try the patience of modern readers" while keeping all the "most famous episodes." An up-dated bibliography including websites and video resources.

481 MALORY, Sir Thomas, *Le Morte Darthur. Selections*, ed. Maureen OKUN. Peterborough, ON: Broadview Press, 2014, 360 p.

A large selection of excerpts from Malory, including the last two tales and most of the material about Lancelot, plus numerous contextual elements, from "Sample Pages of the Winchester Manuscript" to excerpts from the French *Vulgate-Cycle* or from the Stanzaic and Alliterative *Morte Arthure*. Partially modernized text, with a rich array of textual notes. The introduction is short and sticks to the basics.

482 Marie De France, *Poetry*, ed. and trans. Dorothy GILBERT. New York: W.W. Norton, 2015, 432 p.

Includes all of Marie's *lais*, selected fables, and "a generous excerpt" from *Saint Patrick's Purgatory*. The original text of "Bisclavret" and "Yonec" is also provided. Abundant notes, plus a thematically organized section of "Backgrounds and Contexts," that present a number of possible sources or models for Marie's texts. Also, excerpts of scholarly works addressing issues of authorship, identity, and various major themes in the works, by

https://doi.org/10.1515/9783110467499-152

authors ranging from Joseph Bédier to Leo Spitzer, to R. Howard Bloch and Jacques Le Goff. Also available as an e-textbook.

483 *The Romance of Tristran by Beroul and Beroul II. A Diplomatic Edition and a Critical Edition*, ed. and trans. Barbara SARGENT-BAUR. Toronto, ON: University of Toronto Press, 2015, 208 p.

BSB presents, for the first time ever, a diplomatic edition of Béroul's *Tristan*, plus a new critical edition of the text. The volume includes a section of "Rejected Readings," abundant notes, an index of names and an updated bibliography.

484 *The Romance of Tristran by Beroul and Beroul II. Student Edition and English Translation*, ed. and trans. Barbara SARGENT-BAUR. Toronto, ON: University of Toronto Press, 2015, 208 p.

The student's edition includes a translation of the text.

II Critical and Historical Studies

485 ADAMS, Jenny, "Colonizing the Otherworld in *Walewein*," in *Games and Gaming in Medieval Literature*, ed. Serina PATTERSON. New York: Palgrave-Macmillan, 2015, pp. 127–45.

Studies how the chessboard in *Walewein* first appears as a token of the Otherworld, and is progressively appropriated by Arthur's knights and the principles of courtly romance.

486 ADLER, Gillian, "'ȝit þat traytour alls tite teris lete he fall'. Arthur, Mordred, and Tragedy in the *Alliterative Morte Arthure*," *Arthuriana*, 25.3 (2015), 3–21.

In the *Brut* tradition, the narrative of King Arthur's last campaign represents the dying king heroically. However, the late medieval *Alliterative Morte Arthure* differs, from Laȝamon's *Brut* in particular, by connecting Arthur's hyper-masculinity to the collapse of his court. (GA)

487 AMEY, Michael Darin, "Questing the Grail, Questioning Religion. Religion in Modern Grail Narratives," *Arthuriana*, 25.2 (2015), 3–19.

This essay examines how the Grail legend has been re-appropriated by modern storytellers to create competing discourses about religion, spirituality, and doctrine. In particular, this essay explores the role of modern and post-modern Grail narratives in either affirming or challenging specific modes of spirituality. (MDA)

488 ARONSTEIN, Alan, "The *Da Vinci Code* and the Myth of History," in *The Holy Grail on Film: Essays on the Cinematic Quest*, ed. Kevin J. HARTY. Jefferson, NC: McFarland, 2015, pp. 112–27.

AA focuses on the "endless, multi-faceted circus surrounding Dan Brown's" work and shows how the movie tries to reconcile the post-medieval, post-modern conspiracy theories developed in the novel and a more traditionally Christian idea of the quest.

489 ARONSTEIN, Susan, and Jason THOMPSON, "Coding the Grail. *Ready Player One*'s Arthurian Mash-up," *Arthuriana*, 25.4 (2015), 51–65.

Ernest Cline's *Ready Player One* (2011) is a Grail tale for the Twitter-PS4-Wii generation masquerading as a postmodern techno-bildungsroman. (SA & JT)

490 ATKINSON, Stephen, "Meaning 'spryngyth, burgenyth, buddyth, and florysshyth'. Reading Malory's May Passages," *Arthuriana*, 25.3 (2015), 22–32.

After 1947, Malory criticism was derailed by reactions to Vinaver's *Works*, with critics pursuing the phantoms of unity and originality. New developments in critical theory were ignored, and criticism remained fixated on formalist concerns. This essay addresses the May passages through insights from deconstructionism, embracing the May passages' complexities and shifting implications. (SA)

491 BANDLIEN, Bjørn, Stefka Georgieva ERIKSEN, and Sif RIKHARDSDOTTIR, "Arthur of the North. Histories, Emotions, and Imaginations: Introduction," *SS*, 87.1 (2015), 1–7.

Introduction to a special issue of *Scandinavian Studies* devoted specifically to Arthurian literature as it appears in Old Norse, Old Swedish and Icelandic traditions. The authors outline the issue's contributions to the developing scholarship concerning the *Matière Arthurienne* and its representations in Scandinavian countries.

492 BARAGONA, Alan, "Perceval of the Avant-Garde. Rohmer, Blank, and von Trier," in *The Holy Grail on Film: Essays on the Cinematic Quest*, ed. Kevin J. HARTY. Jefferson, NC: McFarland, 2015, pp. 50–66.

AB addresses the Grail matter through the means of its unlikely original Chosen One, Perceval-Parzival. He analyzes three *avant-garde* movies that portray the *nice*, or innocent, but nevertheless flawed character.

493 BLEWETT, Kelly, "An Unfortunate Lily Maid. Transgressive Reading in *Anne of Green Gables*," *Lion & the Unicorn*, 39.3 (2015), 275–93.

Like her heroine, Lucy Maud Montgomery is a booklover, and Anne's love of books helps her negotiate the difficulties of a woman's part in life. The Arthurian references in *Anne of Green Gables* reveal both the author's affinity for romance and her distrust of it.

494 BRADFORD, Clare, and Rebecca HUTTON, "Female Protagonists in Arthurian Television for the Young. Gendering Camelot," in *The Middle Ages in Popular Culture: Medievalism and Genre*, ed. Helen YOUNG. Amherst, NY: Cambria Press, 2015, pp. 11–34.

Explores representations of female agency in three contemporary Arthurian-themed television programs: *The Legend of Prince Valiant*, *Sir Gadabout*, and *Avalon High*.

495 BRANDSMA, Frank, "Where are the Emotions in Scandinavian Arthuriana? Or. How Cool is King Arthur of the North?" *SS*, 87.1 (2015), 95–106.

Using scholarly research about emotive tropes, FB analyzes the portrayal of emotions in secondary and primary characters in Old Norse adaptations of Chrétien de Troyes' romances. Employing theoretical frameworks of "neurological mirroring" demonstrates how medieval audiences would come to display similar emotions to those felt by the characters.

496 Brennan, Joseph, "You Could Shame the Great Arthur Himself. A Queer Reading of Lancelot from BBC's *Merlin* with Respect to the Character in Malory, White, and Bradley," *Arthuriana*, 25.2 (2015), 20–43.

A queer reading of the Lancelot character as he appears in BBC television series *Merlin* (2008–12) and the works of Malory, White, and Bradley, situates the cult series in the long heritage of Arthurian adaptation and reveals a secretive and troubled figure with a personal connection to his adaptors. (JB)

497 Briand, Cédric, "*Kaamelott*'s Paradox. Lancelot between Subjugation and Individuation," *Arthuriana*, 25.1 (2015), 22–43.

In *Kaamelott*, Lancelot rapidly emerges as the only proficient knight of the Round Table. However, while Alexandre Astier's situational and discursive humor form the crux of the series' matter, they also serve to highlight crucial paradoxes in *Kaamelott*, as well as in Lancelot's subjective construction and his progressive development as an unanticipated foe. (CB)

498 Brown, Molly, "King Arthur and the Knights of the Postmodern Fable. Folding the Dead," in *The Middle Ages in Popular Culture: Medievalism and Genre*, ed. Helen Young. Amherst, NY: Cambria Press, 2015, pp. 179–97.

This article analyses two adaptations of the Arthurian legend for young people, Kevin Crossley-Holland's Arthur trilogy and Catherine Fisher's *Corbenic*, as "texts of quotation" (181) that create a "dynamic and dialogic relationship between writer, reader, text, and context" (194).

499 Bruso, Steven P.W, "The Sword and the Scepter. Mordred, Arthur, and the Dual Roles of Kingship in the *Alliterative Morte Arthure*," *Arthuriana*, 25.2 (2015), 44–66.

The poet of the *Alliterative Morte Arthure* complicates the traditional depiction of Mordred-as-traitor in order to show how both Mordred and Arthur struggle to negotiate the dual roles of kings publicly emblematized on coins, seals, and regalia—king-as-warrior and king-as-governor. (SPWB)

500 Cavallaro, Dani, *The Chivalric Romance and the Essence of Fiction*. Jefferson: McFarland, 2015, 229 p.

DC defines chivalric romance as a form that "is tied to historical reality, yet represents the archetype of imaginative literature" and is characterized by "a centerless structure, self-conscious fictionality and a propensity for irony." Chapters 3 and 4 (ca. 100 pages) are more precisely focused on Arthurian works: Chapter 3, "Creative Cornerstones: Chrétien de Troyes and the *Lancelot-Grail Cycle*," considers the variations of the model in France, from Chrétien's 12th-century verse romances to the huge 13th-century prose *Lancelot-Grail* cycle. On the contrary, Chapter 4, "Medieval Masters: Chaucer, Malory, the Lay and the Gawain-Poet," is thoroughly English.

501 CAWSEY, Kathy, "The Once and Future Childslayer. Guy Gavriel Kay's Inversion of Malory's *Morte Darthur*," *Arthuriana*, 25.2 (2015), 67–83.

Guy Gavriel Kay's *Fionavar Tapestry* interprets Arthur's return not as a reward or honor, but as a punishment for killing the children on Mayday. This reinterpretation links the 'Mayday' incident with the famous 'May passages' and provides a rewriting of the *Morte Darthur*'s stance on prophecy, predestination, and free will. (KC)

502 CHAI-ELSHOLZ, Raeleen, and Jean-Marc ELSHOLZ, "John Boorman's Excalibur and the Irrigating Light of the Grail," in *The Holy Grail on Film: Essays on the Cinematic Quest*, ed. Kevin HARTY. Jefferson: McFarland, 2015, pp. 98–111.

The authors focus on the most original and fascinating trait of Boorman's *Excalibur*: its use of light as both substitute and symbol of an otherwise rather vague Grail. They "apply medieval and cinematic theories of light literally to illuminate" the meaning of Boorman's reinterpretation of Malory and other sources.

503 CHANDLER, Erin, "Pendragons at the Chopping Block. Elements of *Sir Gawain and the Green Knight* in the BBC's *Merlin*," *Arthuriana*, 25.1 (2015), 101–12.

The BBC's *Merlin* (2008) borrows elements of *Sir Gawain and the Green Knight* in two of its early episodes, adjusting the thematic content of the poem to appeal to its audience of parents and children by placing the family rather than the court at the center of conflict. (EC)

504 Cirilla, Anthony, "Ghostly Consolation. *Awntyrs off Arthure* as Boethian Memorial," *Enarratio*, 19 (2015), 68–103.

This article uses A.C. Spearing's discussion of *Awntyrs* as a starting point in order to show "The Consolation of Philosophy as a historically relevant intertextual partner to *The Awntyrs off Arthure* and argue that Boethian images and concepts reveal compelling resonance between the two parts of the Arthurian poem" (68).

505 Contzen, Eva von, "Why Medieval Literature Does Not Need the Concept of Social Minds. Exemplarity and Collective Experience," *Narrative*, 23.2 (2015), 140–52.

EvC argues that A. Palmer's concept of "social minds" is not operative in medieval romances, because medieval culture has "an action-oriented rather than a mind-oriented conception of self." She uses examples from *Sir Gawain and the Green Knight* and the *Alliterative Morte Arthure* to prove her point.

506 Curley, Michael J., "Conjuring History. Mother, Nun, and Incubus in Geoffrey of Monmouth's *Historia Regum Britanniae*," *JEGP*, 114.2 (2015), 219–39.

Compares the scenes where Merlin's mother describes Merlin's birth in Geoffrey's *Historia* and in Nennius' *Historia Britonum*. A closer look at the differences serves to "defamiliarize" the scene, helping contemporary scholars to rethink their understanding of how Geoffrey confronted issues of piety and sex during the early twelfth century.

507 Edwards, Jennifer C., "Casting, Plotting, and Enchanting. Arthurian Women in Starz's *Camelot* and the BBC's *Merlin*," *Arthuriana*, 25.1 (2015), 57–81.

The BBC's family drama *Merlin* and Starz's racy *Camelot* offer similar narratives for female characters, especially Morgan(a) and Guinevere. Playing with traditional plots and casting, *Merlin* and *Camelot* tap into passionate attachments viewers have for powerful female television characters, yet preserve traditional notions about women's place in Arthurian society. (JCE)

508 ELLIOT, Andrew B.R., “Arthurian Fragments, Arthurian Mosaics,” *Arthuriana*, 25.4 (2015), 14–24.

Arthurian images are often the result of a composite process of assembly rather than a dogged fidelity to a pre-existent source text. This article analyzes a range of modern Arthurian fragments, exploring them not as wholesale reprisals of individual images but as fragments which hold new meanings for successive generations. (ABRE)

509 ELLIOTT, Andrew B.R., “Our Minds Are in the Gutter, But Some of Us Are Watching Starz... Sex, Violence, and Dirty Medievalism,” in *Fantasy and Science Fiction Medievalisms, from Isaac Asimov to A Game of Thrones*, ed. Helen YOUNG. New York: Cambria Press, 2015, pp. 97–116.

Contemporary medievalism on television often gives the impression of multiplying the scenes of graphic violence or sexuality, making assumptions about the viewers’ idea of the Middle Ages. This article shows that this claim does not apply to all productions, as each chain follows its own policies.

510 ELLIOTT, Andrew B.R., “The Grail as Symbolic Quest in Tarkovsky’s *Stalker*,” in *The Holy Grail on Film: Essays on the Cinematic Quest*, ed. Kevin HARTY. Jefferson: McFarland, 2015, pp. 187–201.

Despite Tarkovsky’s refusal to classify his movie, Stalker may be considered as a spiritual Grail quest, only one where “what is sought is less important than the actual seeking.”

511 ELMES, Melissa Ridley, “Episodic Arthur. ‘Merlin,’ ‘Camelot,’ and the Medieval Romance Tradition,” in *The Middle Ages on Television: Critical Essays*, ed. Karolyn KINANE and Meriem PAGÈS. Jefferson: McFarland, 2015, pp. 99–121.

Using Sir Thomas Malory’s *Le Morte Darthur* as the representative medieval romance for comparison, this essay argues that the medium of television is more appropriate than that of film for the transmission of Arthurian romance into visual media due to its episodic nature, which mimics the medieval Arthurian romance tradition. (MRE)

512 Feinstein, Sandy, "Are You Kidding? *King Arthur and the Knights of Justice*," in *The Middle Ages on Television: Critical Essays*, ed. Karolyn Kinane and Meriem Pagès. Jefferson: McFarland, 2015, pp. 122–38.

Fandom's development, in the late 19th century, informs the construction of the animated *King Arthur and the Knights of Justice* and the genres used to popularize it. The animation remediates the telling of King Arthur's adventures for children with insight into what makes the medieval story matter across time and place. (SF)

513 Finke, Laurie, and Martin B. Shichtman, "*The Waterboy* and Swamp Chivalry. A Grail Knight for American Teens," in *The Holy Grail on Film: Essays on the Cinematic Quest*, ed. Kevin Harty. Jefferson: McFarland, 2015, pp. 202–14.

Explores the general mythopoeic value of sports films and how *The Waterboy*, in particular, seems to make fun of the Grail quest motif while in fact "reinscribing the very myths it seeks to undermine."

514 Flood, Victoria, "Arthur's Return from Avalon. Geoffrey of Monmouth and the Development of the Legend," *Arthuriana*, 25.2 (2015), 84–110.

This article traces the development of the legend of Arthur's return from Avalon from Geoffrey of Monmouth's inception of the motif to its early reception history, exploring its relationship to Welsh and Breton prophetic traditions and the impact of Avalon on subsequent English and French understandings of a constructed genre of pan-British political prophecy. (VF)

515 Foster, Tara, and Jon Sherman, "King Arthur in the Twenty-First Century. *Kaamelott*, BBC's *Merlin*, and Starz's *Camelot*," *Arthuriana*, 25.1 (2015), 3–4.

Introduces *Arthuriana*'s issue devoted to modern cinematographic Arthuriana, with special focus on Alexandre Astier's *Kaamelott* (2005–2009) and the BBC's *Merlin* (2008–2012)—as well as Starz's prematurely cancelled *Camelot* (2011) (TF & JS).

516 Foster, Tara, "Arthur and Gueniève. The Royal Couple of *Kaamelott*," in *The Middle Ages on Television. Critical Essays*, ed. Meriem Pagès and Karolyn Kinane. Jefferson, NC: McFarland, 2015, pp. 174–96.

This article analyzes Alexandre Astier's series from the point of view of male-female roles, in particular those of Arthur and Guinevere, whose distance from the Arthurian tradition results from the satirical aim of the series. Women have supporting roles, but their actions are decisive for the plot.

517 Foster, Tara, "*Kaamelott*'s Global Fifth Century," *Arthuriana*, 25.1 (2015), 5–21.

Despite its fifth-century setting, the wildly popular French television series *Kaamelott* presents spectators with a court that seems familiar and accessible. By lessening the distance between his version of the Arthurian world and his twenty-first-century audience, series creator Alexandre Astier invites viewers to reflect on their own society. (TF)

518 Gautier, Alban, "From Dejection in Winter to Victory in Spring. Aragorn and Alfred, Parallel Episodes?" *Tolkien Studies*, 12 (2015), 95–122.

Argues that Aragorn is not necessarily characterized by Alfred the Great, but may be modeled on King Arthur; however, concludes that Tolkien probably did use an episode from the *Anglo-Saxon Chronicles* regarding Alfred as a template to an Aragorn episode in *The Lord of the Rings*.

519 Gebhardt, Toben R., "Homosexuality in Television Medievalism," in *The Middle Ages on Television. Critical Essays*, ed. Meriem Pagès and Karolyn Kinane. Jefferson, NC: McFarland, 2015, pp. 197–214.

Gebhardt's article analyzes the behaviour of gay characters in TV series, especially *Game of Thrones*, to show the importance of what he calls "provocative entertainment" in neo-medievalism. While the medieval condemnation of homosexuality is not discussed, *Game of Thrones* offers a neo-medieval simulacrum without worrying about historical authenticity.

520 George, Michael W., "Television's Male Gaze. The Male Perspective in TNT's *Mists of Avalon*," in *The Middle Ages on Television. Critical Essays*,

ed. Meriem PAGÈS and Karolyn KINANE. Jefferson, NC: McFarland, 2015, pp. 141–57.

This article analyses the "strong women" in the television adaptation of Marion Zimmer Bradley's fantasy novel *The Mists of Avalon*, which rewrites the Arthurian legend from the point of view of multiple women of the legend.

521 GIL, Steven, "Sword and Science. Science Fiction Interpretations of Medieval Arthurian Literature and Legend in *Stargate SG-1*," in *Fantasy and Science Fiction Medievalisms: From Isaac Asimov to 'A Game of Thrones'*, ed. Helen YOUNG. Amherst, NY: Cambria Press, 2015, pp. 141–58.

Studies how the last two seasons of the science-fiction series *Stargate SG-1* are built around the Arthurian legends, altering them from typical fantasy to science-fiction by divesting characters and objects of their supernatural qualities to imbue them with new, technological ones.

522 GILMORE, Alec, "Steinbeck's Translation of Malory's *Morte d'Arthur*. Success or Failure—An End or a New Beginning?" *Steinbeck Review*, 12.1 (2015), 74–86.

Seeks to refute the common perception that Steinbeck's incomplete translation of Malory's *Morte d'Arthur* is more indicative of a success than of a failure for Steinbeck. AG explores this paradoxical "success" of Steinbeck in terms of his maturity and realization that the value of the "grail" is in one's quest for it.

523 GOERES, Erin Michelle, "Britain as *Sjónhverfing*. Decoding the Landscape in *Strengleikar*," *SS*, 87.1 (2015), 147–66.

Explores the depiction of Anglo-Norman geography through two tales—*Doun* and *Désire*—from the Old Norse *Strengleikar*, and contends that landscapes of the inner parts of Britain remain nebulous and mysterious, despite some basic concrete knowledge of British geography.

524 GRIMBERT, Joan Tasker, "*Lancelot du Lac*. Robert Bresson's Arthurian Realism," in *The Holy Grail on Film: Essays on the Cinematic Quest*, ed. Kevin J. HARTY. Jefferson, NC: McFarland, 2015, pp. 37–49.

JTG studies how Bresson's *Lancelot du Lac*, centered on the total absence of the Grail, attempts to ground Arthurian material in cinematic realism by presenting "not a cinema without symbols, but a cinema with symbols emptied of all their symbolism."

525 HARTY, Kevin J., "Holy Grail, Silent Grail," in *The Holy Grail on Film: Essays on the Cinematic Quest*, ed. Kevin J. HARTY. Jefferson, NC: McFarland, 2015, pp. 7–20.

KJH studies four silent "Grail movies" where the quest is more or less consciously recuperated by conservative ideologies, from the Scout movement to National-Socialism.

526 HOFF, James Dennis, "'Ut Pictora Poesis'. Teaching 'The Lady of Shalott' and Victorian Visual Culture," *CEA Critic*, 77.2 (2015), 223–39.

Argues in favor of contextualizing Tennyson's version of the poem "The Lady of Shalott" within the cultural milieu of early 19th century. Doing so deepens students' understanding of the poem beyond its surface lovelorn tropes. Also insists on the importance of understanding the reciprocal influence between image and text.

527 HOWEY, Ann F., "Arthur and Adaptation," *Arthuriana*, 25.4 (2015), 36–50.

Recent adaptation scholarship theorizes repetition, alteration, and fragmentation—important strategies in the production of Arthuriana. This essay explores intersections of adaptation theory and Arthurian studies, examining representations of Morgan in *Avalon High: Coronation* and BBC's *Merlin* as adaptations to a perceived 'post-feminist' culture. (AFH)

528 JACOBS, Molly A., "'Undir ilmöndum laufum ok nýsprungnum blómstrum'. Sensual Pleasure in Old Norse Arthurian Romance," *SS*, 87.1 (2015), 107–28.

Explores how senses and the pleasures they procure are depicted in Old Norse Arthurian texts. AMJ shows how *Tristrams saga* sets itself apart from other well-known Norse sagas such as the *Ìslendingasögur* and *Konungasögur* through its vivid depictions of various settings, strongly engage the visual sense of Icelandic audiences.

529 Jesson, James, "Parcival in Cooperstown. Arthurian Legend Baseball Mythology and the Mediated Quest in Barry Levinson's *The Natural*," in *The Holy Grail on Film: Essays on the Cinematic Quest*, ed. Kevin J. Harty. Jefferson, NC: McFarland, 2015, pp. 128–42.

JJ shows how, in *The Natural*, "the mythology surrounding the American national pastime mediates the Arthurian quest."

530 Kalinke, Marianne, "Arthur King of Iceland," *SS*, 87.1 (2015), 8–32.

Explores how Geoffey of Monmouth's *Historia regum Britanniae* migrates into Icelandic literature by examining the vestiges of the British Arthur in the *Breta Sögur*. Argues that the source for this text is a late Latin redaction that has already begun the transformation from the chronicle into romance.

531 Kaufman, Amy S., "Introduction: Touching Arthur," *Arthuriana*, 25.4 (2015), 3–13.

The temporary collapse of *Arthurnet* reveals a fraught relationship between scholars and public audiences, but Elizabeth Sklar's work provides solutions for rebuilding broken bridges. (ASK)

532 Kelly, Kathleen Coyne, "Arthurian Things," *Arthuriana*, 25.4 (2015), 94–107.

This article is an object-oriented inquiry into the material but imaginary objects associated with King Arthur and Arthurian legend. (KCK)

533 Larrington, Carolyne, "Learning to Feel in the Old Norse Camelot?" *SS*, 87.1 (2015), 74–94.

Examines emotions as they are portrayed in *le Conte de Graal* versus *Parcevals saga*, focusing on several episodes that serve to illustrate the differences between the original and the Old Norse text.

534 Lindquist, Josefa E., "Medieval Depiction of Spaces. Battle and Tournament Fields in the Tristan and Ysolt Legend," *La corónica: A Journal of Medieval Hispanic Languages, Literatures, and Cultures*, 44.1 (2015), 163–75.

"The primary goal of this article is to examine how the descriptions of the location of battlefields and the tournaments are linked to the *locus eremus* and the *locus amoenus*" in two Spanish versions of Tristan and Ysolt.

535 LINDSAY, Sarah, "The Courteous Monster. Chivalry, Violence, and Social Control in *The Carl of Carlisle*," *JEGP*, 114.3 (2015), 401–18.

Studies how the stanzaic version of *The Carl of Carlisle* tries to disentangle violence and chivalry, with mixed results. Shows how the "monster" is no more—and no less—violent, or courtly, than the ideal knight Gawain himself.

536 LODEN, Sofia, "The Arthurian Legacy in Sweden," *SS*, 87.1 (2015), 62–73.

SL studies the transmission of Arthurian motifs in the generation of narratives coming chronologically after the *Eufemiavisor* (c.1300), and examines how Gauvain and Perceval are transformed from models of courtly behavior to counter-normative characters.

537 LOMBARDI, Elena, "'A Gallehault was the Book' Francesca da Rimini and the Manesse Minnesanger Manuscript," *Med*, 35 (2014), 151–76.

Revisits the very famous episode of Dante's *Hell*, and traces down other associations between love and the act of reading, especially in the *Manesse Manuscript*.

538 MARGINI, Matthew, "The Beast with the Broken Lance. Humanism and Posthumanism in Tennyson's *Idylls of the King*," *Victorian Poetry*, 53.2 (2015), 171–92.

Explores the dialectic of optimistic humanism and a pessimistic awareness of humanism's obsolescence in Tennyson's Arthuriad. Shows how the Victorian poet works to delineate a new, "post-humanist" vision of man as distinct from and superior to the beats within himself.

539 MARSHALL, Adam Bryant, "Sir Lancelot at the Chapel Perelus. Malory's Adaptation of the *Perlesvaus*," *Arthuriana*, 25.3 (2015), 33–48.

This essay examines the differences between Malory's account of Lancelot's adventure at the Chapel Perelus and that of his source-text, the anonymous *Perlesvaus*. Comparison of these two accounts reveals Malory's efforts to make the episode more terrifying, highlighting Lancelot's knightly courage in the face of supernatural danger. (ABM)

540 MARSHALL, David W., "Holy Grail, Schlocky Grail," in *The Holy Grail on Film: Essays on the Cinematic Quest*, ed. Kevin J. HARTY. Jefferson, NC: McFarland, 2015, pp. 215–32.

The last essay in the volume considers 4 little-known B-movies that emphasize the destructive nature of the—sometimes not so Holy— Grail and the unavoidable failure of any quest, whether for a symbol, or for any kind of meaning.

541 MEDIAVILLA, Cindy, "From 'Unthinking Stereotype' to Fearless Antagonist. The Evolution of Morgan le Fay on Television," *Arthuriana*, 25.1 (2015), 44–56.

Although recent fiction has portrayed Morgan le Fay much more sympathetically, on television she has remained, for the most part, an evil caricature. The depictions of Morgan on Starz's *Camelot* and BBC1's *Merlin* stand out as being among the most fully realized versions of her character in any medium. (CM)

542 MELICK, Elizabeth, "Saracens, Graves, and the Formation of National Identity in Sir Thomas Malory's *Le Morte Darthur*," *Enarratio*, 19 (2015), 50–67.

This article argues that because "Malory denies Saracens the opportunity to record their national identity on tombs" and "instead links Saracens to landscape features associated with lack or absence," Malory is able to represent "Saracens as a negation of Christians" (51).

543 MEREDITH, Elysse T., "Gendering Morals, Magic and Medievalism in the BBC's *Merlin*," in *The Middle Ages on Television. Critical Essays*, ed. Meriem PAGÈS and Carolyn KINANE. Jefferson, NC: McFarland, 2015, pp. 158–73.

Meredith analyses the series *Merlin* by concentrating on its representation of the Old Religion, which is inspired by Celtic pagan worship. The article suggests that magic is gendered in the series: while feminine magic is essentially negative (with the exception of Gwen), men are characterized by positive magic use.

544 MILLER, Edmund, "The Date and Occasion of *Sir Gawain and the Green Knight*," *ANQ*, 28.2 (2015), 59–62.

Proposes 1390 as date for *Sir Gawain and the Green Knight*, as being the year of the coming of age and knighting of Roger Mortimer, Earl of March, and in some ways "nephew" to Richard II (as Gawain to Arthur).

545 NAKLEY, Susan, "'Rowned She a Pistel'. National Institutions and Identities According to Chaucer's *Wife of Bath*," *JEGP*, 114.1 (2015), 61–87.

"This essay seeks to explain how Christian nobility crystallizes as a particular form of class-crossing national identity in Chaucer's *Wife of Bath's Tale*, his only Arthurian romance." (SN)

546 NEUFELD, Christine M., "A Dwarf in King Arthur's Court. Perceiving Disability in Arthurian Romance," *Arthuriana*, 25.4 (2015), 25–35.

This article contrasts contemporary and medieval conceptualizations of the dwarf in texts stemming from the French Arthurian tradition in order to draw attention to the critical limitations that ensue from our scholarly tendencies to treat such non-normative bodies as prodigious objects rather than possible subjects. (CMN)

547 NEUFELD, Christine M., "'Lovely Filth'. Monty Python and the Matter of the Holy Grail," in *The Holy Grail on Film: Essays on the Cinematic Quest*, ed. Kevin J. HARTY. Jefferson, NC: McFarland, 2015, pp. 81–97.

CMN discusses "what may arguably be the best-known (and most beloved) Grail film" and argues "that a film about a Quest predicated on questions both asked and unasked leaves us not with a neat, pat set of answers, but rather with a whole new set of questions."

548 PICKENS, Rupert T., *Perceval and Gawain in Dark Mirrors. Reflection and Reflexivity in Chrétien de Troyes's Conte del Graal*. Jefferson, NC: McFarland, 2015, 216 p.

Framed by two Christian quotations, this study reads the *Conte del Graal* through the use and presence of mirrors, metaphorical or real, within the text. It shows how the romance is entirely structured as a series of reflections, and logically concludes that Gauvain is a "dark reflection" of Perceval in the second part of Chrétien's apparently unfinished work: that leads to a suggestion of a "probable" ending for the romance, with Perceval as heir to the "Kingdom of the Grail" and Gauvain as heir to Arthur's Logres. Several intriguing appendixes open deeper vistas on Chrétien's works, including *La Charrette*.

549 RATELIFF, John D., "The lost letter. Seeking the keys to Williams' *Arthuriad*," *Mytl*, 34.1 (2015), 5–36.

Very close reading of a letter by Williams himself, long-believed to have been destroyed by Lewis, that gives precious insights in Williams' Arthurian "finished" texts, *Taliessin Through Logres* and *The Region of the Summer Stars*, as well as what was published under the title *Arthurian Torso*.

550 RUSHTON, Cory James, "Terry Gilliam's *The Fisher King*," in *The Holy Grail on Film: Essays on the Cinematic Quest*, ed. Kevin J. HARTY. Jefferson, NC: McFarland, 2015, pp. 143–57.

CJR studies the "New World Grail" conceived of by Terry Gilliam and shows how Gilliam's usual themes mesh up with probes of medieval aesthetics to depict "a modern reincarnation of the Wasteland in need of healing."

551 RUSHTON, Cory James, "Wrecking It With Camelot," *Arthuriana*, 25.4 (2015), 84–93.

Arthurian studies has some difficulty defining itself and is prone to conflating fidelity and aesthetics. Using a low culture object (the film *Talladega Nights*), this article attempts to raise some questions for the field to consider, including questions of genre and purpose. (CJR)

552 SÉVÈRE, Richard, "Galahad, Percival, and Bors. Grail Knights and the Quest for *Spiritual Friendship*," *Arthuriana*, 25.3 (2015), 49–65.

St. Aelred's *Spiritual Friendship* (dated between 1164 and 1167) serves as a framework through which we can read and better understand the interactions among knights on the Grail Quest. Ultimately, spiritual friendship proves not only an ennobling act in Malory, but also a necessary step in achieving the Grail. (RS)

553 SHERMAN, Jon, "Hans-Jürgen Syberberg's *Parsifal*. Remystifying Kundry," in *The Holy Grail on Film: Essays on the Cinematic Quest*, ed. Kevin J. HARTY. Jefferson, NC: McFarland, 2015, pp. 67–80.

JS analyzes the evolution of the "flawed Grail maiden" Cundrîe from a minor to a major character in the *Parsifal* argument, comparing Wolfram von Eschenbach's tale, and its adaptation by Wagner to the epic film version of the opera by Syberberg.

554 SHERMAN, Jon, "Source, Authority, and Audience in the BBC's *Merlin*," *Arthuriana*, 25.1 (2015), 82–100.

Although *Merlin*'s producers claim to target a young audience, much of the program's appeal is found in intertextual references to and deviations from medieval Arthurian literature. The dynamic tension created between continuity and innovation can only be appreciated by those with some—or even significant—knowledge of *Merlin*'s medieval antecedents. (JS)

555 SPEARING, A. C., "What is a Narrator? Narrator Theory and Medieval Narratives," *Digital Philology: A Journal of Medieval Cultures*, 4.1 (2015), 59–105.

This article questions the "narrator theory of narration" with particular reference to medieval narratives, often retellings of existing stories, and generally neglected by current theory. Part I analyzes the concept of the internal, potentially unreliable narrator, widely regarded as a narratological necessity. Part II examines the history of the term narrator. Part III studies the theories of narration implied by scribal annotations in some medieval manuscripts. Parts IV, V, and VI discuss three medieval cases—Malory's *Morte Darthur*, Chaucer's *Physician's Tale* and the anonymous *Pearl*—in which application of the narrator theory proves to be misleading.

556 STEWART, James T., "Thomas Chestre's *Sir Launfal* and the Knight in Need," *Arthuriana*, 25.2 (2015), 111–28.

This article positions Thomas Chestre's *Sir Launfal* alongside chivalric manuals and histories of nobility in order to highlight the ways in which a knight's attendants and companions support his heroism and social status. (JTS)

557 STØA, Heidi, "The Lover and the Statue. Idolatrous Love in *Tristrams saga ok Ísöndar*," *SS*, 87.1 (2015), 129–46.

HS focuses on the 'Hall of Statues' episode, arguing that this scene, which has been overlooked by previous scholars, provides evidence that Old Norse audiences were, indeed, interested in psychological love.

558 STOCK, Lorraine K., "Reinventing an Iconic Arthurian Moment. The Sword in the Stone in Films and Television," *Arthuriana*, 25.4 (2015), 66–83.

Filmmakers adapting medieval and post-medieval texts devise various modifications of the iconic sword-extraction that reflect their contemporary audiences' cultural issues and concerns. (LKS)

559 STURTEVANT, Paul B., "A Grail or a Mirage? Searching the Wasteland of *The Road Warrior*," in *The Holy Grail on Film: Essays on the Cinematic Quest*, ed. Kevin J. HARTY. Jefferson, NC: McFarland, 2015, pp. 173–86.

Addresses the theoretical question of "what makes a movie a Grail movie?" by suggesting that the Grail is where one wants to find it; the author reads the second movie in the *Mad Max* series as a revival of the Grail myth.

560 SULLIVAN, Joseph M., "A Son, His Father, Some Nazis and the Grail Lance. Lucas and Spielberg's *Indiana Jones and the Last Crusade*," in *The Holy Grail on Film: Essays on the Cinematic Quest*, ed. Kevin J. HARTY. Jefferson, NC: McFarland, 2015, pp. 158–72.

JMS examines the Grail as both a material and an immaterial narrative-driving force in *Indiana Jones and Last Crusade*, and concludes that the quest in the movie is more a quest for a father than a quest for the Grail.

561 SULLIVAN, Joseph, "Arthur of the Northeast. The Old Swedish *Herr Ivan* Redraws the King Arthur of Chrétien's *Yvain*," *SS*, 87.1 (2015), 33–61.

Studies how the first text in the Old Swedish *Eufemiavisor*, *Herr Ivan*, removes the moral and political ambiguity of Chrétien's *Yvain* in order to provide the audience with a "more coherent and positive picture of right rule and the ideal relationships that should exist between individuals" (JS).

562 SWANK, Kris, "The Irish Otherworld Voyage of *Roverandom*," *Tolkien Studies*, 12 (2015), 31–57.

Delineates the influence of the "Voyage to the Otherworld" motif in Irish literature and in Arthurian texts featuring Arthur's departure for Avalon on *Roverandom*, Tolkien's first children's book about the puppy Rover.

563 SWANN, Alaya, "The Once and Future Earth. Ecology and Narrative in Stephen King's Dark Tower Series," *Journal of Popular Culture*, 48.6 (2015), 1327–45.

"In the Dark Tower series [King's Arthurian-inspired cycle about 'the last gunslinger'], King highlights the relationship between narrative, memory, and environment in order to suggest the potential influence of speculative fiction on ecological questions."

564 SWEENEY, Michelle, "Chapter 11 – Lady as Temptress and Reformer in Medieval Romance," *Essays in Medieval Studies*, 30 (2014), 165–78.

Addresses the question of female agency through the ambivalence between sexual transgression (rape) and courtly code in a few medieval romances, among them *Sir Gawain and the Green Knight*, *Lanval*, and *The Knight of the Cart*.

565 TAYLOR, Amanda D., "The Body of Law. Embodied Justice in Sir Thomas Malory's *Morte Darthur*," *Arthuriana*, 25.3 (2015), 66–97.

This article argues that Malory undermines paradigms of divine, sovereign, and common law justice while suggesting embodied justice as a viable alternative that depends upon the agency of the body in debate. It explores the implications for women who gain greater access to judicial process via the mechanism of embodied justice and rejection of prescriptive law. (ADT)

566 *The Holy Grail on Film. Essays on the Cinematic Quest*, ed. Kevin J. HARTY. Jefferson, NC: McFarland, 2015, ix + 245 p.

In line with his previous books on medieval films, KJH gathers this time 15 studies on "American, Australian and European films" that present their own version of the "Holy Vessel."

567 *The Middle Ages in Popular Culture. Medievalism and Genre*, ed. Helen Young. Amherst, NY: Cambria Press, 2015, 240 p.

"Rather than focusing on the medievalism of a single genre, this volume puts multiple genres in dialogue and considers both medievalism and genre to be frameworks from which meaning can be produced. Chapters in it explore works from a wide range of genres—children's and young adult, historical, cyberpunk, fantasy, science fiction, romance, and crime—and across multiple media—fiction, film, television, video games, and music." The first and last chapter are especially devoted to Arthurian forms of medievalism: "Female Protagonists in Arthurian Television for the Young: Gendering Camelot" and "King Arthur and the Knights of the Postmodern Fable: Folding the Dead."

568 Tollerton, David C., "Multiculturalism, Diversity, and Religious Tolerance in Modern Britain and the BBC's *Merlin*," *Arthuriana*, 25.1 (2015), 113–27.

Setting the BBC's *Merlin* in an ahistorical, mythical realm allows the series' creators to reflect key elements of modern rather than medieval British society. As a result, the series explores issues of diversity, multiculturalism, and tolerance in a way which resonates with twenty-first-century viewers. (DCT)

569 Triplette, Stacey, "From Guinevere to Isabel. Rodríguez de Montalvo's Transformations of Oriana in *Amadís de Gaula*," *La corónica: A Journal of Medieval Hispanic Languages, Literatures, and Cultures*, 43.2 (2015), 29–55.

Suggests that the replacement of traditional Arthurian "adultery by youthful disobedience" in *Amadis* does not correspond only to a desire to moralize the romance, but has political implications. Oriana's marriage to Amadis justifies the couple's power on Gaul and Spain, as happens in the case of the *Reyes Catholicos*.

570 WAKEMAN, Rob, "The 'Best Breathed' Knights in a Stertorous Age. Tuberculosis and Sidney Lanier's *The Boy's King Arthur*," *Arthuriana*, 25.3 (2015), 98–114.

Having contracted tuberculosis during the Civil War, Sidney Lanier valorized the 'healthful' qualities of medieval literature in his Reconstruction-era writings. This essay argues that Lanier prescribed his *Boy's King Arthur* as a cure for disease-ridden bodies both politic and personal. (RW)

571 WHETTER, Kevin, "*The Silver Chalice*. The Once and Future Grail," in *The Holy Grail on Film: Essays on the Cinematic Quest*, ed. Kevin J. HARTY. Jefferson, NC: McFarland, 2015, pp. 21–36.

KSW studies the "pre-history" of the Grail, its value as more than an object, and the emergence of Christianity in the little-known movie *The Silver Chalice*, adapted from the 1952 novel with the same title.

572 WOLLER, Megan, "The Lusty Court of *Camelot* (1967). Exploring Sexuality in the Hollywood Adaptation," *Music and the Moving Image*, 8.1 (2015), 3–18.

Shows, through detailed analysis of specific scenes and techniques, how much the Hollywood version of Lerner and Loewe's musical is sexualized.

573 WYATT, Siobhán Mary, "'Gyff me goodly langage, and than my care is paste'. Reproach and Recognition in Malory's *Tale of Sir Gareth*," *Arthuriana*, 25.2 (2015), 129–42.

Damsels who chide in medieval romances reflect the nature of women who scold identified in court records. Malory is unique amongst romance writers in justifying their behavior, and he lends value to their words by illustrating how ill-speaking women can be beneficial to knightly careers. (SMW)

III Reviews

574 *Arthurian Literature*, ed. Elizabeth ARCHIBALD and David F. JOHNSON. Cambridge: D. S. Brewer, 2014, 220 p. (cf. *BIAS*, LXVI, 2014, 375).

Rev. by ARONSTEIN, Susan, *Arthuriana*, 25.1 (2015), 167–68.

575 BATTLES, Dominique, *Cultural Difference and Material Culture in Middle English Romance. Normans and Saxons*. New York, NY: Routledge, 2013, 234 p. Routledge Studies in Medieval Literature and Culture, 3. (cf. *BIAS*, LXVI, 2014, 303).

Rev. by RUSHTON, Cory James, *Spec*, 90.2 (2015), 494–96.

576 BÉDIER, Joseph, *The Romance of Tristan and Iseut*, Edward J. Gallagher. Indianapolis, IN: Hackett Publishing Company, 2013, 210 p. (cf. *BIAS*, LXVI, 2014, 552).

Rev. by TRAXLER, Janina P., *Spec*, 90.1 (2015), 207–09.

577 CALIN, William, *The Lily and the Thistle. The French Tradition and the Older Literature of Scotland – Essays in Criticism*. Toronto: U of Toronto P, 2014, 413 p. (cf. *BIAS*, LXVI, 2014, 566).

Rev. by MANION, Lee, *Spec*, 90.2 (2015), 518–19.

578 CERQUIGLINI-TOULET, Jacqueline, *A New History of Medieval French Literature. Rethinking Theory*. Baltimore, MD: The Johns Hopkins University Press, 2011, 165 p.

Rev. by FRANKLIN-BROWN, Mary, *Spec*, 90.1 (2015), 222–23.

579 CHAUCER, Geoffrey, *A Variorum Edition of the Works of Geoffrey Chaucer, vol. 2: The Canterbury Tales. The Wife of Bath's Prologue and Tale (Parts 5A and 5B)*, ed. Mark ALLEN and John H. FISHER. University of Oklahoma Press: Norman, OK, 2012, 315 p.

Rev. by BARAGONA, Alan, *Spec*, 90.1 (2015), 224–26.

580 CROCKER, Holly A., and D. Vance SMITH, *Medieval Literature. Criticism and Debate*. London / New York, NY: Routledge, 2014, 552 p. (cf. *BIAS*, LXVI, 2014, 320).

Rev. by ROLAND, Meg, *Arthuriana*, 25.2 (2015), 146–47.

581 EDLICH-MUTH, Miriam, *Malory and His European Contemporaries. Adapting Late Arthurian Romance Collections*. Cambridge: D. S. Brewer, 2014, 186 p. Arthurian Studies, 81. (cf. *BIAS*, LXVII, 2015, 388).

Rev. by FRANCIS, Christina, *Arthuriana*, 25.1 (2015), 172–73.
Rev. by HODGES, Kenneth, *TMR*, 2014 (2014), online (14.11.01).
Rev. by MURRIN, Michael, *RQ*, 68.3 (2015), 381–82.

582 EMING, Jutta, Anne-Marie RASMUSSEN, and Kathryn STARKEY, *Visuality and Materiality in the Story of Tristan and Isolde*. Notre Dame, IN: University of Notre Dame Press, 2012, 344 p. (cf. *BIAS*, LXV, 2013, 541).

Rev. by CHINCA, Mark, *Spec*, 90.3 (2015), 803–04.

583 FALETRA, Michael A, *Wales and the Medieval Colonial Imagination. The Matters of Britain in the Twelfth Century*. New York: Palgrave Macmillan, 2014, 243 p. The New Middle Ages. (cf. *BIAS*, LXVII, 2015, 568).

Rev. by BRADY, Lindy, *Arthuriana*, 25.4 (2015), 108–09.
Rev. by MITCHELL, Linda E., *TMR*, 2015 (2015), online (15.01.23).

584 FEIN, Susanna, and Michael JOHNSTON, *Robert Thornton and His Books. Essays on the Lincoln and London Thornton Manuscripts*. Woodbridge, Suffolk / Rochester, NY: York Medieval Press, 2014, 310 p.

Rev. by GORNY, Danny, *Arthuriana*, 25.2 (2015), 147–49.

585 FICHTE, Joerg O., *From Camelot to Obamalot. Essays on Medieval and Modern Arthurian Literature*. Trier: WVT Wissenschaftlicher Verlag Trier, 2010, 202 p.

Rev. by OBERMEIER, Anita, *JEGP*, 114.3 (2015), 453–56.

586 FINDLEY, Brooke H., *Poet Heroines in Medieval French Narrative. Gender and Fictions of Literary Creation*. New York: Palgrave Macmillan, 2012, 267 p.

Rev. by EVANS, Beverly J., *Women in French Studies*, 23 (2015), 156–58.

587 HAINES, John, *Music in Films on the Middle Ages. Authenticity vs. Fantasy*. New York: Routledge, 2014, 239 p.

Rev. by HARTY, Kevin J., *Arthuriana*, 25.1 (2015), 173–75.

588 HANKS, D. Thomas, and Janet JESMOK, *Malory and Christianity. Essays on Sir Thomas Malory's 'Morte Darthur'*. Kalamazoo, MI: Western Michigan University Press, 2013, 244 p. Studies in Medieval Culture, 51. (cf. *BIAS*, LXVI, 2014, 575).

Rev. by RUSHTON, Cory James, *Spec*, 90.3 (2015), 818–19.

589 Hartmann von Aue, *Erec*, Cyril EDWARDS. Cambridge: D.S. Brewer, 2014, 560 p. German Romance, 5. (cf. *BIAS*, LXVII, 2015, 367).

Rev. by MEYER, Evelyn, *TMR*, 2015 (2015), online (15.06.32).

590 HEBERT, Jill M., *Morgan le Fay, Shapeshifter*. New York: Palgrave, 2013, 230 p. Arthurian and Courtly Cultures. (cf. *BIAS*, LXVI, 2014, 340).

Rev. by KAUFMAN, Amy S., *Spec*, 90.1 (2015), 256–57.

591 INNES, Paul, *Epic*. London / New York: Routledge, 2013, 173 p. The New Critical Idiom.

Rev. by ADAMS, Anthony, *Arthuriana*, 25.4 (2015), 114–16.

592 ISHIGURO, Kazuo, *The Buried Giant*. New York: Alfred A. Knopf, 2015, 317 p.

Rev. by LUPACK, Alan, *Arthuriana*, 25.3 (2015), 118–20.

593 KIBLER, William W., and R. Barton PALMER, *Medieval Arthurian Epic and Romance. Eight New Translations*. Jefferson. N.C. / London: McFarland, 2014, 300 p. (cf. *BIAS*, LXVII, 2015, 550).

Rev. by LINDSAY, Sarah, *TMR*, 2015 (2015), online (15.10.08).

594 *'Lancelot-Grail'. The Old French Arthurian Vulgate and Post-Vulgate in Translation*, Norris J. LACY. Paperback edition. Cambridge: D. S. Brewer, 2010, 10 vols.

Rev. by GRIMBERT, Joan Tasker, *Encomia*, 32 (2010), 58–62.

595 LAWRENCE-MATHERS, Anne, *The True History of Merlin the Magician*. New Haven, CT / London: Yale University Press, 2012, 258 p. (cf. *BIAS*, LXV, 2013, 516).

Rev. by PUTTER, Ad, *Clio*, 44.2 (2015), 239–42.

596 LEXTON, Ruth, *Contested Language in Malory's Morte Darthur. The Politics of Romance in Fifteenth-Century England*. New York: Palgrave Macmillan, 2014, 256 p. Arthur and Courtly Cultures. (cf. *BIAS*, LXVII, 2015, 579).

Rev. by PADEN, William D., *MP*, 113.1 (2015), E8–10.

597 *Magistra Doctissima. Essays in Honor of Bonnie Wheeler*, ed. Dorsey ARMSTRONG, Ann W. ASTELL, and Howell CHICKERING. Kalamazoo, MI: Western Michigan University Press, 2013, 281 p.

Rev. by GRIMBERT, Joan Tasker, *Spec*, 90.1 (2015), 198–99.
Rev. by HAUGHT, Leah, *JEGP*, 114.3 (2015), 435–38.

598 MALORY, Sir Thomas, *Morte Darthur*, ed. P. J. C. Field. Cambridge: D. S. Brewer, 2013, 984 p. (cf. *BIAS*, LXVI, 2014, 292).

Rev. by HODGES, Kenneth, *TMR*, 2015 (2015), online (15.02.03).

599 MATTHEWS, David, *Medievalism. A Critical History*. Cambridge: D. S. Brewer, 2015, 211 p.

Rev. by D'ARCENS, Louise, *SAC*, 37 (2015), 301–04.
Rev. by UTZ, Richard, *Arthuriana*, 25.4 (2015), 118–19.

600 MELA, Charles, *Variations sur l'Amour et le Graal*. Geneva: Droz, 2012, 203 p. (cf. *BIAS*, LXV, 2013, 685).

Rev. by PADEN, William D., *Spec*, 90.3 (2015), 839–40.

601 *Middle English Texts in Transition. A Festschrift dedicated to Toshiyuki Takamiya on his 70th birthday*, ed. Simon HOROBIN and Linne R. MOONEY. Woodbridge, Suffolk / Rochester, NY: York Medieval Press, 2014, 335 p.

Rev. by HAUGHT, Leah, *Arthuriana*, 25.4 (2015), 112–14.

602 *'Moult a sans et vallour'. Studies in Medieval French Literature in Honor of William W. Kibler*, ed. Monica L. WRIGHT, Norris J. LACY, and Rupert T. PICKENS. Amsterdam: Rodopi, 2012, 420 p. (cf. *BIAS*, LXV, 2013, 450).

Rev. by CALLAHAN, Christopher, *FR*, 88.3 (2015), 233–34.

603 MURRIN, Michael, *Trade and Romance*. Chicago, IL: University of Chicago Press, 2014, 327 p.

Rev. by FARRAR, Maia, *Com*, 46 (2015), 268–70.
Rev. by HSY, Jonathan, *Arthuriana*, 25.1 (2015), 175–76.

604 *New Directions in Medieval Manuscript Studies and Reading Practices. Essays in Honor of Derek Pearsall*, ed. Kathryn KERBY-FULTON, John J. THOMPSON, and Sarah BAECHLE. Notre Dame, IN: University of Notre Dame Press, 2014, 551 p.

Rev. by WARNER, Lawrence, *Arthuriana*, 25.4 (2015), 116–17.

605 NEWMAN, Barbara, *Medieval Crossover. Reading the Secular against the Sacred*. Notre Dame: University of Notre Dame Press, 2013, 392 p. (cf. *BIAS*, LXVII, 2015, 590).

Rev. by PUCCI, Joseph, *CLS*, 52.3 (2015), 622–24.

606 Perez, Kristina, *The Myth of Morgan la Fey*. New York: Palgrave Macmillan, 2014, 282 p. (cf. *BIAS*, LXVII, 2015, 596).

Rev. by Schiff, Randy P., *Arthuriana*, 25.2 (2015), 155–56.

607 Quinlan, Jessica, *Vater, Tochter, Schwiegersohn. Die erzählerische Ausgestaltung einer familiären Dreierkonstellation im Artusroman französischer und deutscher Sprache um 1200*. Heidelberg: Universitätsverlag Winter, 2013, 308 p. Studien zur historischen Poetik, 7. (cf. *BIAS*, LXVI, 2014, 86).

Rev. by Kerth, Thomas, *JEGP*, 114.2 (2015), 308–11.

608 Radulescu, Raluca L., *Romance and its Contexts in Fifteenth-Century England. Politics, Piety and Penitence*. Woodbridge: D.S. Brewer, 2013, 252 p. (cf. *BIAS*, LXVI, 2014, 362).

Rev. by Denny-Brown, Andrea, *Arthuriana*, 25.1 (2015), 177–78.

609 Richmond, Velma Bourgeois, *Chivalric Stories as Children's Literature. Edwardian Retellings in Words and Pictures*. Jefferson, N.C. / London: McFarland, 2014, 384 p. (cf. *BIAS*, LXVII, 2015, 600).

Rev. by Howey, Ann F., *Arthuriana*, 25.3 (2015), 121–23.

610 Rovang, Paul, *Malory's Anatomy of Chivalry. Characterization in the Morte Darthur*. Madison, NJ: Fairleigh Dickinson University Press, 2014, 224 p. (cf. *BIAS*, LXVII, 2015, 605).

Rev. by Tolhurst, Fiona, *Arthuriana*, 25.4 (2015), 119–21.

611 *Sir Gawain and the Green Knight*, Paul Battles. Peterborough, ON: Broadview Press, 2012, 259 p. (cf. *BIAS*, LXVI, 2014, 551).

Rev. by Sanchez-Marti, Jordi, *TMR*, 2015 (2015), online (15.05.07).

612 Taylor, Jane H.M., *Rewriting Arthurian Romance in Renaissance France. From Manuscript to Printed Book*. Cambridge: Brewer, 2014 (cf. *BIAS*, LXVII, 2015, 414).

Rev. by Brown, Cynthia J., *RQ*, 68.3 (2015), 1124–26.
Rev. by Chase, Carol J. *TMR*, 2015 (2015), online (15.04.18).

613 *The Arthur of the Italians. The Arthurian Legend in Medieval Italian Literature and Culture*, ed. Gloria Allaire and F. Regina Psaki. Cardiff: University of Wales Press, 2014, 352 p. (cf. *BIAS*, LXVII, 2015, 376). (cf. *BIAS*, LXVII, 2015, 376).

Rev. by Grimbert, Joan Tasker, *Arthuriana*, 25.2 (2015), 143–45.

614 *The Holy Grail on Film. Essays on the Cinematic Quest*, ed. Kevin J. Harty. Jefferson, NC: McFarland, 2015, ix + 245 p.

Rev. by Hoffman, Donald L., *Arthuriana*, 25.4 (2015), 109–12.

615 Walter, Philippe, *Dictionnaire de mythologie arthurienne*. Paris: Imago, 2014, 441 p. (cf. *BIAS*, LXVII, 2015, 335).

Rev. by Lacy, Norris J., *Arthuriana*, 25.3 (2015), 123–24.

616 Woods, William F., *The Medieval Filmscape. Reflections of Fear and Desire in a Cinematic Mirror*. Jefferson, NC: McFarland, 2014, 203 p.

Rev. by Finke, Laurie, *TMR*, 2015 (2015), online (15.05.37).

IV Reprints

617 Knight, Stephen, and Merry E. Wiesner-Hanks, *Arthurian Literature and Society*. New York: Palgrave Macmillan, 1983, 229 p. (Paperback edition 2015).

618 Marie de France, *The Lays*, trans. Edward J. Gallagher. Indianapolis: Hackett, 2010, 193 p. (E-book version 2015).

619 Matthews, John, and Pavel Tatamikov, *Arthur of Albion*. Cambridge, MA: Barefoot Books, 2008, 94 p. (Paperback edition 2015).

620 Perez, Kristina, *The Myth of Morgan la Fey*. New York: Palgrave Macmillan, 2014, 282 p. (Paperback edition/ebook 2015).

V Dissertations

621 Berard, Christopher Michael, *Arthurus Redivivus. Arthurian Imitation in Early Plantagenet England, 1154–1307*, PQ DP 10024269 (University of Toronto, 2015).

622 Bolt, Barbara Lee, *Of Wilderness, Forest, and Garden. An Eco-Theory of Genre in Middle English Literature*, PQ DP 3704304 (University of South Carolina, 2015).

623 Cardenas, Joel C., *Sir Gawain. The most complex and enduring knight of Arthur's Round Table*, PQ DP 1596674 (University of Nebraska at Kearney, 2015).

624 Clark, David Eugene, *Masses and Feast Days in the Morte Darthur*, PQ DP 10024269 (Baylor University, 2015).

625 Collins, Wilkie, *Chivalric lieux de mémoire. Nostalgia, communal memory, and the burden of historical consciousness in Sir Thomas Malory's Morte Darthur*, PQ DP 3700600 (Wayne State University, 2015).

626 Curtis, Sarah, *Revealing influence. Exploring British identity, sexual power, and lyric ambiguity in Spenser, Keats, and Tennyson*, PQ DP 1603298 (Southern Illinois University at Carbondale, 2015).

627 Echols, Katherine Barnes, *American radio adaptations of the Robin Hood and King Arthur legends from the 1930s through the late 1950s*, PQ DP 3663754 (University of Houston, 2015).

628 Maloney, Kara Larson, *Future and once. Community and affiliation in King Arthur's court*, PQ DP 3713600 (State University of New York at Binghamton, 2015).

629 Megna, Paul, *Emotional Ethics in Middle English Literature*, PQ DP 3724802 (University of California-Santa Barbara, 2015).

630 MOOTS, Angela, *Perceptions of Syncope in Medieval French Literature of the High Middle Ages. the Function and Cultural History of Fainting*, PQ DP 3706753 (University of Kansas, 2015).

631 OLIVER, Cheyenne, *Which witch? Morgan le Fay as shape-shifter and English perceptions of magic reflected in Arthurian legend*, PQ DP 10096028 (Florida Atlantic University, 2015).

632 SACH, Amy Rowan, *'Of his breast noble poets shall eat; of his blood shall men be drunk'. Nationalism, literature, and Arthurian 'things' in medieval and Early Modern Britain*, PQ DP 3740547 (University of Illinois at Urbana-Champaign, 2015).

633 SNIDER, Katherine A., *Living Landscape. Attitudes Toward the Environment in French Medieval Literature*, PQ DP 10000129 (University of Washington, 2015).

Index of Authors

https://doi.org/10.1515/9783110467499-183

Index of Subject Matter

Titles and medieval terms are in italics. Works are listed under author unless anonymous. Medieval authors are found under their first names (Wolfram von Eschenbach under W), unless traditionally known by their surname (Geoffrey Chaucer under C; Giovanni Boccaccio under B); modern authors under their last names (René Barjavel under B). Works by known authors are listed under their author. All numbers refer to the bibliography.

https://doi.org/10.1515/9783110467499-192